IN THE EYE OF THE STORM

THE APPLAUSE OF HEAVEN

◼

Max Lucado

NASHVILLE DALLAS MEXICO CITY RIO DE JANEIRO BEIJING

Published in Nashville, Tennessee, by Thomas Nelson. Thomas Nelson is a registered trademark of Thomas Nelson, Inc.

Thomas Nelson, Inc., titles may be purchased in bulk for educational, business, fund-raising, or sales promotional use. For information, please e-mail SpecialMarkets@ThomasNelson.com.

In the Eye of the Storm
© 1991, 1995 by Max Lucado

Unless noted otherwise, Scripture quotations are from The Holy Bible: New International Version®. © 1973, 1978, 1984 by International Bible Society. Used by permission of Zondervan Publishing House. Those marked KJV are from the King James Version of the Bible. Those marked TLB are from *The Living Bible.* © 1971. Used by permission of Tyndale House Publishers, Inc., Wheaton, Illinois 60189. Those marked NEB are from the New English Bible, © 1961, 1970 by The Delegates of the Oxford University Press and the Syndics of the Cambridge University Press. Reprinted by permission.

The Applause of Heaven
© 1990, 1996, 1999 by Max Lucado

Unless noted otherwise, Scripture quotations are from The Holy Bible: New International Version®. © 1973, 1978, 1984 by International Bible Society. Used by permission of Zondervan Publishing House. Those marked TLB are from *The Living Bible.* © 1971. Used by permission of Tyndale House Publishers, Inc., Wheaton, Illinois 60189. Those marked NEB are from the New English Bible, © 1961, 1970 by The Delegates of the Oxford University Press and the Syndics of the Cambridge University Press. Reprinted by permission. Those marked PHILLIPS are from J. B. Phillips: The New Testament in Modern English, Revised Edition. © J. B. Phillips 1958, 1960, 1972. Used by permission of Macmillan Publishing Co., Inc. Those marked KJV are from the King James Version of the Bible.

ISBN 978-0-8499-2114-8

Printed in the United States of America

1 2 3 4 5 6 RRD 11 10 09 08

IN THE EYE OF THE STORM

To Robert and Elsie Forcum

two ambassadors with a love for the church
and a burden for the world

CONTENTS

Acknowledgments

Here's a salute to some special friends who made this book possible.

First to the folks at Word Publishing:

Kip Jordon, Byron Williamson, Ernie Owen, Joey Paul, and Roland Lundy—It's a privilege to be on the team.

Dave Moberg, Tom Williams, Susan Russell, Ed Curtis, and Michal Rutledge—Creativity unlimited!

Nancy Norris and Leslie Hughes—We know who really keeps the office working.

Stephen and Amanda Sorenson—You can cross my "t's" and dot my "i's" anytime. Thanks for the great editorial work.

And to my church family at Oak Hills:

Mary Stain—My supersecretary who corrects my mistakes, takes my calls, keeps me prompt, and saves my neck on a daily basis. Thank you so much.

Elsie Clay, Marcelle Le Gallo, and Kathleen McCleery—Our secretarial staff who help Mary so she can help me. Thanks again.

Glen Carter, Jim Toombs, John Tuller, Pat Hile, Jeff Pickens, and Rod Chisholm—Six co-workers who make my work a joy.

Karen Hill, Rod Chisholm, and Allen Dutton, Jr.—Thanks for proofreading the manuscript.

The members of Oak Hills Church—You make every Sunday a homecoming.

And to the Lucado family:

Jenna, Andrea, and Sara—three little girls who've taken my heart hostage.

And most of all, to my wife Denalyn—a decade with you has convinced me: there is a heaven, and you don't have to die to go there.

BEFORE
YOU
BEGIN . . .

CHIPPIE THE PARAKEET NEVER saw it coming. One second he was peacefully perched in his cage. The next he was sucked in, washed up, and blown over.

The problems began when Chippie's owner decided to clean Chippie's cage with a vacuum cleaner. She removed the attachment from the end of the hose and stuck it in the cage. The phone rang, and she turned to pick it up. She'd barely said "hello" when "sssopp!" Chippie got sucked in.

The bird owner gasped, put down the phone, turned off the vacuum, and opened the bag. There was Chippie—still alive, but stunned.

Since the bird was covered with dust and soot, she grabbed him and raced to the bathroom, turned on the faucet, and held Chippie under the running water. Then, realizing that Chippie was soaked and shivering, she did what any compassionate bird owner would do . . . she reached for the hair dryer and blasted the pet with hot air.

Poor Chippie never knew what hit him.

A few days after the trauma, the reporter who'd initially written about the event contacted Chippie's owner to see how the bird was recovering. "Well," she replied, "Chippie doesn't sing much anymore—he just sits and stares."

It's hard not to see why. Sucked in, washed up, and blown over . . . that's enough to steal the song from the stoutest heart.

Can you relate to Chippie? Most of us can. One minute you're seated in familiar territory with a song on your lips, then . . . The pink slip comes. The rejection letter arrives. The doctor calls. The divorce papers are delivered. The check bounces. A policeman knocks on your door.

Sssopp! You're sucked into a black cavern of doubts, doused with the cold water of reality, and stung with the hot air of empty promises.

The life that had been so calm is now so stormy. You're hailstormed by demands. Assailed by doubts. Pummeled by questions. And somewhere in the trauma, you lose your joy. Somewhere in the storm, you lose your song.

Ever found yourself in a storm of life? If so, if Chippie's story is your story, then I'm glad you picked up this book. I wrote it with you in mind. I wrote it because there is a day in the life of Christ that you need to know about.

Aside from the Crucifixion, it is the most stressful day of his life. A roaring sequence of bad news, demanding crowds, and doubting friends. Twenty-four hours in which Jesus faces the same gale-force fears that you and I face. Waves of pressure slam. Winds of anxiety blow. Clouds of darkness billow.

Yet through it all Jesus remains calm. He endures the day without losing his song. I'd like to help you see how he did it.

First we'll consider the *stress of demands*. Jesus handled twelve hours of chaos. What did he do to keep his cool? What did he know that gave him strength? If your days are bookended with deadlines and "chuck-it-all" frustrations—then you'll like this section.

The second section is entitled *Storms of Doubt*. Have you ever found yourself in a storm and wondered why Jesus doesn't pull you out? The disciples did. While Jesus went up the mountain, they went out on the sea. The storm came, their boat bounced, and they were left with a long night of fear and a long list of questions. "Jesus knows we're in a storm. Why doesn't he come?"

Sound familiar?

The final section of the book deals with a third source of anxiety—the *sting of failure*. In the twilight hours of that night we discover a sweet story of grace, Peter's attempt to walk on water. What began as a step of faith ended up as a belly flop of fear. If you've ever wondered what God does when we fail, then read this section and allow the hand that saved Peter to touch you.

Storms come. They come quickly. They pounce ferociously. If you are in one, then you know what I mean. If you're not in one today, you know as well as I—one may be in tomorrow's forecast.

My prayer is that this book will leave you better prepared. My prayer is that you will find some word, some story, some verse, or some thought that will convince you that he is very near. I pray that as you read you will be reminded that the same voice that stilled the rage on the Sea of Galilee can still the storm in your world.

Read on, friend, and be assured—he is closer than you've ever dreamed.

STRESS
OF
DEMANDS

1

FROM
CALM
TO
CHAOS

*M*AYBE YOU CAN RELATE TO the morning I just had. It's Sunday. Sundays are always busy days for me. Sundays are always early days for me. Today promised to be no exception.

With a full slate of activities planned, I got up early and drove to church. There was not much traffic at 6:00 AM I had the roads to myself. The orange of dawn had yet to break the nighttime spell on the summer's black sky. The twilight sparkled. Cool air wafted.

I parked outside my church office and took a minute to enjoy the quietude. I set down my books, picked up my coffee, and leaned against the car.

It was just the star-studded sky and me. Across the city, lights flickered. Shadowed trees slept. The night was calm: no noise, no hurry, no demands. That would all change within a couple of hours. Let a few thousand alarm clocks buzz and a few thousand garage doors open, and the serenity would be invaded as suburbia awakened. But at the moment, suburbia slept.

Life is like that sometimes. There are jaunts in life's journey that are as glassy as a midnight lake on a windless night. No noise. No rushing. No crises. There are measures in our music where the conductor silences the kettledrum, and only the flute is allowed to sing.

And sing she does. Under the spell of her song, dead-lines aren't as deadly. Death is distant. Dear ones are still dear and sometimes near. The eclipsing clouds of fear and debts and angry phone calls have passed. And, for a while, your world is moonlit.

Mine was. I sat on the hood of my car, sipped my coffee, and toasted the stars. They twinkled their response.

It was calm. But calm has a way of becoming chaos.

With a briefcase in one hand and a coffee cup in the other, I walked and whistled across the parking lot to the office door. To enter my office, I had to get past the sleeping dog of the twentieth century: the alarm system. I set down my briefcase and unlocked the door. I picked up my briefcase and walked in.

The code box on the wall was flashing a red light.

I'm not too electronically inclined, but I do know what a red light on an alarm system means: "Punch in the code, buddy, or get ready for the music."

I punched in the code. Nothing happened. I punched in the code again. The little red light kept blinking. I punched it in again. Time was running out. The little light snickered at me. I could hear the message being sent up and down the wires to all the neon-eyed alarm gremlins. "Man your sirens, everybody. Ol' do-do brain is entering his bank-card number again!"

I kept pushing, the clock kept ticking, the light kept flashing, and the gremlins were getting excited. "Get ready! Ten seconds and counting. Ten, nine, eight . . ."

"Oh, no," I groaned, "it's about to hit."

The siren pounced on me like a mountain lion. I thought we were under nuclear attack. Floodlights flash flooded the hallway, and red strobes turned. I kept pushing buttons, and the alarm kept blaring. You'd have thought it was a breakout at Alcatraz.

My pulse raced, my forehead moistened, and my situation was desperate. I raced down the hall to my office, pulled open the lap drawer of my desk, and found the phone number of the alarm company.

I could barely hear what the man said when he answered. When I understood what he said, I could scarcely believe he had said it.

"What do you mean, 'What's the matter?'" I exclaimed. "Can't you hear?"

"Yes, I punched in the code," I screamed. "It didn't do any good!"

The next twenty minutes were loud, demanding, confusing, and aggravating. I was speaking to technicians I couldn't see about equipment I didn't understand trying to understand words I couldn't hear.

That's when the policeman came. He tapped on the window. I opened it. "I can't get the thing to shut off!" I yelled.

"You the preacher here?" he asked.

"Yes," I yelled.

He just shook his head and walked away, probably muttering something about what they don't teach in theology courses.

Finally, for no apparent reason, the siren ceased. The lights shut off. What had been an air-raid shelter became an office again. I walked back to my desk, sat down, and sighed. *What a way to begin the day.* The morning lesson I had prepared was lying on my credenza. I picked it up and read the first line: "When calm becomes chaos."

"Appropriate," I muttered.

Ever happened to you? When was the last time your life went from calm to chaos in half a minute? ("How many examples would you like?" you ask.) When was the last time you found yourself pushing buttons that didn't respond, struggling with instructions you couldn't hear, or operating a system you didn't understand?

You enter the wrong computer code and lose eighteen months worth of ledgers in a matter of seconds. Calm volcanoes into chaos.

A message on your answering machine tells you that the report you are scheduled to give next week is due tomorrow. Good-bye sleep. Hello all-nighter. Good-bye calm. Hello chaos.

The mechanic who promised that the car would be ready today in time for the trip says, "I know I promised, but it's much worse than we thought. Your side axle disjointed, causing the U-joint to descramble the electronic ignition that is hand-assembled in Lower Tasmania and . . ."

"Grrrr."

If you've ever had your spouse call you at the office and say, "Just got a letter from the IRS. They are going to audit . . ."

If your boss has ever begun a conversation with these words: "You're a good worker, but with all this talk about a recession we have to cut back . . ."

If your teenager has ever walked in and asked, "Does our car insurance cover the other guy's car?"

Then you know that life can go from calm to chaos in a matter of moments. No warnings. No announcements. No preparation.

Little red lights blink, and you start pushing buttons. Sometimes you silence the alarm; sometimes it rips the air like a demon. The result can be peace or panic. The result can be calm or chaos.

It all depends on one factor: Do you know the code?

For me, this morning became chaos. Had I been prepared . . . had I known the code . . . had I known what to do when the warning flashed . . . calm would have triumphed.

The next few pages will usher you into a day in Jesus' life when the calm could have become chaos. It has all the elements of anxiety: bad news and a death threat, followed by swarming demands, interruptions, inept disciples, and a blazing temptation to follow the crowd. In twenty-four pressure-packed hours, Jesus was carried from the summit of celebration to the valley of frustration.

It was the second most stressful day of his life. As soon as one alarm was disarmed, another began blinking. The rulers threatened. The crowds pressed. The followers doubted. The people demanded. When you see what he endured that day, you will wonder how he kept his cool.

Somehow, though, he did. Although the people pressed and the problems monsooned, Jesus didn't blow up or bail out. In fact, he did just the opposite. He served people, thanked God, and made cool-headed decisions.

I want to help you see how he did it. I'd like to share with you a few "internal codes" that you desperately need. Equip yourself with these internal codes, punch them in when the red lights of your world start to flash, and you will be amazed at how quickly the alarms will be disarmed.

A few words of explanation:

If you are looking for external adjustments, you won't find them here. I won't say anything about dressing for success or power language or popularity schemes. You can buy many books that will help you externally, but this isn't one of them.

What you will discover in this book are attitudes . . . godly attitudes . . . a way of viewing people and problems as modeled by the Master.

If you want external alteration, look elsewhere. If you want internal development, read on. If you want to see how

God handled—and handles—hassles, then I've got some thoughts to share with you.

Let's do something. Let's take the principles modeled by Jesus into our day-to-day whirlwind of demands and decisions. Let's take a few minutes and observe God under pressure. Let's watch his face. Listen to his words. Observe his choices. And see what we can learn. Let's watch Christ in a pressure-cooker environment and try to answer this question:

What did Jesus know that allowed him to do what he did?

2

GOD UNDER PRESSURE

A DAY IN THE LIFE of Christ.
Call it a tapestry of turmoil, a noisy pictorial in which the golden threads of triumph entwine with the black, frazzled strings of tragedy.

Call it a symphony of emotions, a sunrise-to-sunset orchestration of extremes. One score is brassy with exuberance; the next moans with sorrow. On one page, the orchestra swells in adoration. On the next, Jesus solos the ballad of loneliness.

Whatever you call it, call it real. Call it a day in which Jesus experiences more stress than he will any other day of his life—aside from his crucifixion. Before the morning becomes evening, he has reason to weep . . . run . . . shout . . . curse . . . praise . . . doubt.

From calm to chaos. From peace to perplexity. Within moments his world is turned upside down.

In the tapestry, though, there is one thread that sparkles. In the symphony, there is one song that soars. In the story, there is one lesson that comforts. You've heard it before, but you may have forgotten it. Look closely. Listen intently. Be reminded:

Jesus knows how you feel.

If you've ever had a day in which you've been blitzkrieged by demands, if you've ever ridden the roller coaster of sorrow and celebration, if you've ever wondered if God in heaven can relate to you on earth, then read and reread about this pressure-packed day in the life of Christ.

Take heart. Jesus knows how you feel.

He begins the morning by hearing about the death of John the Baptist: his cousin, his forerunner, his coworker, his friend.[1] The man who came closer to understanding Jesus than any other is dead.

Imagine losing the one person who knows you better than anyone else, and you will feel what Jesus is feeling. Reflect on the horror of being told that your dearest friend has just been murdered, and you will relate to Jesus' sorrow. Consider your reaction if you were told that your best friend had just been decapitated by a people-pleasing, incestuous monarch, and you'll see how the day begins for Christ. His world is beginning to turn upside down.

The emissaries brought more than news of sorrow, however; they brought a warning: "The same Herod who took John's head is interested in yours." Listen to how Luke presents the monarch's madness: "Herod said, 'I beheaded John. Who, then, is this I hear such things about?' *And he tried to see him*"[2] (emphasis mine). Something tells me that Herod wanted more than a social visit.

So, with John's life taken and his own life threatened, Jesus chooses to get away for a while. "When Jesus heard what had happened, he withdrew by boat privately to a solitary place."[3]

But before he can get away, his disciples arrive. The Gospel of Mark states that the "apostles gathered around Jesus and reported to him all they had done and taught."[4]

They return exuberant. Jesus had commissioned them to proclaim the gospel and authenticate it with miracles. "They went out and preached that people should repent. They drove out many demons and anointed many sick people with oil and healed them."[5]

Can you imagine the excitement? Can you envision the scene? A reunion of twelve friends. A reuniting of disciples with their teacher. A homecoming bubbling with testimonies:

• Peter describing a lame man he healed.
• John telling of a crowd he taught.
• Andrew recounting the deliverance of an epileptic.
• James relating to Jesus how the crowds followed him wherever he went.
• Matthew reporting the healing of a blind woman.

Remember, these disciples were ordinary men. They weren't orators, scholars, kings, or saints. They were fishermen and a tax collector, common laborers who, by God's power, had taken a nation by storm. The emotion? Exuberance. In a matter of moments, Jesus' heart goes from the pace of a funeral dirge to the triumphant march of a ticker-tape parade.

And look who follows the disciples to locate Jesus. About five thousand men plus women and children![6] Rivers of people cascade out of the hills and villages. Some scholars estimate the crowd to be as high as twenty-five thousand.[7] They swarm around Jesus, each with one desire: to meet the man who had empowered the disciples.

What had been a calm morning now buzzes with activity. "So many people were coming and going that they did not even have a chance to eat."[8]

I've had people demand my attention. I know what it's like to have a half-dozen kids wanting different things at the same time. I know the feeling of receiving one call with two other people waiting impatiently on other lines. I even know what it's like to be encircled by a dozen or so people, each making a separate request.

But twenty-five thousand? That's larger than many cities! No wonder the disciples couldn't eat. I'm surprised they could breathe!

The morning has been a jungle trail of the unexpected. First Jesus grieves over the death of a dear friend and relative. Then his life is threatened. Next he celebrates the triumphant return of his followers. Then he is nearly suffocated by a brouhaha of humanity. Bereavement . . . jeopardy . . . jubilation. . . bedlam.

Are you beginning to see why I call this the second most stressful day in the life of Christ? And it's far from over.

Jesus decides to take the disciples to a quiet place where they can rest and reflect. He shouts a command over the noise of the crowd. "Come with me by yourselves to a quiet place and get some rest."[9] The thirteen fight their way to the beach and climb into a boat.

And, for a few precious moments, the world is quiet again. The din of the crowd grows distant and the only sound is the slap of the water against the hull. Jesus' heart is weighted by sorrow and buoyed by joy. He watches his followers swapping stories of victory. Then he raises his glance and sees on the horizon Tiberias, the city constructed by John the Baptist's murderer, Herod. Joy suddenly alloyed with indignation causes his fists to clench and his eyes to moisten.

Who would question his desire to get away from the people? He just needs a few hours alone. Just a respite. Just a retreat. Time to pray. Time to ponder. Time to weep. A time without crowds or demands. A campfire wreathed with friends. An evening with those he loves. *The people can wait until tomorrow.*

The people, however, have other ideas. "The crowds learned about it and followed him."[10] It's a six-mile walk around the northeastern corner of the Sea of Galilee, so the crowd takes a hike. When Jesus got to Bethsaida, his desired retreat had become a roaring arena.

"Surprise!"

Add to the list of sorrow, peril, excitement, and bedlam the word *interruption.* Jesus' plans are interrupted. What he has in mind for his day and what the people have in mind for his day are two different agendas. What Jesus seeks and what Jesus gets are not the same.

Sound familiar?

Remember when you sought a night's rest and got a colicky baby? Remember when you sought to catch up at the office and got even further behind? Remember when you sought to use your Saturday for leisure, but ended up fixing your neighbor's sink?

Take comfort, friend. It happened to Jesus, too.

In fact, this would be a good time to pause and digest the central message of this chapter.

Jesus knows how you feel.

Ponder this and use it the next time your world goes from calm to chaos.

His pulse has raced. His eyes have grown weary. His heart has grown heavy. He has had to climb out of bed with a sore throat. He has been kept awake late and has gotten up early. He knows how you feel.

You may have trouble believing that. You probably believe that Jesus knows what it means to endure heavy-duty tragedies. You are no doubt convinced that Jesus is acquainted with sorrow and has wrestled with fear. Most people accept that. But can God relate to the hassles and headaches of my life? Of your life?

For some reason this is harder to believe.

Perhaps that's why portions of this day are recorded in all the Gospel accounts. No other event, other than the Crucifixion, is told by all four Gospel writers. Not Jesus' baptism. Not his temptation. Not even his birth. But all four writers chronicle this day. It's as if Matthew, Mark, Luke, and John knew that you would wonder if God understands. And they proclaim their response in four-part harmony:

Jesus knows how you feel.

A friend of mine was recently trying to teach his six-year-old son how to shoot a basket. The boy would take the basketball and push it as hard as he could toward the goal, but it always fell short. The father would then take the ball and toss it toward the basket, saying something like, "Just do it like this, son. It's easy."

Then the boy would try, and miss, again. My friend would then take the ball and make another basket, encouraging his son to push the ball a bit harder.

After several minutes and many misses, the boy responded to his father's encouragement by saying, "Yeah, but it's easy for you up there. You don't know how hard it is from down here."

You and I can never say that about God. Of the many messages Jesus taught us that day about stress, the first one is this: "God knows how you feel."

Read how J. B. Phillips translates Hebrews 4:15:

For we have no superhuman High Priest to whom our weaknesses are unintelligible—he himself has shared fully in all our experience of temptation, except that he never sinned.

The writer of Hebrews is adamant almost to the point of redundancy. It's as if he anticipates our objections. It's as if he knows that we will say to God what my friend's son said to him: "God, it's easy for you up there. You don't know how hard it is from down here." So he boldly proclaims Jesus' ability to understand. Look at the wording again.

He himself. Not an angel. Not an ambassador. Not an emissary, but Jesus himself.

Shared fully. Not partially. Not nearly. Not to a large degree. Entirely! Jesus shared fully.

In all our experience. Every hurt. Each ache. All the stresses and all the strains. No exceptions. No substitutes. Why? So he could sympathize with our weaknesses.

A politician dons a hardhat and enters the factory like he is one of the employees. A social worker goes to the inner city and spends the night on the streets with the homeless. A general walks into the mess hall and sits down with the soldiers like he is one of the enlisted men.

All three want to communicate the same message: "I identify with you. I can understand. I can relate." There is one problem, though. The factory employees know that the politician's hardhat will come off when the television crew is gone. The derelicts know that the social worker will be in a warm bed tomorrow night. And the soldiers are well aware that for every meal the general eats in the mess hall, he'll eat dozens in the officers' quarters.

Try as they might, these well-meaning professionals don't really understand. Their participation is partial. Jesus' participation, however, was complete. The writer of Hebrews states with double clarity that Jesus "shared *fully* in *all* our experience" (emphasis mine).

A bookstore owner in the Northwest once told me about an angry lady who stomped into his store carrying my book, *God Came Near*. She slammed the book on the counter, said a few less-than-kind things about the book, and then screamed loudly enough for everyone on the block to hear, "My God didn't have pimples!"

I know the paragraph that put the spark in her tinderbox. It reads like this:

> Jesus may have had pimples. He may have been tone-deaf. Perhaps a girl down the street had a crush on him or vice-versa. It could be that his knees were bony. One thing's for sure: He was, while completely divine, completely human.[11]

I can understand why the woman became upset. I can relate to her discomfort. We quickly fix a crack in the stained glass. We rub away any smudges on the altar. There is something *safe* about a God who never had callouses. There is something *awesome* about a God who never felt pain. There is something *majestic* about a God who never scraped his elbow.

But there is also something *cold* about a God who cannot relate to what you and I feel.

If I had a moment with that lady, I would ask her, "Jesus may not have had pimples, but don't you hope that he could have?"

Every page of the Gospels hammers home this crucial principle: God knows how you feel. From the funeral to the factory to the frustration of a demanding schedule. Jesus understands. When you tell God that you've reached your limit, he knows what you mean. When you shake your head at impossible deadlines, he shakes his, too. When your plans are interrupted by people who have other plans, he nods in empathy. He has been there. He knows how you feel.[12]

Before we resume our chronicling of this stressful day in Jesus' life, let me take you to another day—one far more recent, in a place closer to home.

February 15, 1921. New York City. The operating room of the Kane Summit Hospital. A doctor is performing an appendectomy.

In many ways the events leading to the surgery are uneventful. The patient has complained of severe abdominal pain. The diagnosis is clear: an inflamed appendix. Dr. Evan O'Neill Kane is performing the surgery. In his distinguished thirty-seven-year medical career, he has performed nearly four thousand appendectomies, so this surgery will be uneventful in all ways except two.

The first novelty of this operation? The use of local anesthesia in major surgery. Dr. Kane is a crusader against the hazards of general anesthesia. He contends that a local application is far safer. Many of his colleagues agree with him in principle, but in order for them to agree in practice, they will have to see the theory applied.

Dr. Kane searches for a volunteer, a patient who is willing to undergo surgery while under local anesthesia. A volunteer is not easily found. Many are squeamish at the thought of being awake during their own surgery. Others are fearful that the anesthesia might wear off too soon.

Eventually, however, Dr. Kane finds a candidate. On Tuesday morning, February 15, the historic operation occurs. The patient is prepped and wheeled into the operating room. A local anesthetic is applied. As he has done thousands of times, Dr. Kane dissects the superficial tissues and locates the appendix. He skillfully excises it and concludes the surgery. During the procedure, the patient complains of only minor discomfort.

The volunteer is taken into post-op, then placed in a hospital ward. He recovers quickly and is dismissed two days later.

Dr. Kane had proven his theory. Thanks to the willingness of a brave volunteer, Kane demonstrated that local anesthesia was a viable, and even preferable, alternative.

But I said there were two facts that made the surgery unique. I've told you the first: the use of local anesthesia. The second is the patient. The courageous candidate for surgery by Dr. Kane was Dr. Kane.

To prove his point, Dr. Kane operated on himself![13]

A wise move. The doctor became a patient in order to convince the patients to trust the doctor.

I've shared this story with several health professionals. They each gave me the same response: furrowed brow, suspicious grin, and the dubious words, "That's hard to believe."

Perhaps it is. But the story of the doctor who became his own patient is mild compared to the story of the God who became human. But Jesus did. So that you and I would believe that the Healer knows our hurts, he voluntarily became one of us. He placed himself in our position. He suffered our pains and felt our fears.

Rejection? He felt it. Temptation? He knew it. Loneliness? He experienced it. Death? He tasted it.

And stress? He could write a best-selling book about it.

Why did he do it? One reason. So that when you hurt, you will go to him—your Father and your Physician—and let him heal.

3

A
MOTHER'S
LOVE—
A
FRIEND'S
EMPATHY

*T*HERESA BRIONES IS A TENDER, loving mother. She also has a stout left hook that she used to punch a lady in a coin laundry. Why'd she do it?

Some kids were making fun of Theresa's daughter, Alicia.

Alicia is bald. Her knees are arthritic. Her nose is pinched. Her hips are creaky. Her hearing is bad. She has the stamina of a seventy-year-old. And she is only ten.

"Mom," the kids taunted, "come and look at the monster!"

Alicia weighs only twenty-two pounds and is shorter than most preschoolers. She suffers from progeria—a genetic aging disease that strikes one child in eight million. The life expectancy of progeria victims is twenty years. There are only fifteen known cases of this disease in the world.

"She is not an alien. She is not a monster," Theresa defended. "She is just like you and me."

Mentally, Alicia is a bubbly, fun-loving third grader. She has a long list of friends. She watches television in a toddler-sized rocking chair. She plays with Barbie dolls and teases her younger brother.

Theresa has grown accustomed to the glances and questions. She is patient with the constant curiosity. Genuine inquiries she accepts. Insensitive slanders she does not.

The mother of the finger-pointing children came to investigate. "I see 'it,'" she told the kids.

"My child is not an 'it,'" Theresa stated. Then she decked the woman.

Who could blame her? Such is the nature of parental love. Mothers and fathers have a God-given ability to love their children regardless of imperfections. Not because the parents are blind. Just the opposite. They see vividly.

Theresa sees Alicia's inability as clearly as anyone. But she also sees Alicia's value.

So does God.

God sees us with the eyes of a Father. He sees our defects, errors, and blemishes. But he also sees our value.

Two chapters ago, I closed with this question: What did Jesus know that enabled him to do what he did?

Here's part of the answer. He knew the value of people. He knew that each human being is a treasure. And because he did, people were not a source of stress, but a source of joy.

━━━━━━━━━━━━━

When Jesus lands on the shore of Bethsaida, he leaves the Sea of Galilee and steps into a sea of humanity. Keep in mind, he has crossed the sea to get *away* from the crowds. He needs to grieve. He longs to relax with his followers. He needs anything but another crowd of thousands to teach and heal.

But his love for people overcomes his need for rest.

When Jesus landed and saw a large crowd, he had compassion on them and healed their sick.[1]

He had compassion on them, because they were like sheep without a shepherd.[2]

He welcomed them and spoke to them about the kingdom of God, and healed those who needed healing.[3]

It is doubtful that anyone in the crowd thinks to ask Jesus how he is doing. There is no indication that anyone is concerned with how Jesus is feeling. No one has come to give; all have come to take.

═══════════════

In our house we call 5:00 PM the piranha hour. That's the time of day when everyone wants a piece of Mom. Sara, the baby, is hungry. Andrea wants Mom to read her a book. Jenna wants help with her homework. And I—the everloving, ever-sensitive husband—want Denalyn to drop everything and talk to me about my day.

When is your piranha hour? When do people in your world demand much and offer little?

Every boss has had a day in which the requests outnumber the results. There's not a businessperson alive who hasn't groaned as an armada of assignments docks at his or her desk. For the teacher, the piranha hour often begins when the first student enters and ends when the last student leaves.

Piranha hours: parents have them, bosses endure them, secretaries dread them, teachers are besieged by them, and Jesus taught us how to live through them successfully.

When hands extended and voices demanded, Jesus responded with love. He did so because the code within him disarmed the alarm. The code is worth noting: "People are precious."

———————————————

I can hear somebody raising an objection at this point. "Yes, but it was easier for Jesus. He was God. He could do more than I can. After all, he was divine."

True, Jesus was equally God and man. But don't be too quick to dismiss what he did. Consider his loving response from another angle.

Consider that, along with his holy strength, he also had a holy awareness. There were no secrets on the mountain that day; Jesus knew the hearts of each person. He knew why they were there and what they would do.[4]

Matthew writes that Jesus "healed their sick."[5] Not *some* of their sick. Not the *righteous* among the sick. Not the *deserving* among the sick. But *"the sick."*

Surely, among the many thousands, there were a few people unworthy of good health.

The same divinity that gave Jesus the power to heal also gave him the power to perceive. I wonder if Jesus was tempted to say to the rapist, "Heal you? After what you've done?" Or to the child molester, "Why should I restore your health?" Or to the bigot, "Get out of here, buddy, and take your arrogance with you."

And he could see not only their past, he could see their future.

Undoubtedly, there were those in the multitude who would use their newfound health to hurt others. Jesus released tongues that would someday curse. He gave sight to eyes that would lust. He healed hands that would kill.

Many of those he healed would never say "thank you," but he healed them anyway. Most would be more concerned with being healthy than being holy, but he healed them anyway. Some of those who asked for bread today would cry for his blood a few months later, but he healed them anyway.

Jesus chose to do what you and I seldom, if ever, choose to do. He chose to give gifts to people, knowing full well that those gifts could be used for evil.

Don't be too quick to attribute Jesus' compassion to his divinity. Remember both sides. For each time Jesus healed, he had to overlook the future and the past.

Something, by the way, that he still does.

Have you noticed that God doesn't ask you to prove that you will put your salary to good use? Have you noticed that God doesn't turn off your oxygen supply when you misuse his gifts? Aren't you glad that God doesn't give you only that which you remember to thank him for? (Has it been a while since you thanked God for your spleen? Me, too. But I still have one.)

God's goodness is spurred by his nature, not by our worthiness.

Someone asked an associate of mine, "What biblical precedent do we have to help the poor who have no desire to become Christians?"

My friend responded with one word: "God."

God does it daily, for millions of people.

What did Jesus know that allowed him to do what he did? What internal code kept his calm from erupting into chaos? He knew the value of people.

Interestingly, the stress seen that day is not on Jesus' face, but on the faces of the disciples. "Send the crowds away,"[6] they demand. Fair request. "After all," they are saying, "you've taught them. You've healed them. You've accommodated them. And now they're getting hungry. If we don't send them away, they'll want you to feed them, too!"

I wish I could have seen the expression on the disciples' faces when they heard the Master's response. "They do not need to go away. You give them something to eat."[7]

I used to think that this was a rhetorical request. I used to think that Jesus knew the disciples couldn't feed the crowd, but that he asked them anyway. I used to think that it was a "test" to teach them to rely on God for what they couldn't do.

I don't see it like that anymore.

I still think it was a test—not a test to show them what they couldn't do, but a test to demonstrate what they could do. After all, they had just gone on tour achieving the impossible. Jesus is asking them to do it again. "You give them something to eat."[8]

I wish I could tell you that the disciples did it. I wish I could say that they knew God wouldn't ask them to do something he wouldn't empower them to do, so they fed the crowd. I wish I could tell you that the disciples miraculously fed the five thousand men plus women and children.

But I can't . . . because they didn't.

Rather than look to God, they looked in their wallets. "That would take eight months of a man's wages! Are we to go and spend that much on bread and give it to them to eat?"[9]

"Y-y-y-you've got to be kidding."

"He can't be serious."

"It's one of Jesus' jokes."

"Do you know how many people are out there?"

Eyes watermelon-wide. Jaws dangling open. One ear hearing the din of the crowd, the other the command of God.

Don't miss the contrasting views. When Jesus saw the people, he saw an opportunity to love and affirm value. When the disciples saw the people, they saw thousands of problems.

Also, don't miss the irony. In the midst of a bakery—in the presence of the Eternal Baker—they tell the "Bread of Life" that there is no bread.

How silly we must appear to God.

Here's where Jesus should have given up. This is the point in the pressure-packed day where Jesus should have exploded. The sorrow, the life threats, the exuberance, the crowds, the interruptions, the demands, and now this. His own disciples can't do what he asks them. In front of five thousand men, they let him down.

"Beam me up, Father," should have been Jesus' next words. But they weren't. Instead he inquires, "How many loaves do you have?"

The disciples bring him a little boy's lunch. A lunch pail becomes a banquet, and all are fed. No word of reprimand is given. No furrowed brow of anger is seen. No "I-told-you-so" speech is delivered. The same compassion Jesus extends to the crowd is extended to his friends.

Look at this day one more time. Review what our Lord faced.

Intense sorrow—the death of a dear friend and relative.

Immediate threat—his name is on the wanted poster.

Immeasurable joy—a homecoming with his followers.

Immense crowds—a Niagara of people followed him everywhere.

Insensitive interruptions—he sought rest and got people.

Incredible demands—crowds of thousands clamored for his touch.

Inept assistance—the one and only time he asked for help, he got a dozen "you're-pulling-my-leg" expressions.

But the calm within Christ never erupted. The alarm never sounded. What did Jesus know that enabled him to do what he did? He knew the incredible value of people. As a result:

- He didn't stamp his feet and demand his own way.
- He didn't tell the disciples to find another beach where there were no people.
- He didn't ask the crowds why they hadn't brought their own food.
- He didn't send the apostles back into the field for more training.
- Most important, he stayed calm in the midst of chaos. He even paused, in the midst of it all, to pray a prayer of thanks.[10]

A boy went into a pet shop, looking for a puppy. The store owner showed him a litter in a box. The boy looked at the puppies. He picked each one up, examined it, and put it back into the box.

After several minutes, he walked back to the owner and said, "I picked one out. How much will it cost?"

The man gave him the price, and the boy promised to be back in a few days with the money. "Don't take too long," the owner cautioned. "Puppies like these sell quickly."

The boy turned and smiled knowingly, "I'm not worried," he said. "Mine will still be here."

The boy went to work—weeding, washing windows, cleaning yards. He worked hard and saved his money. When he had enough for the puppy, he returned to the store.

He walked up to the counter and laid down a pocketful of wadded bills. The store owner sorted and counted the cash. After verifying the amount, he smiled at the boy and said, "All right, son, you can go get your puppy."

The boy reached into the back of the box, pulled out a skinny dog with a limp leg, and started to leave.

The owner stopped him.

"Don't take that puppy," he objected. "He's crippled. He can't play. He'll never run with you. He can't fetch. Get one of the healthy pups."

"No thank you, sir," the boy replied. "This is exactly the kind of dog I've been looking for."

As the boy turned to leave, the store owner started to speak but remained silent. Suddenly he understood. For extending from the bottom of the boy's trousers was a brace—a brace for his crippled leg.

Why did the boy want the dog? Because he knew how it felt. And he knew it was very special.

What did Jesus know that enabled him to do what he did? He knew how the people felt, and he knew that they were special.

I hope you never forget that.

Jesus knows how you feel. You're under the gun at work? Jesus knows how you feel. You've got more to do than is humanly possible? So did he. You've got children who make a "piranha hour" out of your dinner hour? Jesus knows what that's like. People take more from you than they give? Jesus understands. Your teenagers won't listen? Your students won't try? Your employees give you blank stares when you assign tasks? Believe me, friend, Jesus knows how you feel.

You are precious to him. So precious that he became like you so that you would come to him.

When you struggle, he listens. When you yearn, he responds. When you question, he hears. He has been there. You've heard that before, but you need to hear it again.

He loves you with the love of a Theresa Briones.

He understands you with the compassion of the crippled boy.

Like Theresa, he battles with hell itself to protect you.

And, like the boy, he paid a great price to take you home.

4

WHEN FISHERMEN DON'T FISH

They were like sheep without a shepherd. So he began teaching them many things.[1]

When Jesus landed and saw a large crowd, he had
compassion on them and healed their sick.[2]

*I*T'S A GOOD THING THOSE VERSES weren't written about me.
It's a good thing thousands of people weren't depend-
ing on Max for their teaching and nourishment. Especially
on a day when I'd just heard of the death of a dear friend.
Especially on a day when I wanted to be alone with my
friends. Especially after I'd gotten into a boat to escape
the crowds. Had that been me in Jesus' sandals on that
Bethsaida beach, the verses would read something like:

They were like sheep without a shepherd. So Max told
them to quit grazing on his pasture and to head back
to their pens.

When Max landed and saw a large crowd, he mumbled
something about how hard it was to get a day off and
radioed for the helicopter. Then he and the disciples
escaped to a private retreat.

It's a good thing I wasn't responsible for those people.
I would have been in no mood to teach them, no mood to
help them. I would have had no desire even to be with them.

But, as I think about it, Jesus had no desire to be with them either. After all, he did leave them, didn't he? He had every intention of getting away and being alone. So what happened? Why didn't he tell them to get lost? What made him change his mind and spend the day with the people he was trying to avoid?

Answer? Take a look at five words in Matthew 14:14: "He had compassion on them."

The Greek word used for compassion in this passage is *splanchnizomai*, which won't mean much to you unless you are in the health professions and studied "splanchnology" in school. If so, you remember that "splanchnology" is a study of the visceral parts. Or, in contemporary jargon, a study of the gut.

When Matthew writes that Jesus had compassion on the people, he is not saying that Jesus felt casual pity for them. No, the term is far more graphic. Matthew is saying that Jesus felt their hurt in his gut:

- He felt the limp of the crippled.
- He felt the hurt of the diseased.
- He felt the loneliness of the leper.
- He felt the embarrassment of the sinful.

And once he felt their hurts, he couldn't help but heal their hurts. He was moved in the stomach by their needs. He was so touched by their needs that he forgot his own needs. He was so moved by the people's hurts that he put his hurts on the back burner.

Maybe that's why God brings hurting people into your world, too. All solitude and no service equals selfishness. Some solitude and some service, however, equals perspective.

Here's a story to illustrate my point.

When I was in high school, our family used to fish every year during spring break. One year my brother and my mom couldn't go, so my dad let me invite a friend. I asked Mark. He was a good pal and a great sport. He got permission from his parents, and we began planning our trip.

Days before leaving, we could already anticipate the vacation. We could feel the sun warming our bodies as we floated in the boat. We could feel the yank of the rod and hear the spin of the reel as we wrestled the white bass into the boat. And we could smell the fish frying in an open skillet over an open fire.

We could hardly wait. Days passed like cold molasses. Finally spring break arrived. We loaded our camper and set out for the lake.

We arrived late at night, unfolded the camper, and went to bed—dreaming of tomorrow's day in the sun. But during the night, an unseasonably strong norther blew in. It got cold fast! The wind was so strong that we could barely open the camper door the next morning. The sky was gray. The lake was a mountain range of white-topped waves. There was no way we could fish in that weather.

"No problem," we said. "We'll spend the day in the camper. After all, we have Monopoly. We have *Reader's Digest*. We all know a few jokes. It's not what we came to do, but we'll make the best of it and fish tomorrow."

So, huddled in the camper with a Coleman stove and a Monopoly board, we three fishermen passed the day—indoors. The hours passed slowly, but they did pass. Night finally came, and we crawled into the sleeping bags dreaming of angling.

Were we in for a surprise. The next morning it wasn't the wind that made the door hard to open, it was the ice!

We tried to be cheerful. "No problem," we mumbled. "We can play Monopoly . . . again. We can reread the stories in *Reader's Digest*. And surely we know another joke or two." But as courageous as we tried to be, it was obvious that some of the gray had left the sky and entered our camper.

I began to notice a few things I hadn't seen before. I noticed that Mark had a few personality flaws. He was a bit too cocky about his opinions. He was easily irritated and constantly edgy. He couldn't take any constructive criticism. Even though his socks did stink, he didn't think it was my business to tell him.

"Just looking out for the best interest of my dad's camper," I defended, expecting Dad to come to my aid.

But Dad just sat over in the corner, reading. *Humph*, I thought, *where is he when I need him?* And then, I began to see Dad in a different light. When I mentioned to him that the eggs were soggy and the toast was burnt, he invited me to try my hand at the portable stove. *Touchy, touchy*, I said to myself. *Nothing like being cooped up in a camper with someone to help you see his real nature.*

It was a long day. It was a long, cold night.

When we awoke the next morning to the sound of sleet slapping the canvas, we didn't even pretend to be cheerful. We were flat-out grumpy. Mark became more of a jerk with each passing moment; I wondered what spell of ignorance I must have been in when I invited him. Dad couldn't do anything right; I wondered how someone so irritable could have such an even-tempered son. We sat in misery the whole day, our fishing equipment still unpacked.

The next day was even colder. "We're going home" were my father's first words. No one objected.

I learned a hard lesson that week. Not about fishing, but about people.

When those who are called to fish don't fish, they fight.

When energy intended to be used outside is used inside, the result is explosive. Instead of casting nets, we cast stones. Instead of extending helping hands, we point accusing fingers. Instead of being fishers of the lost, we become critics of the saved. Rather than helping the hurting, we hurt the helpers.

The result? Church Scrooges. "Bah humbug" spirituality. Beady eyes searching for warts on others while ignoring the warts on the nose below. Crooked fingers that bypass strengths and point out weaknesses.

Split churches. Poor testimonies. Broken hearts. Legalistic wars.

And, sadly, poor go unfed, confused go uncounseled, and lost go unreached.

When those who are called to fish don't fish, they fight.

But note the other side of this fish tale: When those who are called to fish, fish—they flourish!

Nothing handles a case of the gripes like an afternoon service project. Nothing restores perspective better than a visit to a hospital ward. Nothing unites soldiers better than a common task.

Leave soldiers inside the barracks with no time on the front line and see what happens to their attitude. The soldiers will invent things to complain about. Bunks will be too hard. Food will be too cold. Leadership will be too tough. The company will be too stale. Yet place those same soldiers in the trench and let them duck a few bullets, and what was a boring barracks will seem like a haven. The beds will feel great. The food will be almost ideal. The leadership will be courageous. The company will be exciting.

When those who are called to fish, fish—they flourish!

Jesus knew that.

When he arrived at Bethsaida, he was sorrowful, tired, and anxious to be alone with the disciples. No one would have blamed him had he dismissed the crowds a second time. No one would have criticized him had he waved away the people. But he didn't. Later he would. Later he would demand their departure and seek solitude.

But not before he "healed their sick"[3] and taught them "many things."[4] Self was forgotten . . . others were served . . . and stress was relieved.

Make a note of that. The next time the challenges "outside" tempt you to shut the door and stay inside, stay long enough to get warm. Then get out. When those who are called to fish don't fish, they fight.

5

THE
JOY
IN
THE
JOURNEY

S HE SAT IN 14E, and I sat in 14D.

She was rural, and I was urban. She was backward, and I was sophisticated. She was homey, and I was "professional." But she could see, and I was blind.

"They sure do put these seats close up against each other, don't they," she said as I sat down.

Her face was ten inches from mine. She had basset-hound cheeks; her eyebrows peaked over her nose; and her jowls sagged. She smiled so widely you could see the cavity on her upper side. Her neck seemed to lean out of her shoulders at a forty-five-degree angle, leaving her head in front of her shoulders rather than above them. She wore a Dutch-bob haircut and a blue, velour pants suit.

I don't know if she was old or just looked old. But I do know one thing: She'd never flown.

"I don't do this too much, do you?"

When I told her I did, her eyes widened. "Oooh, that must be fu-un." (She could add a syllable to any word.)

I groaned to myself. I already had a bad attitude. My week had been hectic. The plane was late and overbooked. I had a toothache and had left the tooth medicine at the hotel. I wanted to sleep, but I had work to do. And now I was sitting next to Gomer Pyle's mother.

"Oooh, boy, look at that one!"

She pointed at the plane ahead of us on the runway.

"Is this one that big?"

"Yes." I hoped my brief response would show her that I wasn't up for chitchat. It didn't.

"I'm going to see my boy in Dallas. Do you ever go to Dallas? I hope he's OK. He had a stomach flu last week. He's got a new dog. I can't wait to see it. It's a Labrador. Do you know what that is? They are big and lovable and . . ."

She was uncanny. Not only could she add a syllable to every word, she could answer her own questions.

As we were taking off, however, she got quiet. For several moments she said nothing. Then she suddenly let out a sound that would have called the pigs for dinner.

"Oooooeeee, those trees down there look like peat moss!"

People seated around us turned and stared like I was E. F. Hutton.

"What river is that?"

I told her I didn't know, so she flagged down a stewardess.

When the drinks came around, I asked for a Coke; she asked for the list.

"Tell me again?" So the stewardess told her again. "Oh, it's so hard to choose," she giggled. But she finally chose.

When they brought her the drink, she exclaimed that she didn't know apple juice came in cans. And when they brought her a sandwich, she opened the box and proclaimed loud enough for the pilot to hear, "Why, they even put mayonnaise in here."

When I pulled out my laptop computer, she was enthralled. "Now isn't that clever."

And that went on . . . the whole flight. She didn't miss a thing. If she wasn't staring out the window, she was amazed by a magazine. If she wasn't talking, she was "ooohing." She played with her fan. She turned her light on and off. She toyed with her seat belt. She savored her lunch. When we went through turbulence, I looked over at her to be sure she was all right, and she was grinning. You'd have thought she was riding the Ferris wheel at the county fair!

It occurred to me, about mid-journey, that she was the only person enjoying the trip.

The rest of us, the "sophisticated," were too mature to have fun. The man in front of me was discussing business trips to Japan, dropping more names than the U.S. Bureau of the Census. The fellow behind me was ordering beers— two at a time. The lady to my right was up to her eyebrows in paperwork. And I was staring at a computer screen—eyes tired, mouth hurting, stressed-out, trying to find a message for stress-filled people and never noticing that the message was sitting beside me.

And I might never have noticed had she not leaned over and said to me at the end of the flight. "Son, I may be out of place in saying this, but you've worked the entire trip. You need to relax, boy. You need to put that machine up and enjoy the journey."

Gulp.

I smiled weakly and mumbled some excuse about needing to get the work done before tomorrow. But she wasn't listening. She was squeezing her hands together in excitement as we landed.

"Wasn't that a fu-un trip?" she asked as we were leaving the plane.

I didn't say anything. I just nodded and smiled. Off she walked, bouncing down the concourse as curious as a six-year-old. I watched her as long as I could, then turned to go to my next flight with a lesson learned.

I resolved to keep my eyes open.

It does little good, I decided, to make the trip and miss the journey.

6

REMARKABLE

SOMETHING HAPPENED A FEW weeks ago that could be filed in the folder labeled "Remarkable."

I was playing basketball at the church one Saturday morning. (A good number of guys show up each week to play.) Some are flat-bellies—guys in their twenties who can touch their toes when they stretch and touch the rim when they jump. The rest of us are fat-bellies—guys who are within eyesight of, if not over the top of, the hill. Touching our toes is no longer an option. Looking down and *seeing* our toes is the current challenge. We never touch the rim when we jump and seldom touch it when we shoot.

But the flat-bellies don't mind if the fat-bellies play. (They don't have a choice. We have the keys to the building.)

Anyway, a few Saturdays back we were in the middle of a game when I went up for a rebound. I must have been pretty slow because, just as I was going up for the ball, someone else was already coming down with it. And the only thing I got from the jump was a finger in the eye.

When I opened my eye, everything was blurry. I knew my contact lens was not where it used to be. I thought I felt it in the corner of my eye, so I waved out of the game and ran to the rest room. But after I looked in the mirror, I realized that it must have fallen out on the floor somewhere.

I ran back onto the court. The guys were at the opposite end, leaving the goal under which I had lost my contact lens vacant.

I hurried out, got down on my knees, and began to search. No luck. When the fellows started bringing the ball downcourt, they saw what I was doing and came to help. All ten of us were down on our knees, panting like puppies and sweating like Pony Express horses.

But no one could find the silly lens.

We were just about to give up when one fellow exclaimed, "There it is." I looked up. He was pointing at a player's shoulder. The same guy whose finger had explored my cornea.

There, on his shoulder, was my lens. It had fallen on him . . . stuck to his skin . . . stayed on his back all the way down the court while he jumped and bounced . . . and then ridden all the way back.

Remarkable.

Even more remarkable when you consider that the contact lens made this round trip on the back of a flat-belly. One of the guys who can touch the rim and his toes. Had it landed on the shoulder of one of the "top-of-the-hill guys," no one would have been impressed. Some of us have the mobility of grazing buffalo. But when you think of the ride the tiny piece of plastic took, when you think of the odds of it being found, you have only one place to put this event: in the folder labeled "Remarkable."

The more I thought about this event, the more remarkable it became.

The more remarkable it became, the more I learned about remarkable things.

I learned that remarkable things usually occur in unremarkable situations, i.e., Saturday morning basketball games.

I also noticed that there are more remarkable things going on than those I usually see. In fact, as I began to look around, I found more and more things that I'd labeled "To be expected" that deserve to be labeled "Well what do you know."

Examples?

My money is in a bank with at least several thousand other folks' money. Who knows how many transactions are made every day? Who knows how much money goes into that place and is taken out? But somehow, if I want some money or just want to know how much money I have, the bank teller can give me what I want.

Remarkable.

Each morning I climb into a truck that weighs half a ton and take it out on an interstate where I—and a thousand other drivers—turn our vehicles into sixty-mile-per-hour missiles. Although I've had a few scares and mishaps, I still whistle while I drive at a speed that would have caused my great-grandfather to pass out.

Remarkable.

Every day I have the honor of sitting down with a book that contains the words of the One who created me. Every day I have the opportunity to let him give me a thought or two on how to live.

If I don't do what he says, he doesn't burn the book or cancel my subscription. If I disagree with what he says, lightning doesn't split my swivel chair or an angel doesn't mark my name off the holy list. If I don't understand what he says, he doesn't call me a dummy.

In fact, he calls me "Son," and on a different page explains what I don't understand.

Remarkable.

At the end of the day when I walk through the house, I step into the bedrooms of three little girls. Their covers are usually kicked off, so I cover them up. Their hair usually hides their faces, so I brush it back. And one by one, I bend over and kiss the foreheads of the angels God has loaned me. Then I stand in the doorway and wonder why in the world he would entrust a stumbling, fumbling fellow like me with the task of loving and leading such treasures.

Remarkable.

Then I go and crawl into bed with a woman far wiser than I . . . a woman who deserves a man much better looking than I . . . but a woman who would argue that fact and tell me from the bottom of her heart that I'm the best thing to come down her pike.

After I think about the wife I have, and when I think that I get to be with her for a lifetime, I shake my head and thank the God of grace for grace and think, *Remarkable*.

In the morning, I'll do it all again. I'll drive down the same road. Go to the same office. Call on the same bank. Kiss the same girls. And crawl into bed with the same woman. But I'm learning not to take these everyday miracles for granted.

Just think, it all came out of a basketball game. Ever since I found that contact, I've seen things a lot clearer.

I'm discovering many things: traffic jams eventually clear up, sunsets are for free, Little League is a work of art, and most planes take off and arrive on time. I'm learning that most folks are good folks who are just as timid as I am about starting a conversation.

I'm meeting people who love their country and their God and their church and would die for any of the three.

I'm learning that if I look . . . if I open my eyes and observe . . . there are many reasons to take off my hat, look at the Source of it all, and just say thanks.

7

THANKS
FOR
THE
BREAD

*D*EAR FRIEND,
    I'm writing to say thanks. I wish I could thank you personally, but I don't know where you are. I wish I could call you, but I don't know your name. If I knew your appearance, I'd look for you, but your face is fuzzy in my memory. But I'll never forget what you did.

There you were, leaning against your pickup in the West Texas oil field. An engineer of some sort. A supervisor on the job. Your khakis and clean shirt set you apart from us roustabouts. In the oil field pecking order, we were at the bottom. You were the boss. We were the workers. You read the blueprints. We dug the ditches. You inspected the pipe. We laid it. You ate with the bosses in the shed. We ate with each other in the shade.

Except that day.

I remember wondering why you did it.

We weren't much to look at. What wasn't sweaty was oily. Faces burnt from the sun; skin black from the grease. Didn't bother me, though. I was there only for the summer. A high-school boy earning good money laying pipe. For me, it was a summer job. For the others, it was a way of life. Most were illegal immigrants from Mexico. Others were drifters, bouncing across the prairie as rootless as tumbleweeds.

We weren't much to listen to, either. Our language was sandpaper coarse. After lunch, we'd light the cigarettes and begin the jokes. Someone always had a deck of cards with lacy-clad girls on the back. For thirty minutes in the heat of the day, the oil patch became Las Vegas—replete with foul language, dirty stories, blackjack, and barstools that doubled as lunch pails.

In the middle of such a game, you approached us. I thought you had a job for us that couldn't wait another few minutes. Like the others, I groaned when I saw you coming.

You were nervous. You shifted your weight from one leg to the other as you began to speak.

"Uh, fellows," you started.

We turned and looked up at you.

"I, uh, I just wanted, uh, to invite . . ."

You were way out of your comfort zone. I had no idea what you might be about to say, but I knew that it had nothing to do with work.

"I just wanted to tell you that, uh, our church is having a service tonight and, uh . . ."

"What?" I couldn't believe it. "He's talking church? Out here? With us?"

"I wanted to invite any of you to come along."

Silence. Screaming silence. The same silence you'd hear if a nun asked a madam if she could use the brothel for a mass. The same silence you'd hear if an IRS representative invited the Mafia to a seminar on tax integrity.

Several guys stared at the dirt. A few shot glances at the others. Snickers rose just inches from the surface.

"Well, that's it. Uh, if any of you want to go . . . uh, let me know."

After you turned and left, we turned and laughed. We called you "reverend," "preacher," and "the pope." We poked fun at each other, daring one another to go. You became the butt of the day's jokes.

I'm sure you knew that. I'm sure you went back to your truck knowing the only good you'd done was to make a good fool out of yourself. If that's what you thought, then you were wrong.

That's the reason for this letter.

I thought of you this week. I thought of you when I read about someone else who took a risk at lunch. I thought of you when I read the story of the little boy who gave his lunch to Jesus.[1]

His lunch wasn't much. In fact, it wasn't anything compared to what was needed for more than five thousand people.

He probably wrestled with the silliness of it all. What was one lunch for so many? He probably asked himself if it was even worth the effort.

How far could one lunch go?

I think that's why he didn't give the lunch to the crowd. Instead he gave it to Jesus. Something told him that if he would plant the seed, God would grant the crop.

So he did.

He summoned his courage, got up off the grass, and walked into the circle of grownups. He was as out of place in that cluster as you were in ours. He must have been nervous. No one likes to appear silly.

Someone probably snickered at him, too.

If they didn't snicker, they shook their heads. "The little fellow doesn't know any better."

If they didn't shake their heads, they rolled their eyes. "Here we have a hunger crisis, and this little boy thinks that a sack lunch will solve it."

But it wasn't the men's heads or eyes that the boy saw; he saw only Jesus.

You must have seen Jesus, too, when you made your decision. Most people would have considered us to be unlikely deacon material. Most would have saved their seeds for softer soil. And they'd have been almost right. But Jesus said to give . . . so you gave.

As I think about it, you and the little boy have a lot in common:

- You both used your lunch to help others.
- You both chose faith over logic.
- You both brought a smile to your Father's face.

There's one difference, though. The boy got to see what Jesus did with his gift, and you didn't. That's why I'm writing. I want you to know that at least one of the seeds fell into a fertile crevice.

Some five years later, a college sophomore was struggling with a decision. He had drifted from the faith given to him by his parents. He wanted to come back. He wanted to come home. But the price was high. His friends might laugh. His habits would have to change. His reputation would have to be overcome.

Could he do it? Did he have the courage?

That's when I thought of you. As I sat in my dorm room late one night, looking for the guts to do what I knew was right, I thought of you.

I thought of how your love for God had been greater than your love for your reputation.

I thought of how your obedience had been greater than your common sense.

I remembered how you had cared more about making disciples than about making a good first impression. And when I thought of you, your memory became my motivation.

So I came home.

I've told your story dozens of times to thousands of people. Each time the reaction is the same: The audience becomes a sea of smiles, and heads bob in understanding. Some smile because they think of the "clean-shirted engineers" in their lives. They remember the neighbor who brought the cake, the aunt who wrote the letter, the teacher who listened . . .

Others smile because they have done what you did. And they, too, wonder if their "lunchtime loyalty" was worth the effort.

You wondered that. What you did that day wasn't much. And I'm sure you walked away that day thinking that your efforts had been wasted.

They weren't.

So I'm writing to say thanks. Thanks for the example. Thanks for the courage. Thanks for giving your lunch to God. He did something with it; it became the Bread of Life for me.

> Gratefully,
> Max

P.S. If by some remarkable coincidence you read this and remember that day, please give me a call. I owe you lunch.

8

MUSINGS
IN
MINNEAPOLIS

*I*T'S A LONG WAY FROM BOSTON, Massachusetts to Edmonton, Canada. No matter how you cut it or route it, it's a long way.

My journey today began around 1:30 PM I spoke where I was supposed to speak and changed into my Reeboks just in time to fight traffic all the way to Logan Airport.

The plane was overbooked; some folks were mad. The plane was also designed by a five-foot, four-inch engineer who hates tall people. (I ate my knees for lunch.) The plane arrived late into Minneapolis, where I was to change planes.

Now, I know I'm not supposed to complain. I've heard myself preach sermons on gratitude. And I know that a million people in the world would love to have the airline peanuts I threw away today. But still, I got off the plane with a cramp in my leg, an empty stomach, a bad attitude, and three more hours of travel to go.

On the way to my next plane, I saw a McDonald's. Looked good. Did I have time? Then I saw something better: a phone.

I walked over, set down my bags, and called home. Denalyn answered. I love it when she answers. She's always glad when I call. When she gets to heaven, Saint Peter will give her the receptionist job at the gate.

We spent twenty minutes talking about major Pentagon-level topics like the weather in New England and the weather in San Antonio. We talked about the fact that Jenna had a friend coming over to spend the night and that Sara might have a fever. I told her about the Canadian, French-speaking English teacher I sat next to on the plane, and she told me about the new elementary school.

We made no decisions. We solved no problems. We re-solved no major conflicts. We just talked. And I felt better.

Jenna got on the phone and asked me when I was coming home, and it felt good to be wanted.

Andrea got on the phone and told me she loved me, and it felt good to be loved.

Jenna put the phone next to baby Sara's ear, and I talked baby talk in the middle of the airport. (Some people turned to stare.) But I didn't care because Sara cooed, and it felt good to be cooed at.

Denalyn got back on the phone and said, "I'm glad you called." And I hung up happy.

Now I'm back on the plane and my attitude is back on track. The plane is delayed because the runway is backed up, which means I'll get into Edmonton an hour later than I planned. I don't know who is going to pick me up, and I can't remember to whom I'm supposed to speak tomorrow. But that's OK.

I can handle being a pilgrim as long as I know that I can call home whenever I want.

Jesus could . . . and he did.

Maybe that's the rationale behind verse 19 of Matthew 14: "Taking the five loaves and the two fish and looking up to heaven, he gave thanks and broke the loaves." I'd always chalked this prayer up to, at best, a good example—at worst, a good habit.

Until now.

Now it occurs to me that Jesus needed to call home in the middle of the hassles as much as I did. He was surrounded by people who wanted food and disciples who wanted a break. His heart was heavy from the death of John the Baptist.

He needed a minute with someone who would understand.

Maybe he, like me, got a bit weary of the hassles of getting a job done in a distant land and needed to call home.

So he did. He chatted with the One he loved. He heard the sound of the home he missed. And he was reminded that when all hell breaks loose, all heaven draws near.

Maybe you should call home, too. God will be glad when you do—but not half as glad as you will be.

9

FENDING OFF THE VOICES

YOU WANT SUCCESS? Here's your model. You want achievement? Here's your prototype. You want bright lights, pageants, and media attention? Consider the front-page, center article of the nation's largest daily newspaper.

It is a caricature of "Miss America." The "vital" data of the fifty-one participants has been compiled to present the perfect woman. She has brown hair. She has brown eyes. She knows how to sing and has a perfect figure: 35–24–35. She is Miss America. She is the ideal.

The message trumpets off the page: "This is the standard for American women." The implication is clear: Do what it takes to be like her. Firm your thighs. Deepen your cleavage. Pamper your hair. Improve your walk.

No reference is made to her convictions . . . to her honesty . . . to her faith . . . or to her God. But you are told her hip size.

In a small photo, four inches to the left, is another woman. Her face is thin. Her skin is wrinkled, almost leathery. No makeup . . . no blush . . . no lipstick. There is a faint smile on her lips and a glint in her eyes.

She looks pale. Perhaps it's my imagination or perhaps it's true. The caption reads, "Mother Teresa: In serious condition."[1]

Mother Teresa. You know her story. When she won the Nobel Peace Prize in 1985, she gave the two hundred

thousand dollars to the poor of Calcutta. When a businessman bought her a new car, she sold it and gave the money
to the underprivileged. She owns nothing. She owes nothing.

Two women: Miss America and Mother Teresa. One
walks the boardwalk; the other works the alley. Two voices.
One promises crowns, flowers, and crowds. The other
promises service, surrender, and joy.

Now, I have nothing against beauty pageants (although
I have my reservations about them). But I do have something against the lying voices that noise our world.

You've heard them. They tell you to swap your integrity
for a new sale. To barter your convictions for an easy deal. To
exchange your devotion for a quick thrill.

They whisper. They woo. They taunt. They tantalize.
They flirt. They flatter. "Go ahead, it's OK." "Just wait until tomorrow." "Don't worry, no one will know." "How could
anything that feels so right be so wrong?"

The voices of the crowd.

Our lives are Wall Streets of chaos, stock markets loud
with demands. Grown men and women barking in a frenzied
effort to get all they can before time runs out. "Buy. Sell.
Trade. Swap. But whatever you do, do it fast—and loud."

A carnival of gray-flannel suits where no one smiles
and everyone dashes.

An endless chorus of booming voices: some offering,
some taking, and all screaming.

What do we do with the voices?

As I work on this manuscript, I'm seated at a desk in
a hotel room. I'm away from home. Away from people who
know me. Away from family members who love me.

Voices that encourage and affirm are distant.

But voices that tantalize and entice are near. Although
the room is quiet, if I listen, their voices are crystal clear.

A placard on my nightstand invites me to a lounge in the lobby, where I can "make new friends in a relaxing atmosphere." An advertisement on top of the television promises me that with the request of a late-night adult movie my "fantasies will come true." In the phone book, several columns of escort services offer "love away from home." An attractive, gold-lettered volume in the drawer of the nightstand beckons: *The Book of Mormon—Another Testament of Jesus Christ.* On television a talk-show host discusses the day's topic: "How to succeed at sex in the office."

Voices. Some for pleasure. Some for power.

Some promise acceptance. Some promise tenderness. But all promise something.

Even the voices that Jesus heard promised something.

"After the people saw the miraculous sign that Jesus did, they began to say, 'Surely this is the Prophet who is to come into the world.'"[2]

To the casual observer, these are the voices of victory. To the untrained ear, these are the sounds of triumph. What could be better? Five thousand men plus women and children proclaiming Christ to be the prophet. Thousands of voices swelling into a roar of revival, an ovation of adulation.

The people have everything they need for a revolution.

They have an enemy: Herod. They have a martyr: John the Baptist. They have leadership: the disciples. They have ample supplies: Jesus the bread maker. And they have a king: Jesus of Nazareth.

Why wait? The time has come. Israel will be restored. God's people have heard God's voice.

"King Jesus!" someone proclaims. And the crowd chimes in.

And don't think for a minute that Christ didn't hear their chant.

A chorus promising power intoxicates. No cross needed. No sacrifice required. An army of disciples at his fingertips. Power to change the world without having to die doing it.

Revenge would be sweet. *The one who took the head of John the Baptist is only a few miles away. I wonder if he has ever felt a cold blade on his neck.*

Yes, Jesus heard the voices. He heard the lurings. But he also heard someone else.

And when Jesus heard him, he sought him.

"Jesus, knowing that they intended to come and make him king by force, withdrew again to a mountain by himself."[3]

Jesus preferred to be alone with the true God rather than in a crowd with the wrong people.

Logic didn't tell him to dismiss the crowds. Conventional wisdom didn't tell him to turn his back on a willing army. No, it wasn't a voice from without that Jesus heard. It was a voice from within.

The mark of a sheep is its ability to hear the Shepherd's voice.

"The sheep listen to his voice. He calls his own sheep by name and leads them out."[4]

The mark of a disciple is his or her ability to hear the Master's voice.

"Here I am! I stand at the door and knock. If anyone hears my voice and opens the door, I will come in and eat with him, and he with me."[5]

The world rams at your door; Jesus taps at your door. The voices scream for your allegiance; Jesus softly and tenderly requests it. The world promises flashy pleasure;

Jesus promises a quiet dinner . . . with God. "I will come in and eat."

Which voice do you hear?

Let me state something important. There is never a time during which Jesus is not speaking. Never. There is never a place in which Jesus is not present. Never. There is never a room so dark . . . a lounge so sensual . . . an office so sophisticated . . . that the ever-present, ever-pursuing, relentlessly tender Friend is not there, tapping gently on the doors of our hearts—waiting to be invited in.

Few hear his voice. Fewer still open the door.

But never interpret our numbness as his absence. For amidst the fleeting promises of pleasure is the timeless promise of his presence.

"Surely I am with you always, to the very end of the age."[6]

"'Never will I leave you; never will I forsake you.'"[7]

There is no chorus so loud that the voice of God cannot be heard . . . if we will but listen.

That's true in this hotel room.

It took me a few minutes to find it, but I did. It wasn't as visible as the lounge placard or the movie advertisement. But it was there. It wasn't as fancy as the Mormon Bible or as attention-grabbing as the escort ads. But I'd give up those lies every time for the peace I've found in this treasure.

A Bible. A simple, hard-covered, Gideon-placed, King James Version Bible. It took me a few minutes to find it, but I did. And when I did, I opened it to one of my favorite voice passages:

> A time is coming when all who are in their graves will hear his voice and come out—those who have done good will rise to live, and those who have done evil will rise to be condemned.[8]

Interesting. A day is coming when everyone will hear his voice. A day is coming when all the other voices will be silenced; his voice—and his voice only—will be heard.

Some will hear his voice for the very first time. It's not that he never spoke, it's just that they never listened. For these, God's voice will be the voice of a stranger. They will hear it once—and never hear it again. They will spend eternity fending off the voices they followed on earth.

But others will be called from their graves by a familiar voice. For they are sheep who know their shepherd. They are servants who opened the door when Jesus knocked.

Now the door will open again. Only this time, it won't be Jesus who walks into our house; it will be we, who walk into his.

10

THE
PHOTO
AND
THE
FILE

*E*ACH JUNE I PUT MY CALENDAR together for the coming year. June is the month of D-Day. I don't mean D-Day as in Normandy invasion. I mean D-Day as in decisions to be made.

This morning I began the process of decision. I opened the "Decision File" and began reading the speaking invitations. A church planter in Wyoming wonders if I could spend time with his church. A church camp in Washington invites me to speak to its campers. A missionary in India has read my books and asks, "If I can come up with the money, can you spend a week with us?"

Something happens as a person fields the invitations of others. He or she begins to feel important.

As I looked at the letters, it dawned on me how vital I was to the progress of humanity.

I wondered how the earth stayed on its axis before I was born. I nodded my head in understanding at the letter that read, "You are the one for this meeting." I put my hand under my shirt and rubbed the S on the red jersey—"Super Max."

I was feeling puffy and proud when I read the last letter. But as I put down the file, I noticed another request. One that didn't make it into the folder. One that was lying on my desk.

It had no date, no signature, no deadline. It wasn't a letter or a phone message. It was a photograph—a photograph so recent that it had no frame. It was a portrait of a mom and a dad encircled by three little girls. Our family portrait.

The positioning of the photo and the file struck me. There was something symbolic about the way I'd unintentionally placed the letters next to the family picture. The singular photo lying in the shadow of the stack of requests seemed to whisper a question that only I could answer:

"Max, who will win?"

There is only so much sand in the hourglass. Who gets it?

You know what I'm talking about, don't you? Since you don't stockpile your requests until June, your situation may not be as graphic as mine. But it's every bit as real.

"The PTA needs a new treasurer. With your background and experience and talent and wisdom and love for kids and degree in accounting, YOU are the perfect one for the job!"

"There's going to be some shuffling in the ranks. With the retirement of the branch manager, *somebody* will move up. The company is looking for a bright, young salesman—someone like you—who is willing to demonstrate his dedication to the organization by taking on some extra projects . . . and working some late hours."

"I apologize that I have to ask you again, but you are such a good Sunday-school teacher. If you could only take one more quarter . . ."

"I just lost my hygienist. Will you come back to work for me? I know you don't want to go back to work until your children start school. But it's only four hours a day and there's a day-care center just a few blocks from my office now. Wouldn't the extra money be nice?"

"Would I be willing to serve as chapter president? Well, to be honest, I was going to sit out this term because our youngest goes to college next fall. Yes, I realize this is a critical year for the organization. . . . Oh, no, I wouldn't want the club to falter. . . . Yes, we have made great progress over the last few months. It's just that . . ."

It's tug-of-war, and you are the rope.

On one side are the requests for your time and energy. They call. They compliment. They are valid and good. Great opportunities to do good things. If they were evil, it'd be easy to say no. But they aren't, so it's easy to rationalize.

On the other side are the loved ones in your world. They don't write you letters. They don't ask you to consult your calendar. They don't offer to pay your expenses. They don't use terms like "appointment," "engagement," or "do lunch." They don't want you for what you can do for them; they want you for who you are.

Clovis Chappell, a minister from a century back, used to tell the story of two paddleboats. They left Memphis about the same time, traveling down the Mississippi River to New Orleans. As they traveled side by side, sailors from one vessel made a few remarks about the snail's pace of the other.

Words were exchanged. Challenges were made. And the race began. Competition became vicious as the two boats roared through the Deep South.

One boat began falling behind. Not enough fuel. There had been plenty of coal for the trip, but not enough for a race. As the boat dropped back, an enterprising young sailor took some of the ship's cargo and tossed it into the ovens. When the sailors saw that the supplies burned as well as the coal, they fueled their boat with the material they had been assigned to transport. They ended up winning the race, but burned their cargo.

God has entrusted cargo to us, too: children, spouses, friends. Our job is to do our part in seeing that this cargo reaches its destination.

Yet when the program takes priority over people, people often suffer.

How much cargo do we sacrifice in order to achieve the number one slot? How many people never reach the destination because of the aggressiveness of a competitive captain?

A world of insight is hidden in four words in Matthew 14:22: "He dismissed the crowd." This wasn't just *any* crowd that Jesus dismissed.

These weren't casually curious.

These weren't coincidental bystanders.

This was a multitude with a mission. They had heard the disciples. They had left their homes. They had followed Jesus around the sea. They had heard him teach and had seen him heal. They had eaten the bread. And they were ready to make him king.

Surely Jesus will commandeer the crowd and focus their frenzy. Surely he will seize the chance to convert the thousands. Surely he will spend the night baptizing the willing followers. No one would turn down an opportunity to minister to thousands of people, right?

Jesus did.

"He dismissed the crowd." Why? Read verse 23: "After he had dismissed them, he went up on a mountainside by himself to pray."

He said no to the important in order to say yes to the vital.

He said no to a good opportunity in order to say yes to a better opportunity. It wasn't a selfish decision. It was a deliberate choice to honor priorities. If Jesus thought it necessary to say no to the demands of the crowds in order to pray, don't you think you and I should, too?

"Blessed are the meek,"[1] Jesus said. The word *meek* does not mean weak. It means focused. It is a word used to describe a domesticated stallion. Power under control. Strength with a direction.

Blessed are those who are harnessed. Blessed are those who recognize their God-given responsibilities. Blessed are those who acknowledge that there is only one God and have quit applying for his position. Blessed are those who know what on earth they are on earth to do and set themselves about the business of doing it. Blessed are those who are able to "discern what is best."[2]

As I looked at the photo and the file, I decided to try something. I decided to make a list of what I would lose by saying no to my family one night. It wasn't hard to do; I just made a list of what I would have missed by not being home with my family last night.

I could have been out of town this week. I had an invitation to be in the Midwest at a church. I turned it down. What if I hadn't? If I had gone, I would have had the attention of a thousand people for an hour. I would have had the opportunity to speak about Jesus to some people who don't know him. Is a Tuesday evening at home with three children and a spouse more important than preaching to an audience?

Read my list of what I would have missed. Then you decide.

I would have missed a trip to the swimming pool in which I saw Jenna climb onto her inner tube for the first time.

I would have missed fifteen minutes of bouncing up and down in the shallow end of the pool, with Andrea clinging to my neck singing the theme from "Sleeping Beauty."

I would have missed seeing Denalyn get sentimental as she unpacked a box of baby clothes.

I wouldn't have gone on a walk with the girls during which Jenna found ten "special" rocks.

I wouldn't have been there to hold Andrea when her finger got slammed in the door.

I wouldn't have been there to answer Jenna's question: "Daddy, what is a handicapped person?"

I would have missed seeing Andrea giggle as she took Jenna's straw when Jenna's back was turned.

I wouldn't have heard Jenna tell the story of Jesus on the cross during our family devotional (when she assured us, "But he didn't stay dead!").

I wouldn't have seen Andrea make a muscle with her arm and sing, "Our God is so BIIIIIIIG!"

What do you think? I know my vote. There are a hundred speakers who could have addressed that crowd, but my girls just have one daddy.

After I made my list, just for the fun of it I picked up the phone and called the church that had asked me to come and speak this week. The minister wasn't in, but his secretary was. "Isn't this the week of your seminar?" I asked.

"Oh, yes! It has been a wonderful success!"

They didn't even miss me.

Now I've got a better idea what to do with my stack of requests.

STORMS
OF
DOUBT

11

SEEING GOD THROUGH SHATTERED GLASS

*T*HERE IS A WINDOW IN YOUR heart through which you can see God. Once upon a time that window was clear. Your view of God was crisp. You could see God as vividly as you could see a gentle valley or hillside. The glass was clean, the pane unbroken.

You knew God. You knew how he worked. You knew what he wanted you to do. No surprises. Nothing unexpected. You knew that God had a will, and you continually discovered what it was.

Then, suddenly, the window cracked. A pebble broke the window. A pebble of pain.

Perhaps the stone struck when you were a child and a parent left home—forever. Maybe the rock hit in adolescence when your heart was broken. Maybe you made it into adulthood before the window was cracked. But then the pebble came.

Was it a phone call? "We have your daughter at the station. You'd better come down."

Was it a letter on the kitchen table? "I've left. Don't try to reach me. Don't try to call me. It's over. I just don't love you anymore."

Was it a diagnosis from the doctor? "I'm afraid our news is not very good."

Was it a telegram? "We regret to inform you that your son is missing in action."

Whatever the pebble's form, the result was the same—a shattered window. The pebble missiled into the pane and shattered it. The crash echoed down the halls of your heart. Cracks shot out from the point of impact, creating a spider web of fragmented pieces.

And suddenly God was not so easy to see. The view that had been so crisp had changed. You turned to see God, and his figure was distorted. It was hard to see him through the pain. It was hard to see him through the fragments of hurt.

You were puzzled. God wouldn't allow something like this to happen, would he? Tragedy and travesty weren't on the agenda of the One you had seen, were they? Had you been fooled? Had you been blind?

The moment the pebble struck, the glass became a reference point for you. From then on, there was life before the pain and life after the pain. Before your pain, the view was clear; God seemed so near. After your pain, well, he was harder to see. He seemed a bit distant . . . harder to perceive. Your pain distorted the view—not eclipsed it, but distorted it.

Maybe these words don't describe your situation. There are some people who never have to redefine or refocus their view of God. Most of us do.

Most of us know what it means to feel disappointed by God.

Most of us have a way of completing this sentence: "If God is God, then . . ." Call it an agenda, a divine job description. Each of us has an unspoken, yet definitive, expectation of what God should do. "If God is God, then . . ."

• There will be no financial collapse in my family.

• My children will never be buried before me.

- People will treat me fairly.
- This church will never divide.
- My prayer will be answered.

These are not articulated criteria. They are not written down or notarized. But they are real. They define the expectations we have of God. And when pain comes into our world—when the careening pebble splinters the window of our hearts—these expectations go unmet and doubts may begin to surface.

We look for God, but can't find him. Fragmented glass hinders our vision. He is enlarged through this piece and reduced through that one. Lines jigsaw their way across his face. Large sections of shattered glass opaque the view.

And now you aren't quite sure what you see.

———————————

The disciples weren't sure what they saw, either.

Jesus failed to meet their expectations. The day Jesus fed the five thousand men he didn't do what they wanted him to do.

The Twelve returned from their mission followed by an army. They finished their training. They recruited the soldiers. They were ready for battle. They expected Jesus to let the crowds crown him as king and attack the city of Herod. They expected battle plans . . . strategies . . . a new era for Israel.

What did they get?

Just the opposite.

Instead of weapons, they got oars. Rather than being sent to fight, they were sent to float. The crowds were sent away. Jesus walked away. And they were left on the water with a storm brewing in the sky.

What kind of Messiah would do this?

Note carefully the sequence of the stormy evening as Matthew records it:

> Immediately Jesus made the disciples get into the boat and go on ahead of him to the other side, while he dismissed the crowd. After he had dismissed them, he went up on a mountainside by himself to pray. *When evening came* [emphasis mine], he was there alone, but the boat was already a considerable distance from land, buffeted by the waves because the wind was against it.[1]

Matthew is specific about the order of events. Jesus sent the disciples to the boat. Then he dismissed the crowd and ascended a mountainside. It was evening, probably around 6:00 PM. The storm struck immediately. The sun had scarcely set before typhoon-like winds began to roar.

Note that Jesus sent the disciples out into the storm *alone.* Even as he was ascending the mountainside, he could feel and hear the gale's force. Jesus was not ignorant of the storm. He was aware that a torrent was coming that would carpet-bomb the sea's surface. But he didn't turn around. The disciples were left to face the storm . . . alone.

The greatest storm that night was not in the sky; it was in the disciples' hearts. The greatest fear was not from seeing the storm-driven waves; it came from seeing the back of their leader as he left them to face the night with only questions as companions.

It was this fury that the disciples were facing that night. Imagine the incredible strain of bouncing from wave to wave in a tiny fishing vessel. One hour would weary you. Two hours would exhaust you.

Surely Jesus will help us, they thought. They'd seen him still storms like this before. On this same sea, they had awakened him during a storm, and he had commanded the skies to be silent. They'd seen him quiet the wind and soothe the waves. *Surely he will come off the mountain.*

But he doesn't. Their arms begin to ache from rowing. Still no sign of Jesus. Three hours. Four hours. The winds rage. The boat bounces. Still no Jesus. Midnight comes. Their eyes search for God—in vain.

By now the disciples have been on the sea for as long as six hours.

All this time they have fought the storm and sought the Master. And, so far, the storm is winning. And the Master is nowhere to be found.

"Where is he?" cried one.

"Has he forgotten us?" yelled another.

"He feeds thousands of strangers and yet leaves us to die?" muttered a third.

The Gospel of Mark adds compelling insight into the disciples' attitude. "They had not understood about the loaves; their hearts were hardened."[2]

What does Mark mean? Simply this. The disciples were mad. They began the evening in a huff. Their hearts were hardened toward Jesus because he fed the multitude. Their preference, remember, had been to "send the crowds away."[3] And Jesus had told them to feed the people. But they wouldn't try. They said it couldn't be done. They told Jesus to let the people take care of themselves.

Also keep in mind that the disciples had just spent some time on center stage. They'd tasted stardom. They were celebrities. They had rallied crowds. They had recruited an army. They were, no doubt, pretty proud of themselves. With chests a bit puffy and heads a bit swollen, they'd told Jesus, "Just send them away."

Jesus didn't. Instead, he chose to bypass the reluctant disciples and use the faith of an anonymous boy. What the disciples said couldn't be done was done—in spite of them, not through them.

They pouted. They sulked. Rather than being amazed at the miracle, they became mad at the Master. After all, they had felt foolish passing out the very bread they said could not be made. Add to that Jesus' command to go to the boat when they wanted to go to battle, and it's easier to understand why these guys are burning!

"Now what is Jesus up to, leaving us out on the sea on a night like this?"

It's 1:00 AM, no Jesus.

It's 2:00 AM, no Jesus.

Peter, Andrew, James, and John have seen storms like this. They are fishermen; the sea is their life. They know the havoc the gale-force winds can wreak. They've seen the splintered hulls float to shore. They've attended the funerals. They know, better than anyone, that this night could be their last. "Why doesn't he come?" they sputter.

Finally, he does. "During the fourth watch of the night [3:00 to 6:00 AM] Jesus went out to them, walking on the lake."[4]

Jesus came. He finally came. But between verse 24—being buffeted by waves—and verse 25—when Jesus appeared—a thousand questions are asked.

Questions you have probably asked, too. Perhaps you know the angst of being suspended between verses 24 and 25. Maybe you're riding a storm, searching the coastline for a light, a glimmer of hope. You know that Jesus knows what you are going through. You know that he's aware of your storm. But as hard as you look to find him, you can't see him. Maybe your heart, like the disciples' hearts, has been hardened by unmet expectations. Your pleadings for help are salted with angry questions.

The first section of this book spoke of stress; the second is about storms. Stress attacks your nerves. Storms attack your faith. Stress interrupts. Storms destroy. Stress comes like a siren. Storms come like a missile. Stress clouds the day. Storms usher in the night.

The question of stress is, *"How can I cope?"* The question of storms is, *"Where* is God and *why* would he do this?"*

The second section of this book is for you if the pebble of pain has struck the window of your heart, if you've known the horror of looking for God's face and seeing only his back as he ascends a mountainside.

In the following pages, you will discover hopeful chronicles to help you deal with your doubts. Let me introduce you to a few friends who learned to see through shattered glass.

- An entrepreneur, stripped of treasures, who found one treasure that no one could take.
- A father who learned of trust during a six-hour drive with three children.
- A mother superior in New Mexico who discovered that prayer—her last resort—was her best resort.
- A woodsman who taught a village the virtue of patience.
- God's son—dog-tired and heartsore—who found strength through heaven's friends.

Some stories are fiction, some are fact. Some are legendary, others are biblical. Some are humorous, others are serious. But all have a message for those who know the anxiety of searching for God in a storm.

The message? When you can't see him, trust him. The figure you see is not a ghost. The voice you hear is not the wind.

Jesus is closer than you've ever dreamed.

12

TWO FATHERS, TWO FEASTS

I DROVE THE FAMILY TO Grandma's last night for Thanksgiving. Three hours into the six-hour trip, I realized that I was in a theology lab.

A day with a car full of kids will teach you a lot about God. Transporting a family from one city to another is closely akin to God transporting us from our home to his. And some of life's stormiest hours occur when the passenger and the Driver disagree on the destination.

A journey is a journey, whether the destination be the Thanksgiving table or the heavenly one. Both demand patience, a good sense of direction, and a driver who knows that the feast at the end of the trip is worth the hassles in the midst of the trip.

The fact that my pilgrims were all under the age of seven only enriched my learning experience.

As minutes rolled into hours and our car rolled through the hills, I began to realize that what I was saying to my kids had a familiar ring. I had heard it before—from God. All of a sudden, the car became a classroom. I realized that I was doing for a few hours what God has done for centuries: encouraging travelers who'd rather rest than ride.

I shared the idea with Denalyn. We began to discover similarities between the two journeys. Here are a few we noted.

In order to reach the destination, we have to say no to some requests.

Can you imagine the outcome if a parent honored each request of each child during a trip? We'd inch our bloated bellies from one ice-cream store to the next. Our priority would be popcorn and our itinerary would read like a fast-food menu. "Go to the Cherry Malt and make a right. Head north until you find the Chili Cheeseburger. Stay north for 1,300 calories and bear left at the Giant Pizza. When you see the two-for-one Chili Dog Special, take the Pepto-Bismol Turnpike east for five convenience stores. At the sixth toilet . . ."

Can you imagine the chaos if a parent indulged every indulgence?

Can you imagine the chaos if God indulged each of ours?

No is a necessary word to take on a trip. Destination has to reign over Dairy Deluxe Ice Cream Sundae.

"For God has not *destined* us [emphasis mine] to the terrors of judgement, but to the full attainment of salvation through our Lord Jesus Christ."[1]

Note God's destiny for your life. Salvation.

God's overarching desire is that you reach that destiny. His itinerary includes stops that encourage your journey. He frowns on stops that deter you. When his sovereign plan and your earthly plan collide, a decision must be made. Who's in charge of this journey?

If God must choose between your earthly satisfaction and your heavenly salvation, which do you hope he chooses?

Me, too.

When I'm in the driver's seat as the father of my children, I remember that I'm in charge. But when I'm in the passenger's seat as a child of my Father, I forget that he's in charge. I forget that God is more concerned with my destiny than my belly (although my belly hasn't done too badly). And I complain when he says no.

The requests my children made last night on the road to Grandma's weren't evil. They weren't unfair. They weren't rebellious. In fact, we had a couple of cones and Cokes. But most of the requests were unnecessary.

My four-year-old daughter would argue that fact. From her viewpoint, another soft drink is indispensable to her happiness. I know otherwise, so I say no.

A forty-year-old adult would argue that fact. From his standpoint, a new boss is indispensable to his happiness. God knows otherwise and says no.

A thirty-year-old woman would argue that fact. From her standpoint, *that* man with *that* job and *that* name is exactly who she needs to be happy. Her Father, who is more concerned that she arrive at his City than at the altar, says, "Wait a few miles. There's a better option down the road."

"Wait!" she protests. "How long do I have to wait?"

Which takes us to a second similarity between the two journeys.

———————————————

Children have no concept of minutes or miles.
"We'll be there in three hours," I said.

"How long is three hours?" Jenna asked. (How do you explain time to a child who can't tell time?)

"Well, it's about as long as three Sesame Streets," I ventured.

The children groaned in unison. "Three Sesame Streets?! That's forever!"

And to them, it is.

And to us, it seems that way, too.

He who "lives forever"[2] has placed himself at the head of a band of pilgrims who mutter, "How long, O Lord? How long?"[3]

"How long must I endure this sickness?"

"How long must I endure this spouse?"

"How long must I endure this paycheck?"

Do you really want God to answer? He could, you know. He could answer in terms of the here and now with time increments we know. "Two more years on the illness." "The rest of your life in the marriage." "Ten more years for the bills."

But he seldom does that. He usually opts to measure the *here and now* against the *there and then*. And when you compare *this* life to *that* life, this life ain't long.

Our days on earth are like a shadow.[4]

Each man's life is but a breath.[5]

You are a mist that appears for a little while and then vanishes.[6]

As for man, his days are like grass, he flourishes like a flower of the field; the wind blows over it and it is gone, and its place remembers it no more.[7]

"It's a short journey," I offer to the children. "We're almost there."

I know. I've been there before. I've driven this road. I've covered this territory. For me, it's no challenge. Ah, but for the children, it's eternal.

So I try another approach. "Just think how good it will be," I depict. "Turkey, dressing, pie . . . I promise you, when you get there, the trip will have been worth it."

But they still groan.

Which takes us to the third similarity.

━━━━━━━━━━━━

Children can't envision the reward.

For me, six hours on the road is a small price to pay for my mom's strawberry cake. I don't mind the drive because I know the reward. I have three decades of Thanksgivings under my belt, literally. As I drive, I can taste the turkey. Hear the dinner-table laughter. Smell the smoke from the fireplace.

I can endure the journey because I know the destiny.

My daughters have forgotten the destiny. After all, they are young. Children easily forget. Besides, the road is strange, and the dark night has come. They can't see where we're going. It's my job, as their father, to guide them.

I try to help them see what they can't see.

I tell them how we'll feed the ducks at the lake. How we'll play on the swings. How they can spend the night with their cousins. We speak of sleeping on the floor in sleeping bags and staying up late since there is no school.

And it seems to work. Their grumbling decreases as their vision clears—as their destiny unfolds.

Perhaps that's how the apostle Paul stayed motivated. He had a clear vision of the reward.

> Therefore we do not lose heart. Though outwardly we are wasting away, yet inwardly we are being renewed

day by day. For our light and momentary troubles are
achieving for us an eternal glory that far outweighs
them all. So we fix our eyes not on what is seen, but
on what is unseen.[8]

It's not easy to get three girls under the age of seven to
see a city they can't see. But it's necessary.

It's not easy for us to see a City we've never seen, either,
especially when the road is bumpy . . . the hour is
late . . . and companions are wanting to cancel the trip and
take up residence in a motel. It's not easy to fix our eyes on
what is unseen. But it's necessary.

One line in the 2 Corinthians passage you just read
makes me smile: "our light and momentary troubles."

I wouldn't have called them that if I were Paul. Read
what he called *light and momentary,* and I think you'll
agree:

- Imprisoned.
- Beaten with a whip five times.
- Faced death.
- Beaten with rods three times.
- Stoned once.
- Shipwrecked three times.
- Stranded in the open sea.
- Left homeless.
- In constant danger.
- Hungry and thirsty.[9]

Long and trying ordeals, perhaps. *Arduous and deadly afflictions,* OK. But *light and momentary troubles?* How could Paul describe endless trials with that phrase?

He tells us. He could see "an eternal glory that far out-weighs them all."

———————————————

Can I speak candidly for a few lines?

For some of you, the journey has been long. Very long and stormy. In no way do I wish to minimize the difficulties that you have had to face along the way. Some of you have shouldered burdens that few of us could ever carry. You have bid farewell to life-long partners. You have been robbed of life-long dreams. You have been given bodies that can't sustain your spirit. You have spouses who can't tolerate your faith. You have bills that outnumber the paychecks and challenges that outweigh the strength.

And you are tired.

It's hard for you to see the City in the midst of the storms. The desire to pull over to the side of the road and get out entices you. You want to go on, but some days the road seems so long.

Let me encourage you with one final parallel between your life's journey and the one our family took last night.

———————————————

It's worth it.

As I write, the Thanksgiving meal is over. My legs are propped up on the hearth. My tablet is on my lap.

I have every intention of dozing off as soon as I finish this chapter.

The turkey has been attacked. The giblet gravy has been gobbled. The table is clear. The kids are napping. And the family is content.

As we sat around the table today, no one spoke of the long trip to get here. No one mentioned the requests I didn't honor. No one grumbled about my foot being on the accelerator when their hearts were focused on the banana splits. No one complained about the late hour of arrival.

Yesterday's challenges were lost in today's joy.

That's what Paul meant. God never said that the journey would be easy, but he did say that the arrival would be worthwhile.

Remember this: God may not do what you want, but he will do what is right . . . and best. He's the Father of forward motion. Trust him. He will get you home. And the trials of the trip will be lost in the joys of the feast.

Now, if you'll excuse me, I'll close my eyes. I'm a bit tired from the journey, and it feels good to rest.

13

DOUBTSTORMS

*T*HERE ARE SNOWSTORMS. There are hailstorms. There are rainstorms. And there are doubtstorms.

Every so often a doubtstorm rolls into my life, bringing with it a flurry of questions and gale-force winds of fear. And, soon after it comes, a light shines through it.

Sometimes the storm comes after the evening news. Some nights I wonder why I watch it. Some nights it's just too much. From the steps of the Supreme Court to the steppes of South Africa, the news is usually gloomy . . . thirty minutes of bite-sized tragedies. A handsome man in a nice suit with a warm voice gives bad news. They call him the anchorman. Good title. One needs an anchor in today's tempestuous waters.

Sometimes I wonder, *How can our world get so chaotic?*

Sometimes the storm comes when I'm at work. Story after story of homes that won't heal and hearts that won't melt. Always more hunger than food. More needs than money. More questions than answers. On Sundays I stand before a church with a three-point outline in my hand, thirty minutes on the clock, and a prayer on my lips. I do my best to say something that will convince a stranger that an unseen God still hears.

And I sometimes wonder why so many hearts have to hurt.

Do you ever get doubtstorms? Some of you don't, I know. I've talked to you. Some of you have a "Davidish" optimism that defies any Goliath. I used to think that you were naive at best and phony at worst.

I don't think that anymore.

I think you are gifted. You are gifted with faith. You can see the rainbow before the clouds part. If you have this gift, then skip this chapter. I won't say anything you need to hear.

But others of you wonder . . .

You wonder what others know that you don't. You wonder if you are blind or if they are. You wonder why some proclaim "Eureka" before the gold is found. You wonder why some shout "Land ho" before the fog has cleared. You wonder how some people believe so confidently while you believe so reluctantly.

As a result, you are a bit uncomfortable on the padded pew of blind belief. Your Bible hero is Thomas. Your middle name is Caution. Your queries are the bane of every Sunday school teacher.

"If God is so good, why do I sometimes feel so bad?"

"If his message is so clear, why do I get so confused?"

"If the Father is in control, why do good people have gut-wrenching problems?"

You wonder if it is a blessing or a curse to have a mind that never rests. But you would rather be a cynic than a hypocrite, so you continue to pray with one eye open and wonder:

- about starving children
- about the power of prayer
- about the depths of grace
- about Christians in cancer wards
- about who you are to ask such questions anyway.

Tough questions. Throw-in-the-towel questions. Questions the disciples must have asked in the storm.

All they could see were black skies as they bounced in the battered boat. Swirling clouds. Wind-driven white caps. Pessimism that buried the coastline. Gloom that swamped the bow. What could have been a pleasant trip became a white-knuckled ride through a sea of fear.

Their question—What hope do we have of surviving a stormy night?

My question—Where is God when his world is stormy?

Doubtstorms: turbulent days when the enemy is too big, the task too great, the future too bleak, and the answers too few.

Every so often a storm will come, and I'll look up into the blackening sky and say, "God, a little light, please?"

The light came for the disciples. A figure came to them walking on the water. It wasn't what they expected. Perhaps they were looking for angels to descend or heaven to open. Maybe they were listening for a divine proclamation to still the storm. We don't know what they were looking for. But one thing is for sure, they weren't looking for Jesus to come walking on the water.

"'It's a ghost,' they said and cried out in fear" (Matt. 14:26).

And since Jesus came in a way they didn't expect, they almost missed seeing the answer to their prayers.

And unless we look and listen closely, we risk making the same mistake. God's lights in our dark nights are as numerous as the stars, if only we'll look for them.

Can I share a few lights with you that have illuminated my world recently?

A friend and I sat in front of my house in his car and talked about his dilemma. His chief client pulled out on him, leaving him big bills and few solutions. What the client did wasn't right, but he did it anyway. The client's company was big and my friend's was small, and there wasn't a lot he could do. My friend was left with a den of hungry lions wanting six figures' worth of satisfaction.

"I called my uncle and told him what had happened. I told him I was thinking of filing for bankruptcy."

"What did he say?" I asked.

"He didn't say anything," my friend responded. "After he was silent for a long time, I said it for him. 'We don't do it like that, do we?'"

"'No, we don't,' he told me. So I'll pay the bills. If I have to sell my house, I'll pay my bills."

I was encouraged. Somebody still believed that if he did what was right, God would do what was best. There was still some we-don't-do-it-like-that faith in the world. The sky began to clear.

Light number two came from a cancer ward.

"We will celebrate forty-four years tomorrow," Jack said, feeding his wife.

She was bald. Her eyes were sunken, and her speech was slurred. She looked straight ahead, only opening her mouth when he brought the fork near. He wiped her cheek. He wiped his brow.

"She has been sick for five years," he told me. "She can't walk. She can't take care of herself. She can't even feed herself, but I love her. And," he spoke louder so she could hear, "we are going to beat this thing, aren't we, Honey?"

He fed her a few bites and spoke again, "We don't have insurance. When I could afford it, I thought I wouldn't need it. Now I owe this hospital more than $50,000." He was quiet for a few moments as he gave her a drink. Then he continued. "But they don't pester me. They know I can't pay, but they admitted us with no questions asked. The doctors treat us like we are their best-paying patients. Who would've imagined such kindness?"

I had to agree with him. Who would've imagined such kindness? In a thorny world of high-tech, expensive, often criticized health care, it was reassuring to find professionals who would serve two who had nothing to give in return.

Jack thanked me for coming, and I thanked God that once again a sinew of light reminded me of the sun behind the clouds.

Then, a few days later, another light.

Larry Brown is the coach of the San Antonio Spurs, the local professional basketball team. I don't know him personally (although rumor has it that he wants me to sign a multi-year contract and play point guard for the team . . . nice fantasy).

Coach Brown recently spent an afternoon at a local men's store, signing autographs. He was scheduled to spend two hours, but ended up spending three. Pencil-and-pad-toting kids besieged the place, asking him questions and shaking his hand.

When he was finally able to slip out, he climbed into his car, only to notice a touching sight. A late-arriving youngster pedaled up, jumped off his bike, and ran to the window to see if the coach was still in the store. When he saw he wasn't, he turned slowly and sadly, walked over to his bike, and began to ride off.

Coach Brown turned off the ignition, climbed out of the car, and walked over to the boy. They chatted a few minutes, went next door to a drugstore, sat down at a table, and had a soft drink.

No reporters were near. No cameras were on. As far as these two knew, no one knew. I'm sure Larry Brown had other things to do that afternoon. No doubt he had other appointments to keep. But it's doubtful that anything he might have done that afternoon was more important than what he did.

In a world of big-bucked, high-glossed professional sports, it did me good to hear of one coach who is still a coach at heart. Hearing what he did was enough to blow away any lingering clouds of doubt and to leave me warmed by God's light . . . his gentle light.

Gentle lights. God's solutions for doubtstorms. Gold-flecked glows that amber hope into blackness. Not thunderbolts. Not explosions of light. Just gentle lights. A businessman choosing honesty. A hospital choosing compassion. A celebrity choosing kindness.

Visible evidence of the invisible hand.

Soft reminders that optimism is not just for fools.

Funny. None of the events were "religious." None of the encounters occurred in a ceremony or a church service. None will make the six o'clock news.

But such is the case with gentle lights.

When the disciples saw Jesus in the middle of their stormy night, they called him a ghost. A phantom. A hallucination. To them, the glow was anything but God.

When we see gentle lights on the horizon, we often have the same reaction. We dismiss occasional kindness as apparitions, accidents, or anomalies. Anything but God.

"When Jesus comes," the disciples in the boat may have thought, "he'll split the sky. The sea will be calm. The clouds will disperse."

"When God comes," we doubters think, "all pain will flee. Life will be tranquil. No questions will remain."

And because we look for the bonfire, we miss the candle. Because we listen for the shout, we miss the whisper.

But it is in burnished candles that God comes, and through whispered promises he speaks: "When you doubt, look around; I am closer than you think."

14

THE
MIRACLE
OF
THE
CARPENTER

*I*T'S NO ACCIDENT THAT NEW MEXICO is called the "Land of Enchantment." Sprawling deserts spotted with sage. Purple mountains wreathed with clouds. Adobe homes hidden on hillsides. Majestic pines. Endless artifacts. A cloverleaf of cultures from the conquistador to the Comanche to the cowboy. New Mexico enchants.

And in this land of enchantment, there is a chapel of wonder.

A block south of the La Fonda Hotel in Santa Fe, on the corner of Water Street and Old Santa Fe Trail, you will find Loretto Chapel. As you step through its iron gate, you enter more than a chapel courtyard. You enter another era. Pause for a moment under the sprawling branches of the ancient trees. Imagine what it was like when the Mexican carpenters completed the chapel in 1878.

Can you see the settlers stomping through the muddy streets? Can you hear the donkeys braying? The wagon wheels groaning? And can you see the early morning sun spotlighting this gothic chapel—so simple, so splendid—as it sits against the backdrop of the desert hills?

Loretto Chapel took five years to complete. Modeled after the Sainte-Chapelle in Paris, its delicate sanctuary contains an altar, a rose window, and a choir loft.

The choir loft is the reason for wonder.

Were you to stand in the newly built chapel in 1878, you might see the Sisters of Loretto looking forlornly at the balcony. Everything else was complete: the doors had been hung, the pews had been placed, the floor had been laid. Everything was finished. Even the choir loft. Except for one thing. No stairs.

The chapel was too small to accommodate a conventional stairway. The best builders and designers in the region shook their heads when consulted. "Impossible," they murmured. There simply wasn't enough room. A ladder would serve the purpose, but mar the ambiance.

The Sisters of Loretto, whose determination had led them from Kentucky to Santa Fe, now faced a challenge greater than their journey: a stairway that couldn't be built.

What they had dreamed of and what they could do were separated by fifteen impossible feet.

So what did they do? The only thing they could do. They ascended the mountain. Not the high mountains near Santa Fe. No, they climbed even higher. They climbed the same mountain that Jesus climbed 1,800 years earlier in Bethsaida. They climbed the mountain of prayer.

"He went up on a mountainside by Himself to pray."[1]

Jesus faced an impossible task. More than five thousand people were ready to fight a battle he had not come to fight. How could he show them that he didn't come to be a king, but to be a sacrifice? How could he take their eyes off an earthly kingdom so that they would see the spiritual one? How could they see the eternal when they only had eyes for the temporal?

The Miracle of the Carpenter

What Jesus dreamed of doing and what he seemed able to do were separated by an impossible gulf. So Jesus prayed.

We don't know what he prayed about. But I have my guesses:

- He prayed that eyes blinded by power could see God's truth.

- He prayed that disciples dizzied by success could endure failure.

- He prayed that leaders longing for power would follow him to a cross.

- He prayed that people desiring bread for the body would hunger for bread for the soul.

He prayed for the impossible to happen.

Or maybe I'm wrong. Maybe he didn't ask for anything. Maybe he just stood quietly in the presence of Presence and basked in the Majesty. Perhaps he placed his war-weary self before the throne and rested.

Maybe he lifted his head out of the confusion of earth long enough to hear the solution of heaven. Perhaps he was reminded that hard hearts don't faze the Father. That problem people don't perturb the Eternal One.

We don't know what he did or what he said. But we do know the result. The hill became a steppingstone; the storm became a path. And the disciples saw Jesus as they had never seen him before.

During the storm, Jesus prayed. The sky darkened. The winds howled. Yet he prayed. The people grumbled. The disciples doubted. Yet he prayed. When forced to choose between the muscles of men and the mountain of prayer, he prayed.

Jesus did not try to do it by himself. Why should you?

127

There are crevasses in your life that you cannot cross alone. There are hearts in your world that you cannot change without help. There are mountains that you cannot climb until you climb His mountain.

Climb it. You will be amazed.

The Sisters of Loretto were.

As the story goes, the nuns prayed for nine days. On the last day of the novena, a Mexican carpenter with a beard and a wind-burned face appeared at the convent. He explained that he had heard they needed a stairway to a chapel loft. He thought he could help.

The mother superior had nothing to lose, so she gave him permission.

He went to work with crude tools, painstaking patience, and uncanny skill. For eight months he worked.

One morning the Sisters of Loretto entered the chapel to find their prayers had been answered. A masterpiece of carpentry spiraled from the floor to the loft. Two complete three-hundred-sixty-degree turns. Thirty-three steps held together with wooden pegs and no central support. The wood is said to be a variety of hard fir, one nonexistent in New Mexico!

When the sisters turned to thank the craftsman, he was gone. He was never seen again. He never asked for money. He never asked for praise. He was a simple carpenter who did what no one else could do so singers could enter a choir loft and sing.

See the stairway for yourself, if you like. Journey into the land of Enchantment. Step into this chapel of amazement and witness the fruit of prayer.

Or, if you prefer, talk to the Master Carpenter yourself. He has already performed one impossible feat in your world. He, like the Santa Fe carpenter, built a stairway no one else could build. He, like the nameless craftsman, used material from another place. He, like the visitor to Loretto, came to span the gap between where you are and where you long to be.

Each year of his life is a step. Thirty-three paces. Each step of the stair is an answered prayer. He built it so you can climb it.

And sing.

15

THE WOODCUTTER'S WISDOM

W OULD YOU BUY A HOUSE IF you were only allowed to see one of its rooms? Would you purchase a car if you were permitted to see only its tires and a taillight? Would you pass judgment on a book after reading only one paragraph?

Nor would I.

Good judgment requires a broad picture. Not only is that true in purchasing houses, cars, and books, it's true in evaluating life. One failure doesn't make a person a failure; one achievement doesn't make a person a success.

"The end of the matter is better than its beginning,"[1] penned the sage.

"Be . . . patient in affliction,"[2] echoed the apostle Paul.

"Don't judge a phrase by one word," stated the woodcutter.

The woodcutter? Oh, you may not know him. Let me present him to you.

I met him in Brazil. He was introduced to me by a friend who knew that I needed patience. Denalyn and I were six months into a five-year stint in Brazil, and I was frustrated. My fascination with Rio de Janeiro had turned into exasperation with words I couldn't speak and a culture I didn't understand.

"Tenha paciência," Maria would tell me. "Just be patient." She was my Portuguese instructor. But, more than that, she was a calm voice in a noisy storm. With maternal persistence, she corrected my pronunciation and helped me learn to love her homeland.

Once, in the midst of a frustrating week of trying to get our goods out of customs (which eventually took three months), she gave me this story as a homework assignment. It helped my attitude far more than it helped my Portuguese.

It's a simple fable. Yet for those of us who try to pass judgment on life with only one day's evidence, the message is profound. I've done nothing to embellish it; I've only translated it. I pray that it will remind you, as it did me, that patience is the greater courage.

Once there was an old man who lived in a tiny village. Although poor, he was envied by all, for he owned a beautiful white horse. Even the king coveted his treasure. A horse like this had never been seen before—such was its splendor, its majesty, its strength.

People offered fabulous prices for the steed, but the old man always refused. "This horse is not a horse to me," he would tell them. "It is a person. How could you sell a person? He is a friend, not a possession. How could you sell a friend?" The man was poor and the temptation was great. But he never sold the horse.

One morning he found that the horse was not in the stable. All the village came to see him. "You old fool," they scoffed, "we told you that someone would steal your horse. We warned you that you would be robbed. You are so poor.

How could you ever hope to protect such a valuable animal? It would have been better to have sold him. You could have gotten whatever price you wanted. No amount would have been too high. Now the horse is gone, and you've been cursed with misfortune."

The old man responded, "Don't speak too quickly. Say only that the horse is not in the stable. That is all we know; the rest is judgment. If I've been cursed or not, how can you know? How can you judge?"

The people contested, "Don't make us out to be fools! We may not be philosophers, but great philosophy is not needed. The simple fact that your horse is gone is a curse."

The old man spoke again. "All I know is that the stable is empty, and the horse is gone. The rest I don't know. Whether it be a curse or a blessing, I can't say. All we can see is a fragment. Who can say what will come next?"

The people of the village laughed. They thought that the man was crazy. They had always thought he was a fool; if he wasn't, he would have sold the horse and lived off the money. But instead, he was a poor woodcutter, an old man still cutting firewood and dragging it out of the forest and selling it. He lived hand to mouth in the misery of poverty. Now he had proven that he was, indeed, a fool.

After fifteen days, the horse returned. He hadn't been stolen; he had run away into the forest. Not only had he returned, he had brought a dozen wild horses with him. Once again the village people gathered around the woodcutter and spoke. "Old man, you were right and we were wrong. What we thought was a curse was a blessing. Please forgive us."

The man responded, "Once again, you go too far. Say only that the horse is back. State only that a dozen horses returned with him, but don't judge. How do you know if this is a blessing or not? You see only a fragment. Unless you know the whole story, how can you judge? You read only one page of a book. Can you judge the whole book? You read only one word of a phrase. Can you understand the entire phrase?

"Life is so vast, yet you judge all of life with one page or one word. All you have is a fragment! Don't say that this is a blessing. No one knows. I am content with what I know. I am not perturbed by what I don't."

"Maybe the old man is right," they said to one another. So they said little. But down deep, they knew he was wrong. They knew it was a blessing. Twelve wild horses had returned with one horse. With a little bit of work, the animals could be broken and trained and sold for much money.

The old man had a son, an only son. The young man began to break the wild horses. After a few days, he fell from one of the horses and broke both legs. Once again the villagers gathered around the old man and cast their judgments.

"You were right," they said. "You proved you were right. The dozen horses were not a blessing. They were a curse. Your only son has broken his legs, and now in your old age you have no one to help you. Now you are poorer than ever."

The old man spoke again. "You people are obsessed with judging. Don't go so far. Say only that my son broke his legs. Who knows if it is a blessing or a curse? No one knows. We only have a fragment. Life comes in fragments."

It so happened that a few weeks later the country engaged in war against a neighboring country. All the young men of the village were required to join the army. Only the son of the old man was excluded, because he was injured. Once again the people gathered around the old man, crying and screaming because their sons had been taken. There was little chance that they would return. The enemy was strong, and the war would be a losing struggle. They would never see their sons again.

"You were right, old man," they wept. "God knows you were right. This proves it. Your son's accident was a blessing. His legs may be broken, but at least he is with you. Our sons are gone forever."

The old man spoke again. "It is impossible to talk with you. You always draw conclusions. No one knows. Say only this: Your sons had to go to war, and mine did not. No one knows if it is a blessing or a curse. No one is wise enough to know. Only God knows."

———————————————

The old man was right. We only have a fragment. Life's mishaps and horrors are only a page out of a grand book. We must be slow about drawing conclusions. We must reserve judgment on life's storms until we know the whole story.

I don't know where the woodcutter learned his patience. Perhaps from another woodcutter in Galilee. For it was the Carpenter who said it best:

"Do not worry about tomorrow, for tomorrow will worry about itself."[3]

He should know. He is the Author of our story. And he has already written the final chapter.

16

LAWS
OF
THE
LIGHTHOUSE

*T*HE FIRST OF THE YEAR IS known for three things: black-eyed peas, bowl games, and lists. Some don't eat black-eyed peas. Others hate football. But everybody likes lists.

Lists are reassuring. They comfort us. They suggest that the crazy, zooming, blooming chaos of the universe can be mastered and tamed within the cage of a tidy column. To list is to understand, solve, and even control. For that reason we can't resist the urge, at the end of the year, to spew out lists like Washington, D.C. spews out documents.

We list the best movies . . . the best books . . . the worst dressed . . . the most used . . . the least popular . . . the most mysterious . . . the highest paid. We salute the good. We satire the bad. And we sum up the year on lists—"end-list" lists.

Although New Year's Day ranks at the top of the list of list-producing days, the rest of the year is by no means "list-less."

- Your grocery list makes a trip to the market manageable.

- Your calendar probably has a "to do" space, where you organize and number things you'd like to do but probably won't.

- Your syllabus tells you which books to buy.

- Your itinerary tells you which plane to take.
- Your telephone book tells you which numbers to dial.

The Bible certainly has its share of lists. Moses brought one down from the mountain. Noah might have used one as he loaded the ark. Jesus gave a list of principles in the Sermon on the Mount. (Paul gave his version in Romans 12.) Matthew and Luke listed the genealogies of Jesus. John listed the splendors of heaven.

There are lists of the gifts of the Spirit. Lists of good fruit and bad. Lists of salutations and greetings. Even the disciples' boat got into the action as it listed in the stormy Sea of Galilee. (If you smiled at that, then I've got a list of puns you'd enjoy.)

But the greatest day of lists is still New Year's Day. And the number one list is the list I call the Laws of the Lighthouse.

The Laws of the Lighthouse list contains immutable, immovable truths. Candidates for this inventory only qualify if they have lighthouse characteristics:

- They warn you of potential danger.
- They signal safe harbor.
- They are stronger than the storm.
- They shine brightest in the fog.

The Laws of the Lighthouse contain more than good ideas, personal preferences, and honest opinions. They are God-given, time-tested truths that define the way you should navigate your life. Observe them and enjoy secure passage. Ignore them and crash against the ragged rocks of reality.

In *U.S. Naval Institute Proceedings,* the magazine of the Naval Institute, Frank Koch illustrates the importance of obeying the Laws of the Lighthouse.[1]

Two battleships assigned to the training squadron had been at sea on maneuvers in heavy weather for several days. I was serving on the lead battleship and was on watch on the bridge as night fell. The visibility was poor with patchy fog, so the captain remained on the bridge keeping an eye on all activities.

Shortly after dark, the lookout on the wing reported, "Light, bearing on the starboard bow."

"Is it steady or moving astern?" the captain called out.

The lookout replied, "Steady, Captain," which meant we were on a dangerous collision course with that ship.

The captain then called to the signalman, "Signal that ship: 'We are on a collision course, advise you change course twenty degrees.'"

Back came the signal, "Advisable for you to change course twenty degrees."

The captain said, "Send: 'I'm a captain, change course twenty degrees.'"

"I'm a seaman second-class," came the reply. "You had better change course twenty degrees."

By that time the captain was furious. He spat out, "Send: 'I'm a battleship. Change course twenty degrees.'"

Back came the flashing light, "I'm a lighthouse."

We changed course.

Smart move. The wise captain shifts the direction of his craft according to the signal of the lighthouse. A wise person does the same.

Herewith, then, are the lights I look for and the signals I heed:

- Love God more than you fear hell.
- Once a week, let a child take you on a walk.
- Make major decisions in a cemetery.
- When no one is watching, live as if someone is.
- Succeed at home first.
- Don't spend tomorrow's money today.
- Pray twice as much as you fret.
- Listen twice as much as you speak.
- Only harbor a grudge when God does.
- Never outgrow your love of sunsets.
- Treat people like angels; you will meet some and help make some.
- 'Tis wiser to err on the side of generosity than on the side of scrutiny.
- God has forgiven you; you'd be wise to do the same.
- When you can't trace God's hand, trust his heart.
- Toot your own horn and the notes will be flat.
- Don't feel guilty for God's goodness.
- The book of life is lived in chapters, so know your page number.
- Never let the important be the victim of the trivial.

- Live your liturgy.

To sum it all up:
Approach life like a voyage on a schooner. Enjoy the view. Explore the vessel. Make friends with the captain. Fish a little. And then get off when you get home.

17

HE
SPEAKS
THROUGH
THE
STORM

I HAD HEARD ABOUT YOU BEFORE, *but now I have seen you."*[1] It all happened in one day. One day he could choose his tee time at the nicest golf course in the country; the next he couldn't even be the caddie. One day he could Lear jet across the country to see the heavyweight bout at the Las Vegas Mirage. The next he couldn't afford a city bus across town.

Talk about calm becoming chaos . . .

The first thing to go is his empire. The market crashes; his assets tumble. What is liquid goes dry. What has been up goes down. Stocks go flat, and Job goes broke. There he sits in his leather chair and soon-to-be-auctioned-off mahogany desk when the phone rings with news of calamity number two:

The kids were at a resort for the holidays when a storm blew in and took them with it.

Shell-shocked and dumbfounded, Job looks out the window into the sky that seems to be getting darker by the minute. He starts praying, telling God that things can't get any worse . . . and that's exactly what happens. He feels a pain in his chest that is more than last night's ravioli. The next thing he knows, he is bouncing in an ambulance with wires stuck to his chest and needles stuck in his arm.

He ends up tethered to a heart monitor in a community hospital room. Next to him lies an illegal immigrant who can't speak English.

Not, however, that Job lacks for conversation.

First there is his wife. Who could blame her for being upset at the week's calamities? Who could blame her for telling Job to curse God? But to curse God *and die?* If Job doesn't already feel abandoned, you know he does the minute his wife tells him to pull the plug and be done with it.

Then there are his friends. They have the bedside manner of a drill sergeant and the compassion of a chainsaw killer. A revised version of their theology might read like this: "Boy, you must have done something really bad! We know that God is good, so if bad things are happening to you, then you have been bad. Period."

Does Job take that lying down? Not hardly.

"You are doctors who don't know what they are doing," he says. "Oh, please be quiet! That would be your highest wisdom."[2]

Translation? "Why don't you take your philosophy back to the pigpen where you learned it."

"I'm not a bad man," Job argues. "I paid my taxes. I'm active in civic duties. I'm a major contributor to United Way and a volunteer at the hospital bazaar."

Job is, in his eyes, a good man. And a good man, he reasons, deserves a good answer.

"Your suffering is for your own good," states Elihu, a young minister fresh out of seminary who hasn't lived long enough to be cynical and hasn't hurt enough to be quiet. He paces back and forth in the hospital room, with his Bible under his arm and his finger punching the air.

"God does all these things to a man—twice, even three times—to turn back his soul from the pit, that the light of life may shine on him."[3]

Job follows his pacing like you'd follow a tennis player, head turning from side to side. What the young man says isn't bad theology, but it isn't much comfort, either. Job steadily tunes him out and slides lower and lower under the covers. His head hurts. His eyes burn. His legs ache. And he can't stomach any more hollow homilies.

Yet his question still hasn't been answered:

"God, why is this happening to me?"

So God speaks.

Out of the thunder, he speaks. Out of the sky, he speaks. For all of us who would put ditto marks under Job's question and sign our names to it, he speaks.

- For the father who holds a rose taken off his son's coffin, he speaks.

- For the wife who holds the flag taken off her husband's casket, he speaks.

- For the couple with the barren womb and the fervent prayers, he speaks.

- For any person who has tried to see God through shattered glass, he speaks.

- For those of us who have dared to say, "If God is God, then . . . ," God speaks.

He speaks out of the storm and into the storm, for that is where Job is. That is where God is best heard.

God's voice thunders in the room. Elihu sits down. Job sits up. And the two will never be the same again.

"Who is this that darkens my counsel with words without knowledge?"[4]

Job doesn't respond.

"Brace yourself like a man; I will question you, and you shall answer me."[5]

"Where were you when I laid the foundations of the earth? Tell me, if you know so much."[6]

One question would have been enough for Job, but it isn't enough for God.

"Do you know how its dimensions were determined and who did the surveying?" God asks. "What supports its foundations, and who laid its cornerstone, as the morning stars sang together and all the angels shouted for joy?"[7]

Questions rush forth. They pour like sheets of rain out of the clouds. They splatter in the chambers of Job's heart with a wildness and a beauty and a terror that leave every Job who has ever lived drenched and speechless, watching the Master redefine who is who in the universe.

> Have you ever once commanded the morning to appear, and caused the dawn to rise in the east? Have you ever told the daylight to spread to the ends of the earth, to end the night's wickedness?[8]

God's questions aren't intended to teach; they are intended to stun. They aren't intended to enlighten; they are intended to awaken. They aren't intended to stir the mind; they are intended to bend the knees.

> Has the location of the gates of Death been revealed to you? Do you realize the extent of the earth? Tell me about it if you know! Where does the light come from, and how do you get there? Or tell me about the darkness. Where does it come from? Can you find its boundaries, or go to its source? But of course you know all this! For you were born before it was all created, and you are so very experienced![9]

Finally Job's feeble hand lifts, and God stops long enough for him to respond. "I am nothing—how could I ever find the answers? I lay my hand upon my mouth in silence. I have said too much already."[10]

God's message has connected:

- Job is a peasant, telling the King how to run the kingdom.
- Job is an illiterate, telling e. e. cummings to capitalize his personal pronouns.
- Job is the bat boy, telling Babe Ruth to change his batting stance.
- Job is the clay, telling the potter not to press so hard.

"I owe no one anything," God declares in the crescendo of the wind. "Everything under the heaven is mine."[11]

Job couldn't argue. God owes no one anything. No explanations. No excuses. No help. God has no debt, no outstanding balance, no favors to return. God owes no man anything.

Which makes the fact that he gave us everything even more astounding.

How you interpret this holy presentation is key. You can interpret God's hammering speech as a divine "in-your-face" tirade if you want. You can use the list of unanswerable questions to prove that God is harsh, cruel, and distant. You can use the Book of Job as evidence that God gives us questions and no answers. But to do so, you need some scissors. To do so, you need to cut out the rest of the Book of Job.

For that is not how Job heard it. All his life, Job had been a good man. All his life, he had believed in God. All his life, he had discussed God, had notions about him, and had prayed to him.

But in the storm Job sees him!

He sees Hope. Lover. Destroyer. Giver. Taker. Dreamer. Deliverer.

Job sees the tender anger of a God whose unending love is often received with peculiar mistrust. Job stands as a blade of grass against the consuming fire of God's splendor. Job's demands melt like wax as God pulls back the curtain and heaven's light falls uneclipsed across the earth.

Job sees God.

God could turn away at this point. The gavel has been slammed, the verdict has been rendered. The Eternal Judge has spoken.

Ah, but God is not angry with Job. Firm? Yes. Direct? No doubt. Clear and convincing? Absolutely. But angry? No.

God is never irritated by the candle of an honest seeker.

If you underline any passage in the Book of Job, underline this one: "I had heard about you before, but now I have seen you."[12]

Job sees God—and that is enough.

But it isn't enough for God.

The years to come find Job once again sitting behind his mahogany desk with health restored and profits up. His lap is once again full of children and grandchildren and great-grandchildren—for four generations!

If Job ever wonders why God doesn't bring back the children he had taken away, he doesn't ask. Maybe he doesn't ask because he knows that his children could never be happier than they are in the presence of this One he has seen so briefly.

Something tells me that Job would do it all again, if that's what it took to hear God's voice and stand in the Presence. Even if God left him with his bedsores and bills, Job would do it again.

For God gave Job more than Job ever dreamed. God gave Job Himself.

18

PILGRIM
PONDERINGS

After six days Jesus took with him Peter, James and John the brother of James, and led them up a high mountain by themselves. There he was transfigured before them. His face shone like the sun, and his clothes became as white as the light. Just then there appeared before them Moses and Elijah, talking with Jesus.

Peter said to Jesus, "Lord, it is good for us to be here. If you wish, I will put up three shelters—one for you, one for Moses, and one for Elijah." While he was still speaking, a bright cloud enveloped them, and a voice from the cloud said, "This is my Son, whom I love; with him I am well pleased. Listen to him!"[1]

---

*T*HE YOUNG WOMAN, EIGHT MONTHS heavy with child, waddles into her mother's house. Flops onto the sofa. Kicks off her tennis shoes. Props her puffy feet on the coffee table. And groans, "I don't think I can make it."

Wise from the years, the mother picks up a photo album and sits down beside her daughter. She opens the album to photos of her children in diapers and ankle-high walking shoes. Slowly the two turn the memory-filled pages. They smile at the kids blowing out candles and sitting in front of Christmas trees.

As the mother sees yesterday, the daughter sees tomorrow.

And, for just a moment, the daughter is changed. The *here and now* becomes the *there and then.* Her child is born. She sees the first stumbling step taken. She hears the first word, discernible only to Mommy. She places the shiny, black, patent-leather shoes on the stockinged feet and Karo-syrups a ribbon on the nearly bald but ever-so-precious head.

A transformation occurs. The pain in her back is now overshadowed by the joy approaching. The hand that had rubbed the neck now rests on her stomach. For the first time that day, she smiles.

A snowstorm in Chicago. Stranded at O'Hare. No place to sit in the lobby, so he walks to the coffee shop. No place to sit in the coffee shop, so he buys a cup to go, wanders back to the lobby, sits on his briefcase, and drapes his overcoat over his lap.

He looks at his watch. *Should I go to a hotel for the night?* he wonders. *It's nearly midnight! I should be halfway home by now. Who knows when I'll be able to leave?*

He sighs, leans back against a wall, and waits. He unbuttons his collar. Loosens his tie. Rubs his whiskered neck. His thoughts drift back over the week. Many calls made. Few orders placed. Blame it on the economy. Blame it on the system. Blame it on God. But blame doesn't put money in the bank.

There's an executive lobby across the hall with empty couches, snacks, and a television. In better times, he could afford the membership; now that money goes toward college tuition and braces for the kids.

A flight is announced. He pulls his boarding pass out of his overcoat breast pocket. The flight isn't his. He sticks the pass back into the coat that stretches across his lap. A leather calendar tumbles out. He picks it up and, for no real reason, looks inside.

There, amidst taxi receipts and credit cards, is a laminated photo of a family—his family. Teenage daughter with eyes like her mom's and the metallic smile. College-bound son wearing a necktie and blue jeans, mid-step between adolescence and adulthood. And his wife. My, has it been twenty-five years? Take away a few wrinkles and pounds, and he can see her in the white gown again.

For just a moment, he is home. The television is off. The kids are in bed. The dog is outside. The doors are locked. The fire is golden. His wife is asleep on the couch. For just a moment, the world of O'Hare, hotels, and sales calls are a world away. He is where it's all worthwhile. He is home.

Someone taps him on the shoulder, and he hears a kind voice. "Is that your flight?" He looks up into the half-empty lobby . . . sees the line forming at the gate . . . and smiles.

"Yeah," the salesman says, standing. "It's my flight home."

———————————————

Four people snake their way up the mountain. The trip has been long; the hour is late. A level place on the hillside is reached, and they sit down. They're tired. Their muscles hurt. The grayness of twilight settles over them like a soft cloth.

The quartet of pilgrims longs to sleep, but only three do.

The fourth sits in the shadows. Legs crossed. Face skyward. The stars wink at their Maker. Winds waft over the shoulders of their Designer, cooling his neck. He slips off his sandals and rubs his sore feet and reflects on the wildness of it all.

A God with sore legs? Holiness with hunger? Divinity with thirst? A World Maker made weary by his world?

His thoughts drift homeward. *Nazareth. How good it would be to be home again.*

The memories surface so easily. Sawdust-covered workbench. Friends stopping to talk. Dinner-table laughter. Wrestling with his brothers. The synagogue. The house. The home.

What I'd give to go home.

But Nazareth would never be home again. They tried to kill him the last time he was there. Neighbors, friends, teachers, schoolmates . . . they squeezed the stones intended for his body. Even his brothers and sisters considered him insane. They wanted to hide him, to put him away. They were ashamed to be known as his family.

No, Nazareth can never be home again.

What about Galilee? He could go back to Galilee. There the crowds listened. There the people followed. But he shook his head. *As long as I made them bread . . . As long as I said what they wanted to hear . . .* He remembered the crowds as they turned away. He heard their jeering. He felt their rejection.

No, I can never go back to Galilee.

He thinks of Jerusalem. She offers no comfort. He knows what she will do to him. A foreboding pain stabs his wrists. He winces at the slicing of his brow. He sees the world around him growing darker, darker . . . *My God!* a premonition inside him cries.

He shakes his head and breathes a staggered breath. His thoughts return to the present.

He plucks a shoot of grass, puts it into his mouth, and sits in the shadow of his fear.

He looks at his followers, as asleep as they are naive. They have no idea. They just can't understand. He speaks of suffering; they think of conquering. He speaks of sacrifice; they think of celebration. He's an artist painting for the color-blind. He's a singer singing for the deaf. They nod their heads and clap their hands. They think they see. They think they hear. But they don't.

They can't see. No one sees.

Part of him knew it would be like this. And part of him never knew it would be so bad.

Part of him wonders, *Would it be so bad to give up?* After all, there might be a better era. There will be other generations . . . other people.

He has given his best, and what does he have? A ragged band of good-hearted but hardheaded followers who are destined to fall face-flat over promises they can't keep. He puts his face into his cupped hands and closes his eyes and prays. It's all he knows to do.

Sounds familiar, doesn't it, seeker? Was it so long ago that you were on a quest for truth—Galahad in search of the grail? But the forest of questions was deep. The thicket of perplexities thick. It was easier to say nothing than to ask why. So you stopped.

Sounds familiar, doesn't it, dreamer? You wanted so badly to change the world. Sure the mountain was high, but you were brave. Then the winds came. Sharp rocks of reality cut your feet, breaking your stride . . . breaking your heart. And you found that the role of the cynic was less costly than the role of the dreamer. So you sat down.

You need to know something: Jesus sat down, too.

Oh, sure, there were moments when he stood tall. There were hours of splendor. There were dynamic days during which the lepers leapt and the dead came alive and the people worshiped. Those days came.

But his plateaus of popularity were gorged by canyons of isolation.

And on this day, the crevasse is deep. Steep walls mock an easy escape. Rocky abutments imprison his vision. His strength has reached its solstice.

He sits down and puts a tear-streaked face into cupped palms and prays. It's all he can do.

And when his Father sees him, it's all his Father can take.

From another dimension, a light comes. It enters the solitary figure and glows.

"As he was praying," Luke writes, "the appearance of his face changed, and his clothes became as bright as a flash of lightning."[2]

Jesus implodes with glory. For just a moment, he is transfigured; a roaring radiance pours from him. He becomes as he was before he came. For one brief, shining moment, the burden of his humanity is lifted. "Decarnation" occurs. He is elevated above earth's horizon and escorted into the eternal. He is home again. Familiar sounds surround him. Those who understand welcome him. And the One who sent him . . . holds him.

Dusty trails and hard hearts are, literally, a world away.

The One who felt weary is reminded: the weariness will soon pass.

Moses and Elijah, aflame with eternal robes, stand beside their King. When Jesus was preparing himself in the desert for the work of life, angels came to encourage him. Now, on the mountain, preparing himself for the work of death, Moses and Elijah draw near: Moses, the Lawgiver whose grave no man knew; Elijah, the prophet who side-stepped death in a fiery chariot.

The One who saw death is reminded: the grave is impotent.

And then, the voice thunders. God inhabits a cloud. It becomes a bonfire, puffy with brilliance. It consumes the shadows. It transforms the nightened mountain into a shining monument. And from the belly of the cloud, the Father speaks:

"This is my Son, whom I love; with him I am well pleased. Listen to him!"[3]

The One who had despaired is affirmed. "What people think doesn't matter," God shouts. "What I think does. And I'm proud."

By now Jesus is standing. By now the apostles are awake.

For Peter, James, and John, the scene is bizarre: dazzling white clouds, a voice from the sky, living images from the past. But for Jesus, it is a view of home. A view into yesterday. A glimpse into tomorrow.

He is the mother—pregnant with new life, dreading the pains of childbirth.

He is the father—on a long journey in a cold place.

He is—as they were, as we are—given a glimpse of home.

And tomorrow's dream becomes today's courage.

19

OUR STORM WAS HIS PATH

*S*UPPOSE ONE OF JESUS' DISCIPLES *kept a journal. And suppose that disciple made an entry in the journal on the morning after the storm. And suppose we discovered that journal. Here is how it would read . . . I suppose.*

Only minutes before, chaos had erupted.

Oh, how the storm roared. Stars were hidden by a black ceiling. Clouds billowed like smoke. Bolts of lightning were the conductor's baton that cued the kettledrums of thunder to rumble.

And rumble they did. The clouds seemed to rise as a bear on hind legs and growl. The booms shook everything: the heavens, the earth, and—most of all—the sea. It was as if the Sea of Galilee were a bowl in the hands of a dancing giant. From the bowels of the lake the waves came, turning the glassy surface into a mountain range of snow-topped waves. Five, ten, even fifteen feet into the air they mounted, rising and falling like swallows chasing mosquitoes.

In the midst of the sea, our boat bounced. The waves slapped it as easily as children would a ball. Our straining at the oars scarcely budged it. We were at the storm's mercy. The waves lifted us up so high that we felt like we were in midair. Then down into the valley we plunged.

We were a twig in a whirlpool . . . a leaf in the wind. We were helpless.

That's when the light appeared. At first I thought it was a reflection of the moon, a gleam on the surface of the water. But the night held no moon. I looked again. The light was moving toward us, not over the waves but through them. I wasn't the only one who saw it.

"A ghost," someone screamed. Fear of the sea was eclipsed by a new terror. Thoughts raced as the specter drew near. *Was it a figment of our imagination? Was it a vision? Who? How? What was this mystical light that appeared so . . . ?*

A flash of lightning illuminated the sky. For a second I could see its face . . . his face. A second was all I needed.

It was the Master!

He spoke:

"Take courage! It is I. Don't be afraid."[1]

Nothing had changed. The storm still raged. The wind still shrieked. The boat still pitched. The thunder still boomed. The rain still slapped. But in the midst of the tumult, I could hear his voice. Although he was still far away, it was like he was by my side. The night was ferocious, yet he spoke as though the sea were placid and the sky silent.

And, somehow, courage came.

"Lord, if it's you, . . . tell me to come to you on the water."[2]

The voice was Peter's. He wasn't being cocky. He wasn't demanding proof. He was scared. Like me, he knew what this storm could do. He knew that the boat would soon go down. He knew that Jesus was standing up. And he knew where he wanted to be . . . where we all wanted to be.

"Come on," Jesus invited.

So Peter climbed over the side and stepped onto the sea. Before him opened a trail through a forest of waves. He stepped quickly. Water splashed. But he kept going. This path to Jesus was a ribbon of calm. It was peaceful. Serene.

Jesus radiated light at the end of the trail. Smiling.

Peter stepped toward the light like it was his only hope. He was halfway there when we all heard the thunder. It boomed, and he stopped. I saw his head turn. He looked up at the sky. He looked up at the clouds. He felt the wind. And down he went.

Boy did he yell!

A hand came through the water sheets and grabbed Peter. Lightning flashed again, and I could see the face of Jesus. I noticed that his smile was gone. Hurt covered his face. It was like he couldn't believe that we couldn't believe. Danger to us was just a detour to him. I wanted to ask him, "Aren't you afraid, Jesus? Aren't you afraid?"

But I said nothing. Before I knew it, he was in the boat with us.

The sea stilled as silk.

The winds hushed.

A canyon opened in the clouds; soft moonlight fell over the water.

It happened instantaneously. It didn't take the rest of the night. It didn't take an hour. It didn't take a minute. It happened in a blink.

From chaos to calm. From panic to peace. The sky was so suddenly silent that I could hear my heart pounding. I thought I was dreaming. Then I saw the wide eyes of the others and felt my clothing soaked against my skin. This was no dream. I looked at the water. I looked at Peter. I looked at the others. And then I looked at him.

And I did the only thing I could have done. With the stars as my candles and the stilled boat as my altar, I fell at his feet and worshiped.

There are times in a person's life when, even in the midst of them, you know you'll never be the same. Moments that forever serve as journey posts. This was one.

I had never seen Jesus as I saw him then. I had seen him as powerful. I had seen him as wise. I had witnessed his authority and marveled at his abilities. But what I witnessed last night, I know I'll never forget.

I saw God. The God who can't sit still when the storm is too strong. The God who lets me get frightened enough to need him and then comes close enough for me to see him. The God who uses my storms as his path to come to me.

I saw God. It took a storm for me to see him. But I saw him. And I'll never be the same.

20

THEY'D
DO
IT
AGAIN

*T*HEY'D DO IT AGAIN. I'm confident they would. The disciples would get into the same boat and ride through the same storm. They'd do it again in a heartbeat. Why?

Because through the storm they saw the Savior.

Read this verse: "Then those who were in the boat worshiped him, saying, 'Truly you are the Son of God.'"[1]

After the storm, they worshiped him. They had never, as a group, done that before. Never. Check it out. Open your Bible. Search for a time when the disciples corporately praised him.

You won't find it.

You won't find them worshiping when he heals the leper. Forgives the adulteress. Preaches to the masses. They were willing to follow. Willing to leave family. Willing to cast out demons. Willing to be in the army.

But only after the incident on the sea did they worship him. Why?

Simple. This time, they were the ones who were saved. This time, their necks were removed from the noose. Their bodies were plucked from the deep. One minute, they were dangling over the edge of the abyss, staring into the throat of the slack-jawed canyon. The next, they were bottom-plopped and wide-eyed on the deck of a still boat on a placid sea.

So they worshiped. They did the only thing that they could do when their death sentence was stayed at the eleventh hour: They looked to the Eternal Governor who gave the pardon and thanked him.

━━━━━━━━━━━━━━━

When you recognize God as Creator, you will admire him. When you recognize his wisdom, you will learn from him. When you discover his strength, you will rely on him. But only when he saves you will you worship him.

It's a "before and after" scenario. Before your rescue, you could easily keep God at a distance. Comfortably dismissed. Neatly shelved. Sure he was important, but so was your career. Your status. Your salary. He was high on your priority list, but he shared the spot with others.

Then came the storm . . . the rage . . . the fight . . . the ripped moorings . . . the starless night. Despair fell like a fog; your bearings were gone. In your heart, you knew there was no exit.

Turn to your career for help? Only if you want to hide from the storm . . . not escape it. Lean on your status for strength? A storm isn't impressed with your title. Rely on your salary for rescue? Many try . . . many fail.

Suddenly you are left with one option: God.

And when you ask . . . genuinely ask . . . he will come.

And from that moment on, he is not just a deity to admire, a teacher to observe, or a master to obey. He is the Savior. The Savior to be worshiped.

That's why I'm convinced that the disciples would do it again. They'd endure the storm another night . . . a thousand other nights . . . if that's what it took.

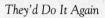
They'd Do It Again

A season of suffering is a small price to pay for a clear view of God.

STING
OF
FAILURE

21

CASTLES
OF
SORROW

S ARAH WAS RICH. SHE HAD inherited twenty million dollars. Plus she had an additional income of one thousand dollars a day.

That's a lot of money any day, but it was immense in the late 1800s.

Sarah was well known. She was the belle of New Haven, Connecticut. No social event was complete without her presence. No one hosted a party without inviting her.

Sarah was powerful. Her name and money would open almost any door in America. Colleges wanted her donations. Politicians clamored for her support. Organizations sought her endorsement.

Sarah was rich. Well known. Powerful. And miserable.

Her only daughter had died at five weeks of age. Then her husband had passed away. She was left alone with her name, her money, her memories, . . . and her guilt.

It was her guilt that caused her to move west. A passion for penance drove her to San Jose, California. Her yesterdays imprisoned her todays, and she yearned for freedom.

She bought an eight-room farmhouse plus one hundred sixty adjoining acres. She hired sixteen carpenters and put them to work. For the next thirty-eight years, craftsmen labored every day, twenty-four hours a day, to build a mansion.

Observers were intrigued by the project. Sarah's instructions were more than eccentric . . . they were eerie.

The design had a macabre touch. Each window was to have thirteen panes, each wall thirteen panels, each closet thirteen hooks, and each chandelier thirteen globes.

The floor plan was ghoulish. Corridors snaked randomly, some leading nowhere. One door opened to a blank wall, another to a fifty-foot drop. One set of stairs led to a ceiling that had no door. Trapdoors. Secret passageways. Tunnels. This was no retirement home for Sarah's future; it was a castle for her past.

The making of this mysterious mansion only ended when Sarah died. The completed estate sprawled over six acres and had six kitchens, thirteen bathrooms, forty stairways, forty-seven fireplaces, fifty-two skylights, four hundred sixty-seven doors, ten thousand windows, one hundred sixty rooms, and a bell tower.

Why did Sarah want such a castle? Didn't she live alone? "Well, sort of," those acquainted with her story might answer. "There were the visitors . . ."

And the visitors came each night.

Legend has it that every evening at midnight, a servant would pass through the secret labyrinth that led to the bell tower. He would ring the bell . . . to summon the spirits. Sarah would then enter the "blue room," a room reserved for her and her nocturnal guests. Together they would linger until 2:00 AM, when the bell would be rung again. Sarah would return to her quarters; the ghosts would return to their graves.

Who comprised this legion of phantoms?

Indians and soldiers killed on the U.S. frontier. They had all been killed by bullets from the most popular rifle in America—the Winchester. What had brought millions of dollars to Sarah Winchester had brought death to them.

So she spent her remaining years in a castle of regret, providing a home for the dead.

You can see this poltergeist place in San Jose, if you wish. You can tour its halls and see its remains.

But to see what unresolved guilt can do to a human being, you don't have to go to the Winchester mansion. Lives imprisoned by yesterday's guilt are in your own city. Hearts haunted by failure are in your own neighborhood. People plagued by pitfalls are just down the street . . . or just down the hall.

There is, wrote Paul, a "worldly sorrow" that "brings death."[1] A guilt that kills. A sorrow that's fatal. A venomous regret that's deadly.

How many Sarah Winchesters do you know? How far do you have to go to find a soul haunted by ghosts of the past? Maybe not very far.

Maybe Sarah's story is your story.

If so, I'm especially grateful that this book has made its way into your hands. This final section has been written with you in mind. In these final chapters, I have assembled thoughts on failure and forgiveness.

For in the twilight hours during the storm's black night, there is a story of grace.

It is the story of Peter: recognizing the Master's voice . . . seeing the Master's face . . . scrambling to safety from the storm.

It is also another story of Peter: hearing the winds . . . seeing the torrent . . . sinking into the water.

But most of all, it is the story of Jesus. It is the story of God extending his hand during stormy seas. It is the answer to the question every person asks: "What does God do when I fail?"

The answers to guilt's questions are not found in a new house.

The answer is found in the foundation of the one you have.

22

FEAR
THAT
BECOMES
FAITH

"They saw Jesus . . . walking on the water; and they were terrified."[1]

*F*AITH IS OFTEN the child of fear.

Fear propelled Peter out of the boat. He'd ridden these waves before. He knew what these storms could do. He'd heard the stories. He'd seen the wreckage. He knew the widows. He knew the storm could kill. And he wanted out.

All night he wanted out. For nine hours he'd tugged on sails, wrestled with oars, and searched every shadow on the horizon for hope. He was soaked to the soul and bone weary of the wind's banshee wail.

Look into Peter's eyes and you won't see a man of conviction. Search his face and you won't find a gutsy grimace. Later on, you will. You'll see his courage in the garden. You'll witness his devotion at Pentecost. You'll behold his faith in his epistles.

But not tonight. Look into his eyes tonight and see fear—a suffocating, heart-racing fear of a man who has no way out.

But out of this fear would be born an act of faith, for faith is often the child of fear.

"The fear of the Lord is the beginning of wisdom,"[2] wrote the wise man.

Peter could have been his sermon illustration.

If Peter had seen Jesus walking on the water during a calm, peaceful day, do you think that he would have walked out to him?

Nor do I.

Had the lake been carpet smooth and the journey pleasant, do you think that Peter would have begged Jesus to take him on a stroll across the top of the water? Doubtful.

But give a man a choice between sure death and a crazy chance, and he'll take the chance . . . every time.

Great acts of faith are seldom born out of calm calculation.

It wasn't logic that caused Moses to raise his staff on the bank of the Red Sea.[3]

It wasn't medical research that convinced Naaman to dip seven times in the river.[4]

It wasn't common sense that caused Paul to abandon the Law and embrace grace.[5]

And it wasn't a confident committee that prayed in a small room in Jerusalem for Peter's release from prison.[6] It was a fearful, desperate, band of backed-into-a-corner believers. It was a church with no options. A congregation of have-nots pleading for help.

And never were they stronger.

At the beginning of every act of faith, there is often a seed of fear.

———

Biographies of bold disciples begin with chapters of honest terror. Fear of death. Fear of failure. Fear of loneliness. Fear of a wasted life. Fear of failing to know God.

Faith begins when you see God on the mountain and you are in the valley and you know that you're too weak to make the climb. You see what you need . . . you see what you have . . . and what you have isn't enough to accomplish anything.

Peter had given it his best. But his best wasn't enough.

Moses had a sea in front and an enemy behind. The Israelites could swim or they could fight. But neither option was enough.

Naaman had tried the cures and consulted the soothsayers. Traveling a long distance to plunge into a muddy river made little sense when there were clean ones in his backyard. But what option did he have?

Paul had mastered the Law. He had mastered the system. But one glimpse of God convinced him that sacrifices and symbols were not enough.

The Jerusalem church knew that they had no hope of getting Peter out of prison. They had Christians who would fight, but too few. They had clout, but too little. They didn't need muscle. They needed a miracle.

So does Peter. He is aware of two facts: He is going down, and Jesus is staying up. He knows where he would rather be.

There's nothing wrong with this response. Faith that begins with fear will end up nearer the Father.

I went to West Texas some time back to speak at the funeral of a godly, family friend. He had raised five children. One son, Paul, told a story about his earliest memory of his father.

It was spring in West Texas—tornado season. Paul was only three or four years old at the time, but he remembers vividly the day that a tornado hit their small town.

His father hustled the kids indoors and had them lie on the floor while he laid a mattress over them. But his father didn't climb under the protection. Paul remembers peeking out from under the mattress and seeing him standing by an open window, watching the funnel cloud twist and churn across the prairie.

When Paul saw his father, he knew where he wanted to be. He struggled out of his mother's arms, crawled out from under the mattress, and ran to wrap his arms around his dad's leg.

"Something told me," Paul said, "that the safest place to stand in a storm was next to my father."

Something told Peter the same thing.

"Lord, if it's you," Peter says, "tell me to come to you on the water."[7]

Peter is not testing Jesus; he is pleading with Jesus. Stepping onto a stormy sea is not a move of logic; it is a move of desperation.

Peter grabs the edge of the boat. Throws out a leg . . . follows with the other. Several steps are taken. It's as if an invisible ridge of rocks runs beneath his feet. At the end of the ridge is the glowing face of a never-say-die friend.

We do the same, don't we? We come to Christ in an hour of deep need. We abandon the boat of good works. We realize, like Moses, that human strength won't save us. So we look to God in desperation. We realize, like Paul, that all the good works in the world are puny when laid before the Perfect One. We realize, like Peter, that spanning the gap between us and Jesus is a feat too great for our feet.

So we beg for help. Hear his voice. And step out in fear, hoping that our little faith will be enough.

Faith is not born at the negotiating table where we barter our gifts in exchange for God's goodness. Faith is not an award given to the most learned. It's not a prize given to the most disciplined. It's not a title bequeathed to the most religious.

Faith is a desperate dive out of the sinking boat of human effort and a prayer that God will be there to pull us out of the water. Paul wrote about this kind of faith in the letter to the Ephesians:

"For it is by grace you have been saved, through faith— and this not from yourselves, it is the gift of God—not by works, so that no one can boast."[8]

Paul is clear. The supreme force in salvation is God's grace. Not our works. Not our talents. Not our feelings. Not our strength.

Salvation is God's sudden, calming presence during the stormy seas of our lives. We hear his voice; we take the step.

We, like Paul, are aware of two things: We are great sinners and we need a great Savior.

We, like Peter, are aware of two facts: We are going down and God is standing up. So we scramble out. We leave behind the *Titanic* of self-righteousness and stand on the solid path of God's grace.

And, surprisingly, we are able to walk on water. Death is disarmed. Failures are forgivable. Life has real purpose. And God is not only within sight, he is within reach.

With precious, wobbly steps, we draw closer to him. For a season of surprising strength, we stand upon his promises. It doesn't make sense that we are able to do this. We don't claim to be worthy of such an incredible gift. When people ask how in the world we can keep our balance during such stormy times, we don't boast. We don't brag. We point unabashedly to the One who makes it possible. Our eyes are on him.

"Nothing in my hand I bring; Simply to Thy cross I cling,"[9] we sing.

"Dressed in His righteousness alone, Faultless to stand before the throne,"[10] we declare.

" 'Twas grace that taught my heart to fear, And grace my fears relieved,"[11] we explain.

Some of us, unlike Peter, never look back.

Others of us, like Peter, feel the wind and are afraid.[12]

Maybe we face the wind of pride: "I'm not such a bad sinner after all. Look at what I can do."

Perhaps we face the wind of legalism: "I know that Jesus is doing part of this, but I have to do the rest."

Most of us, though, face the wind of doubt: "I'm too bad for God to treat me this well. I don't deserve such a rescue."

And downward we plunge. Heavied by mortality's mortar, we sink. Gulping and thrashing, we fall into a dark, wet world. We open our eyes and see only blackness. We try to breathe, and no air comes. We kick and fight our way back to the surface.

With our heads barely above the water, we have to make a decision.

The prideful ask: "Do we 'save face' and drown in pride? Or do we scream for help and take God's hand?"

The legalists ask: "Do we sink under the lead-heavy weight of the Law? Or do we abandon the codes and beg for grace?"

The doubters ask: "Do we nurture doubt by mumbling, 'I've really let him down this time?' Or do we hope that the same Christ who called us out of the boat will call us out of the sea?"

We know Peter's choice.

"[As he was] beginning to sink, [he] cried out, 'Lord, save me!'"[13]

"Immediately Jesus reached out his hand and caught him."[14]

We also know the choice of another sailor in another storm.

Although separated by seventeen centuries, this sailor and Peter are drawn together by several striking similarities:

- Both made their living on the sea.
- Both met their Savior after a nine-hour battle in a storm.
- Both met the Father in fear and then followed him in faith.
- Both walked away from their boats and became preachers of the Truth.

You know the story of Peter, the first sailor. Let me tell you about the second, whose name was John.

He had served on the seas since he was eleven years old. His father, an English shipmaster in the Mediterranean, took him aboard and trained him well for a life in the Royal Navy.

Yet what John gained in experience, he lacked in discipline. He mocked authority. Ran with the wrong crowd. Indulged in the sinful ways of a sailor. Although his training would have qualified him to serve as an officer, his behavior caused him to be flogged and demoted.

In his early twenties, he made his way to Africa, where he became intrigued with the lucrative slave trade. At age twenty-one, he made his living on the *Greyhound,* a slave ship crossing the Atlantic Ocean.

John ridiculed the moral and poked fun at the religious. He even made jokes about a book that would eventually help reshape his life: *The Imitation of Christ.* In fact, he was degrading that book a few hours before his ship sailed into an angry storm.

That night the waves pummeled the *Greyhound,* spinning the ship one minute on the top of a wave. Plunging her the next into a watery valley.

John awakened to find his cabin filled with water. A side of the *Greyhound* had collapsed. Ordinarily such damage would have sent a ship to the bottom in a matter of minutes. The *Greyhound,* however, was carrying buoyant cargo and remained afloat.

John worked at the pumps all night. For nine hours, he and the other sailors struggled to keep the ship from sinking. But he knew that it was a losing cause. Finally, when his hopes were more battered than the vessel, he threw himself on the saltwater-soaked deck and pleaded, "If this will not do, then Lord have mercy on us all."

John didn't deserve mercy, but he received it. The *Greyhound* and her crew survived.

John never forgot God's mercy shown on that tempestuous day in the roaring Atlantic. He returned to England where he became a prolific composer. You've sung his songs, like this one:

> Amazing grace! how sweet the sound,
> That saved a wretch like me!
> I once was lost, but now am found,
> was blind, but now I see.[15]

This slave-trader-turned-songwriter was John Newton.

Along with his hymn writing, he also became a powerful pulpiteer. For nearly fifty years, he filled pulpits and churches with the story of the Savior who meets you and me in the storm.

A year or two before his death, people urged him to give up preaching because of his failing sight. "What!" he explained. "Shall the old African blasphemer stop while he can yet speak?"

He wouldn't stop. He couldn't stop. What had begun as a prayer of fear resulted in a lifetime of faith. During his last years, someone asked him about his health. He confessed that his powers were failing. "My memory is almost gone," he said, "but I remember two things: I am a great sinner, and Jesus is a great Savior."

What more do you and I need to remember?

———————————————

Two sailors and two seas. Two vessels in two storms. Two prayers of fear and two lives of faith. Uniting them is one Savior—one God who'll walk through hell or high water to extend a helping hand to a child who cries for help.

23

WHY
GOD
SMILES

I HAVE A SKETCH OF JESUS LAUGHING. It hangs on the wall across from my desk.

It's quite a drawing. His head is back. His mouth is open. His eyes are sparkling. He isn't just grinning. He isn't just chuckling. He's roaring. He hasn't heard or seen one like that in quite a while. He's having trouble catching his breath.

It was given to me by an Episcopal priest who carries cigars in his pocket and collects portraits of Jesus smiling. "I give them to anyone who might be inclined to take God too seriously," he explained as he handed me the gift.

He pegged me well.

I'm not one who easily envisions a smiling God. A weeping God, yes. An angry God, OK. A mighty God, you bet. But a chuckling God? It seems too . . . too . . . too unlike what God should do—and be. Which just shows how much I know—or don't know—about God.

What do I think he was doing when he stretched the neck of the giraffe? An exercise in engineering? What do I think he had in mind when he told the ostrich where to put his head? Spelunking? What do I think he was doing when he designed the mating call of an ape? Or the eight legs of the octopus? And what do I envision on his face when he saw Adam's first glance at Eve? A yawn?

Hardly.

As my vision improves and I'm able to read without my stained glasses, I'm seeing that a sense of humor is perhaps the only way God has put up with us for so long.

Is that him with a smile as Moses does a double take at the burning bush that speaks?

Is he smiling again as Jonah lands on the beach, dripping gastric juices and smelling like whale breath?

Is that a twinkle in his eye as he watches the disciples feed thousands with one boy's lunch?

Do you think that his face is deadpan as he speaks about the man with a two-by-four in his eye who points out a speck in a friend's eye?

Can you honestly imagine Jesus bouncing children on his knee with a somber face?

No, I think that Jesus smiled. I think that he smiled a bit at people and a lot with people.

Let me explain with an example.

We don't know a thing about her. We don't know her name . . . her background . . . her looks . . . her hometown. She came from nowhere and went nowhere. She disappeared the same way that she appeared, like a puff of smoke.

But what a delightful puff she was.

The disciples, during two years of training, hadn't done what she did in a few moments of conversing. She impressed God with her faith. The disciples' hearts may have been good. Their desire may have been sincere. But their faith didn't turn God's head.

Hers did. For all we don't know about her, we do know one remarkable truth: She impressed God with her faith. After that, anything else she ever did was insignificant.

"Woman, you have great faith!"[1] Jesus stated.

Some statement. Especially when you consider God said it. The God who can put a handful of galaxies into his palm. The One who creates Everests as a hobby. The One who paints rainbows without a canvas. The One who can measure the thickness of mosquito wings with one hand and level a mountain with the other.

One would think that the Creator would not be easily impressed. But something about this woman brought a sparkle to his eyes and . . . most likely . . . a smile to his face.

Matthew called her a "Canaanite woman" and, in doing so, called strikes one and two. Strike one? A Canaanite. An outsider. A foreigner. An apple in a family tree of oranges. Strike two? A woman. Might as well have been a junkyard dog. She lived in a culture that had little respect for women outside the bedroom and kitchen.

But she met the Teacher, who had plenty of respect for her.

Oh, it doesn't appear that way. In fact, the dialogue between the two seems harsh. It's not an easy passage to understand unless you're willing to concede that Jesus knew how to smile. If you have trouble with the sketch of the smiling Jesus hanging in my office, you'll have trouble with this story. But if you don't, if the thought of God smiling brings you a bit of relief, then you'll like the next few paragraphs.

Here's my interpretation.

The woman is desperate. Her daughter is demon possessed.

The Canaanite woman has no right to ask anything of Jesus. She is not a Jew. She is not a disciple. She offers no money for the ministry. She makes no promises to devote herself to missionary service. You get the impression that she knows as well as anybody that Jesus doesn't owe her anything, and she is asking him for everything. But that doesn't slow her down. She persists in her plea.

"Have mercy on me!"[2]

Matthew notes that Jesus says nothing at first. Nothing. He doesn't open his mouth. Why?

To test her? Most commentators suggest this. Maybe, they say, he is waiting to see how serious she is about her plea. My dad used to make me wait a week from the day I asked him for something to the day he gave me his answer. Most of the time, I forgot that I ever made the request. Time has a way of separating whims from needs. Is Jesus doing that?

I have another opinion. I think that he was admiring her. I think that it did his heart good to see some spunky faith for a change. I think that it refreshed him to see someone asking him to do the very thing he came to do—give great gifts to unworthy children.

How strange that we don't allow him to do it more often for us.

Perhaps the most amazing response to God's gift is our reluctance to accept it. We want it. But on our terms. For some odd reason, we feel better if we earn it. So we create religious hoops and hop through them—making God a trainer, us his pets, and religion a circus.

The Canaanite woman knew better. She had no resume. She claimed no heritage. She had no earned degrees. She knew only two things: Her daughter was weak, and Jesus was strong.

———————

The disciples are annoyed. As Jesus sits in silence, they grow more smug. "Send her away," they demand. The spotlight is put on Jesus. He looks at the disciples, then looks at the woman. And what follows is one of the most intriguing dialogues in the New Testament.

"I was sent only to the lost sheep of Israel,"[3] he says.

"Lord, help me!"[4]

"It is not right to take the children's bread and toss it to their dogs,"[5] he answers.

"But even the dogs eat the crumbs that fall from their masters' table,"[6] she responds.

Is Jesus being rude? Is he worn-out? Is he frustrated? Is he calling this woman a dog? How do we explain this dialogue?

Bible commentaries give us three options.

Some say that Jesus was trapped. He could not help the woman because he had been sent first to the lost sheep of Israel. Neat theory, but full of problems. One is the Samaritan woman. Another is the centurion. Jesus had already helped Gentiles and stayed faithful to the focus of his mission. So why couldn't he do it now?

Others think that Jesus was rude. Who can blame him? He was tired. It had been a long trip. The disciples were coming along pretty slowly. And this request was the straw that broke the camel's back.

Like that explanation? I don't either. The one who had had compassion on the five thousand men . . . who had wept over the city of Jerusalem . . . who had come to seek and save ones like this one . . . would not snap so abruptly at such a needy woman.

The most popular theory is that he was testing her . . . again. Just to be sure that she was serious about her request. Just to make sure that her faith was real.

But by insinuating that she was a dog?

I don't think Jesus would do that, either. Let me suggest another alternative.

Could it be that Jesus' tongue is poking his cheek? Could it be that he and the woman are engaging in satirical banter? Is it wry exchange in which God's unlimited grace is being highlighted? Could Jesus be so delighted to have found one who is not bartering with a religious system or proud of a heritage that he can't resist a bit of satire?

He knows he can heal her daughter. He knows he isn't bound by a plan. He knows her heart is good. So he decides to engage in a humorous moment with a faithful woman. In essence, here's what they said:

"Now, you know that God only cares about Jews," he says smiling.

And when she catches on, she volleys back, "But your bread is so precious, I'll be happy to eat the crumbs."

In a spirit of exuberance, he bursts out, "Never have I seen such faith! Your daughter is healed."

This story does not portray a contemptuous God. It portrays a willing One who delights in a sincere seeker.

Aren't you glad he does?

The story is told about the time Napoleon's steed got away from him. An alert private jumped on his own horse and chased down the emperor's horse. When he presented the reins of the animal to Napoleon, the ruler took them, smiled at this willing private, and said, "Thank you, Captain."

The soldier's eyes widened at what he had heard. He then straightened. Saluted. And snapped, "Thank you, sir!"

He immediately went to the barracks. Got his bags. Moved into the officers' quarters. Took his old uniform to the quartermaster and exchanged it for that of a captain. By the emperor's word, he had become a private-turned-commissioned officer.[7] He didn't argue. He didn't shrug. He didn't doubt. He knew that the one who had the power to do it had done it. And he accepted that.

If only we would do the same. If only we would have the faith of the private and the trust of the Canaanite woman. If only, when God smiles and says we are saved, we'd salute him, thank him, and live like those who have just received a gift from the commander in chief.

We seldom do that, though. We prefer to get salvation the old-fashioned way: We earn it. To accept grace is to admit failure, a step we are hesitant to take. We opt to impress God with how good we are rather than confessing how great he is. We dizzy ourselves with doctrine. Burden ourselves with rules. Think that God will smile on our efforts.

He doesn't.

God's smile is not for the healthy hiker who boasts that he made the journey alone. It is, instead, for the crippled leper who begs God for a back on which to ride.

Such were the woman's words. She knew that her request was ludicrous. But she also knew that Jesus was Lord.

Daniel's words could have been hers: "We do not make requests of you because we are righteous, but because of your great mercy."[8]

She came, banking on the hope that Jesus would answer her prayer based on his goodness and not her worthiness.

And he did. With a smile.

When I think about the prayers God has answered for me in spite of the life I've lived, I think he must be smiling still.

So I think I'll keep his picture on the wall.

24

THE
SACRIFICIAL
VISITOR

*L*ET ME DESCRIBE A SCENE to you and then ask you to come back to it at the end of the chapter.

An old man walks down a Florida beach. The sun sets like an orange ball on the horizon. The waves slap the sand. The smell of saltwater stings the air. The beach is vacant. No sun to entice the sunbathers. Not enough light for the fishermen. So, aside from a few joggers and strollers, the gentleman is alone.

He carries a bucket in his bony hand. A bucket of shrimp. It's not for him. It's not for the fish. It's for the sea gulls.

He walks to an isolated pier cast in gold by the setting sun. He steps out to the end of the pier. The time has come for the weekly ritual.

He stands and waits.

Soon the sky becomes a mass of dancing dots. The evening silence gives way to the screeching of birds. They fill the sky and then cover the moorings. They are on a pilgrimage to meet the old man.

For a half hour or so, the bushy-browed, shoulder-bent gentleman will stand on the pier, surrounded by the birds of the sea, until his bucket is empty.

But even after the food is gone, his feathered friends still linger. They linger as if they're attracted to more than just food. They perch on his hat. They walk on the pier. And they all share a moment together.

Got the scene? Now put it on the back burner for a few minutes.

─────────────────

Jesus left there and went along the Sea of Galilee. Then he went up on a mountainside and sat down. Great crowds came to him, bringing the lame, the blind, the crippled, the mute and many others, and laid them at his feet; and he healed them. The people were amazed when they saw the mute speaking, the crippled made well, the lame walking and the blind seeing. And they praised the God of Israel.

Jesus called his disciples to him and said, "I have compassion for these people; they have already been with me three days and have nothing to eat. I do not want to send them away hungry, or they may collapse on the way."[1]

This is not the day that Jesus fed the five thousand men; it is the day he fed the *four* thousand. Although the events have much in common, they are different in several respects:

- When Jesus fed the five thousand, he was with Jews. When he fed the four thousand (plus women and children), he was in Decapolis, a Gentile region.

- When Jesus fed the five thousand, he taught and healed them. When he was with the four thousand, there is no record that he taught—only that he healed.

- When Jesus was with the five thousand, he was with them for one afternoon. When he was with

the four thousand, he was with them for three
days.

And for three days he did a most remarkable thing: He
healed them. "The lame, the blind, the crippled, the mute
and many others" came to him, Matthew wrote, "and he
healed them."

Many times I wish that the New Testament writers had
been a bit more descriptive. This is one of those times. "And
he healed them" is too short a phrase to describe what must
have been an astonishing sight.

Let your imagination go. Can you see the scene?

Can you see the blind husband seeing his wife for the
first time? His eyes gazing into her tear-filled ones like she
was the queen of the morning?

Envision the man who had never walked, now walking! Don't you know that he didn't want to sit down? Don't
you know that he ran and jumped and did a dance with the
kids?

And what about the mute who could speak? Can you
picture him sitting by the fire late into the night and talking? Saying and singing everything and anything that he
had ever wanted to say and sing.

And the deaf woman who could now hear. What was it
like when she heard her child call her "Mamma" for the
first time?

For three days it went on. Person after person. Mat
after mat. Crutch after crutch. Smile after smile. No record
is given of Jesus preaching or teaching or instructing or
challenging. He just healed.

"The people," Matthew wrote, "were amazed when they
saw the mute speaking, the crippled made well, the lame
walking and the blind seeing." Four thousand amazed
people, each telling a story grander than the other. In the

midst of them all is Jesus. Not complaining. Not postponing. Not demanding. Just enjoying every minute.

Then Matthew, still the great economizer of words, gave us another phrase on which I wish he would have elaborated:

"They praised the God of Israel."

I wonder how they did that? I feel more certain of what they *didn't* do than of what they did do. I feel confident that they didn't form a praise committee. I feel confident that they didn't make any robes. I feel confident that they didn't sit in rows and stare at the back of each other's heads.

I doubt seriously if they wrote a creed on how they were to praise this God they had never before worshiped. I can't picture them getting into an argument over technicalities. I doubt if they felt it had to be done indoors.

And I know they didn't wait until the Sabbath to do it.

In all probability, they just did it. Each one—in his or her own way, with his or her own heart—just praised Jesus. Perhaps some people came and fell at Jesus' feet. Perhaps some shouted his name. Maybe a few just went up on the hillside, looked into the sky, and smiled.

I can picture a mom and dad standing speechless before the Healer as they hold their newly healed baby.

I can envision a leper staring in awe at the One who took away his terror.

I can imagine throngs of people pushing and shoving. Wanting to get close. Not to request anything or demand anything, but just to say "thank you."

Perhaps some tried to pay Jesus, but what payment would have been sufficient?

Perhaps some tried to return his gift with another, but what could a person give that would express the gratitude?

All the people could do was exactly what Matthew said they did. "They praised the God of Israel."

However they did it, they did it. And Jesus was touched, so touched that he insisted they stay for a meal before they left.

Without using the word *worship,* this passage defines it. Worship is when you're aware that what you've been given is far greater than what you can give. Worship is the awareness that were it not for his touch, you'd still be hobbling and hurting, bitter and broken. Worship is the half-glazed expression on the parched face of a desert pilgrim as he discovers that the oasis is not a mirage.

Worship is the "thank you" that refuses to be silenced.

We have tried to make a science out of worship. We can't do that. We can't do that any more than we can "sell love" or "negotiate peace."

Worship is a voluntary act of gratitude offered by the saved to the Savior, by the healed to the Healer, and by the delivered to the Deliverer. And if you and I can go days without feeling an urge to say "thank you" to the One who saved, healed, and delivered us, then we'd do well to remember what he did.

━━━━━━━━━━━━━━

The old man on the pier couldn't go a week without saying "thank you."

His name was Eddie Rickenbacker. If you were alive in October 1942, you probably remember the day that he was reported missing at sea.

He had been sent on a mission to deliver a message to Gen. Douglas MacArthur. With a handpicked crew in a B-17 known as the "Flying Fortress," he set off across the South Pacific. Somewhere the crew became lost, the fuel ran out, and the plane went down.

All eight crew members escaped into the life rafts. They battled the weather, the water, the sharks, and the sun. But most of all, they battled the hunger. After eight days, their rations were gone. They ran out of options. It would take a miracle for them to survive.

And a miracle occurred.

After an afternoon devotional service, the men said a prayer and tried to rest. As Rickenbacker was dozing with his hat over his eyes, something landed on his head. He would later say that he knew it was a sea gull. He didn't know how he knew; he just knew. That gull meant food . . . if he could catch it. And he did.

The flesh was eaten. The intestines were used as fish bait. And the crew survived.

What was a sea gull doing hundreds of miles away from land?

Only God knows.

But whatever the reason, Rickenbacker was thankful. As a result, every Friday evening this old captain walked to the pier, his bucket full of shrimp and his heart full of thanks.

We'd be wise to do the same. We've much in common with Rickenbacker. We, too, were saved by a Sacrificial Visitor.

We, too, were rescued by One who journeyed far from only God knows where.

And we, like the captain, have every reason to look into the sky . . . and worship.

25

HOLINESS IN A BATHROBE

W HEN YOUR WORLD TOUCHES God's world, the result is a holy moment. When God's high hope kisses your earthly hurt, that moment is holy. That moment might happen on a Sunday during Communion or on a Thursday night at the skating rink. It might occur in a cathedral or in a subway, by a burning bush or by a feed trough. When and where don't matter. What matters is that holy moments occur. Daily. And I'd like to talk to you about the holiest of those moments—I'd like to talk to you about the holiest moment of your life.

No, not your birth. Not your wedding. Not the birth of a child. I'm talking about *the* holiest moment of your life. Those other moments are special. They sparkle with reverence. But compared to this moment, they are about as holy as a burp.

I'm talking about the sacred hour.

No, not your baptism or your christening. Not your first Communion or your first confession or even your first date. I know those moments are precious and certainly sacrosanct, but I've a different moment in mind.

It happened this morning. Right after you awoke. Right there in your house. Did you miss it? Let me recreate the scene.

The alarm rings. Your wife pokes you or your husband nudges you or your mom or dad shakes you. And you wake up.

You've already hit the sleeper button three times; hit it again and you'll be late. You've already asked for five more minutes . . . five different times; ask again and you'll get water poured on your head.

The hour has come. Daybreak has broken. So, with a groan and a grunt, you throw back the covers and kick a warm foot out into a cold world. It's followed by a reluctant companion.

You lean up and sit on the edge of the bed and stare at the back of your eyelids. You tell them to open, but they object. You pry them apart with your palms and peek into the room.

(The moment isn't holy yet, but it's almost here.)

You stand. At that moment, everything that will hurt during the course of the day hurts. It's as if the little person in your brain that's in charge of pain needs to test the circuits before you make it to the bathroom.

"Back pain?"

"Check."

"Stiff neck?"

"Check."

"High school football knee injury."

"Still hurting."

"Flaky scalp?"

"Still itching."

"Hay fever reaction?"

"Achoo!"

With the grace of a pregnant elephant, you step toward the bathroom. You wish there is some way to turn on the light slowly, but there isn't. So you slap on the spotlight, blink as your eyes adjust, and step up to the bathroom sink.

You are approaching the sacred. You may not know it, but you have just stepped on holy tile. You are in the inner sanctum. The burning bush of your world.

The holiest moment of your life is about to occur. Listen. You'll hear the fluttering of angels' wings signaling their arrival. Trumpets are poised on heaven's lips. A cloud of majesty encircles your bare feet. Heaven's hosts cease all motion as you raise your eyes and . . .

(Get ready. Here it comes. The holy moment is nigh.)

Cymbals clash. Trumpets echo in sacred halls. Heaven's children race through the universe scattering flower petals. Stars dance. The universe applauds. Trees sway in choreographed adulation. And well they should, for the child of the King has awakened.

Look in the mirror. Behold the holy one. Don't turn away. The image of perfection is looking back at you. The holy moment has arrived.

I know what you are thinking. *You call that "holy"? You call that "perfect"? You don't know what I look like at 6:30 AM.*

No, but I can guess. Hair matted. Pajamas or nightgown wrinkled. Chunks of sleep stuck in the corners of your eyes. Belly bulging. Dried-out lips. Pudgy eyes. Breath that could stain a wall. A face that could scare a dog.

"Anything but holy," you say. "Give me an hour and I'll look holy. Give me some coffee, some makeup. Give me a toothbrush and a hairbrush, and I'll make this body presentable. A little perfume . . . a splash of cologne. Then take me into the Holy of Holies. Then I'll make heaven smile."

Ah, but there's where you're wrong. You see, what makes the morning moment so holy is its honesty. What makes the morning mirror hallowed is that you are seeing exactly who God sees.

And who God loves.

No makeup. No pressed shirts. No power ties. No matching shoes. No layers of images. No status jewelry. Just unkempt honesty.

Just you.

If people love you at 6:30 in the morning, one thing is sure: They love *you.* They don't love your title. They don't love your style. They don't love your accomplishments. They just love you.

"Love," wrote one forgiven soul, "covers over a multitude of sins."[1]

Sounds like God's love.

"He has made perfect forever those who are being made holy," wrote another.[2]

Underline the word *perfect.* Note that the word is not *better.* Not *improving.* Not *on the upswing.* God doesn't improve; he perfects. He doesn't enhance; he completes. What does the perfect person lack?

Now I realize that there's a sense in which we're imperfect. We still err. We still stumble. We still do exactly what we don't want to do. And that part of us is, according to the verse, "being made holy."

But when it comes to our position before God, we're perfect. When he sees each of us, he sees one who has been made perfect through the One who is perfect—Jesus Christ.

"All of you who were baptized into Christ have clothed yourselves with Christ."[3]

This morning I "put on" clothing to hide the imperfections I'd rather not display. When you see me, fully clothed, you can't see my moles, scars, or bumps. Those are hidden.

When we choose to be baptized, by lifestyle as much as by symbol, into Christ, the same shielding occurs. Our sins and faults are lost beneath the sheer radiance of his covering. "For you died, and your life is now hidden with Christ in God."[4] Please, don't miss the impact of this verse. When God sees us, he also sees Christ. He sees perfection! Not perfection earned by us, mind you, but perfection paid for by him.

Reflect on these words for a moment:

"God made him who had no sin to be sin for us so that *in him* [emphasis mine] we might become the righteousness of God."[5]

Now read these words in the Phillips translation:

"For God caused Christ, who himself knew nothing of sin, actually to *be* sin for our sakes, so that in Christ we might be made good with the goodness of God."

Note the last four words: "the goodness of God." God's goodness is your goodness. You are absolute perfection. Flawless. Without defects or mistakes. Unsullied. Unrivaled. Unmarred. Peerless. Virgin pure. Undeserved yet unreserved perfection.

No wonder heaven applauds when you wake up. A masterpiece has stirred.

"Shh," whisper the stars, "look at the wonder of that child."

"My!" gasp the angels, "what a prodigy God has created."

So while you groan, eternity gasps with wonder. As you stumble, angels are star struck. What you see in the mirror as morning disaster is, in reality, a morning miracle. Holiness in a bathrobe.

Go ahead and get dressed. Go ahead and put on the

He has already seen you as you really are. And in his book, you are perfect.

26

THE CHOICE

W HY DO I WANT TO DO BAD?" my daughter asked me, unknowingly posing a question asked by many seekers
of truth. "Why do I do the thing I hate? What is this ape
that gibbers within?" Or, perhaps a more basic question is
being asked. "If sin separates me from God, why doesn't
God separate me from sin? Why doesn't he remove from me
the option to sin?"

To answer that, let's go to the beginning.

Let's go to the Garden and see the seed that both blessed
and cursed. Let's see why God gave man . . . the choice.

Behind it all was a choice. A deliberate decision. An
informed move. He didn't have to do it. But he chose to. He
knew the price. He saw the implications. He was aware of
the consequences.

We don't know when he decided to do it. We can't know.
Not just because we weren't there. Because time was not
there. *When* did not exist. Nor did *tomorrow* or *yesterday*
or *next time.* For there was no time.

We don't know when he thought about making the
choice. But we do know that he made it. He didn't have to
do it. He chose to.

He chose to create.

"In the beginning God created . . ."[1]

With one decision, history began. Existence became measurable.

Out of nothing came light.

Out of light came day.

Then came sky . . . and earth.

And on this earth? A mighty hand went to work.

Canyons were carved. Oceans were dug. Mountains erupted out of flatlands. Stars were flung. A universe sparkled.

Our sun became just one of millions. Our galaxy became just one of thousands. Planets invisibly tethered to suns roared through space at breakneck speeds. Stars blazed with heat that could melt our planet in seconds.

The hand behind it was mighty. He is mighty.

And with this might, he created. As naturally as a bird sings and a fish swims, he created. Just as an artist can't not paint and a runner can't not run, he couldn't not create. He was the Creator. Through and through, he was the Creator. A tireless dreamer and designer.

From the pallet of the Ageless Artist came inimitable splendors. Before there was a person to see it, his creation was pregnant with wonder. Flowers didn't just grow; they blossomed. Chicks weren't just born; they hatched. Salmons didn't just swim; they leaped.

Mundaneness found no home in his universe.

He must have loved it. Creators relish creating. I'm sure his commands were delightful! "Hippo, you won't walk . . . you'll waddle!" "Hyena, a bark is too plain. Let me show you how to laugh!" "Look, raccoon, I've made you a mask!" "Come here, giraffe, let's stretch that neck a bit." And on and on he went. Giving the clouds their puff. Giving the oceans their blue. Giving the trees their sway.

Giving the frogs their leap and croak. The mighty wed with the creative, and creation was born.

He was mighty. He was creative.

And he was love. Even greater than his might and deeper than his creativity was one all-consuming characteristic:

Love.

Water must be wet. A fire must be hot. You can't take the wet out of water and still have water. You can't take the heat out of fire and still have fire.

In the same way, you can't take the love out of this One who lived before time and still have him exist. For he was . . . and is . . . Love.

Probe deep within him. Explore every corner. Search every angle. Love is all you find. Go to the beginning of every decision he has made and you'll find it. Go to the end of every story he has told and you'll see it.

Love.

No bitterness. No evil. No cruelty. Just love. Flawless love. Passionate love. Vast and pure love. He is love.

As a result, an elephant has a trunk with which to drink. A kitten has a mother from which to nurse. A bird has a nest in which to sleep. The same God who was mighty enough to carve out the canyon is tender enough to put hair on the legs of the Matterhorn Fly to keep it warm. The same force that provides symmetry to the planets guides the baby kangaroo to its mother's pouch before the mother knows it is born.

And because of who he was, he did what he did.

He created a paradise. A sinless sanctuary. A haven before fear. A home before there was a human dweller. No time. No death. No hurt. A gift built by God for his ultimate creation. And when he was through, he knew "it was very good."[2]

But it wasn't enough.

His greatest work hadn't been completed. One final masterpiece was needed before he would stop.

Look to the canyons to see the Creator's splendor. Touch the flowers and see his delicacy. Listen to the thunder and hear his power. But gaze on this—the zenith—and witness all three . . . and more.

Imagine with me what may have taken place on that day.

He placed one scoop of clay upon another until a form lay lifeless on the ground.

All of the Garden's inhabitants paused to witness the event. Hawks hovered. Giraffes stretched. Trees bowed. Butterflies paused on petals and watched.

"You will love me, nature," God said. "I made you that way. You will obey me, universe. For you were designed to do so. You will reflect my glory, skies, for that is how you were created. But this one will be like me. This one will be able to choose."

All were silent as the Creator reached into himself and removed something yet unseen. A seed. "It's called 'choice.' The seed of choice."

Creation stood in silence and gazed upon the lifeless form.

An angel spoke, "But what if he . . ."

"What if he chooses not to love?" the Creator finished. "Come, I will show you."

Unbound by today, God and the angel walked into the realm of tomorrow.

"There, see the fruit of the seed of choice, both the sweet and the bitter."

The angel gasped at what he saw. Spontaneous love. Voluntary devotion. Chosen tenderness. Never had he seen anything like these. He felt the love of the Adams. He heard the joy of Eve and her daughters. He saw the food and the burdens shared. He absorbed the kindness and marveled at the warmth.

"Heaven has never seen such beauty, my Lord. Truly, this is your greatest creation."

"Ah, but you've only seen the sweet. Now witness the bitter."

A stench enveloped the pair. The angel turned in horror and proclaimed, "What is it?"

The Creator spoke only one word: "Selfishness."

The angel stood speechless as they passed through centuries of repugnance. Never had he seen such filth. Rotten hearts. Ruptured promises. Forgotten loyalties. Children of the creation wandering blindly in lonely labyrinths.

"This is the result of choice?" the angel asked.

"Yes."

"They will forget you?"

"Yes."

"They will reject you?"

"Yes."

"They will never come back?"

"Some will. Most won't."

"What will it take to make them listen?"

The Creator walked on in time, further and further into the future, until he stood by a tree. A tree that would be fashioned into a cradle. Even then he could smell the hay that would surround him.

With another step into the future, he paused before another tree. It stood alone, a stubborn ruler of a bald hill. The trunk was thick, and the wood was strong. Soon it would be cut. Soon it would be trimmed. Soon it would be mounted on the stony brow of another hill. And soon he would be hung on it.

He felt the wood rub against a back he did not yet wear.

"Will you go down there?" the angel asked.

"I will."

"Is there no other way?"

"There is not."

"Wouldn't it be easier to not plant the seed? Wouldn't it be easier to not give the choice?"

"It would," the Creator spoke slowly. "But to remove the choice is to remove the love."

He looked around the hill and foresaw a scene. Three figures hung on three crosses. Arms spread. Heads fallen forward. They moaned with the wind.

Men clad in soldiers' garb sat on the ground near the trio. They played games in the dirt and laughed.

Men clad in religion stood off to one side. They smiled. Arrogant, cocky. They had protected God, they thought, by killing this false one.

Women clad in sorrow huddled at the foot of the hill. Speechless. Faces tear streaked. Eyes downward. One put her arm around another and tried to lead her away. She wouldn't leave. "I will stay," she said softly. "I will stay."

All heaven stood to fight. All nature rose to rescue. All eternity poised to protect. But the Creator gave no command.

"It must be done . . . ," he said, and withdrew.

But as he stepped back in time, he heard the cry that he would someday scream: "My God, my God, why have you forsaken me?"[3] He wrenched at tomorrow's agony.

The angel spoke again. "It would be less painful . . ."

The Creator interrupted softly. "But it wouldn't be love."

They stepped into the Garden again. The Maker looked earnestly at the clay creation. A monsoon of love swelled up within him. He had died for the creation before he had made him. God's form bent over the sculptured face and breathed. Dust stirred on the lips of the new one. The chest rose, cracking the red mud. The cheeks fleshened. A finger moved. And an eye opened.

But more incredible than the moving of the flesh was the stirring of the spirit. Those who could see the unseen gasped.

Perhaps it was the wind who said it first. Perhaps what the star saw that moment is what has made it blink ever since. Maybe it was left to an angel to whisper it:

"It looks like . . . it appears so much like . . . it is him!"

The angel wasn't speaking of the face, the features, or the body. He was looking inside—at the soul.

"It's eternal!" gasped another.

Within the man, God had placed a divine seed. A seed of his self. The God of might had created earth's mightiest. The Creator had created, not a creature, but another creator. And the One who had chosen to love had created one who could love in return.

Now it's our choice.

27

CAUGHT WITH YOUR PANTS DOWN, BUT YOUR HEAD UP

STEVE LYONS WILL BE REMEMBERED as the player who dropped his pants.

He could be remembered as an outstanding infielder . . . as the player who played every position for the Chicago White Sox . . . as the guy who always dove into first base . . . as a favorite of the fans who high fived the guy who caught the foul ball in the bleachers. He could be remembered as an above-average player who made it with average ability.

But he won't. He'll be remembered as the player who dropped his pants on July 16, 1990.

The White Sox were playing the Tigers in Detroit. Lyons bunted and raced down the first-base line. He knew it was going to be tight, so he dove at the bag. Safe! The Tiger's pitcher disagreed. He and the umpire got into a shouting match, and Lyons stepped in to voice his opinion.

Absorbed in the game and the debate, Lyons felt dirt trickling down the inside of his pants. Without missing a beat he dropped his britches, wiped away the dirt, and . . . uh oh . . . twenty thousand jaws hit the bleachers' floor.

And, as you can imagine, the jokes began. Women behind the White Sox dugout waved dollar bills when he came onto the field. "No one," wrote one columnist, "had ever dropped his drawers on the field. Not Wally Moon. Not Blue

Moon Odom. Not even Heinie Manush."[1] Within twenty-four hours of the "exposure," he received more exposure than he'd gotten his entire career: seven live television and approximately twenty radio interviews.

"We've got this pitcher, Melido Perez, who earlier this month pitched a no-hitter," Lyons stated, "and I'll guarantee you he didn't do two live television shots afterwards. I pull my pants down, and I do seven. Something's pretty skewed toward the zany in this game."

Fortunately, for Steve, he was wearing sliding pants under his baseball pants. Otherwise the game would be rated "R" instead of "PG-13."

Now, I don't know Steve Lyons. I'm not a White Sox fan. Nor am I normally appreciative of men who drop their pants in public. But I think Steve Lyons deserves a salute.

I think anybody who dives into first base deserves a salute. How many guys do you see roaring down the baseline of life more concerned about getting a job done than they are about saving their necks? How often do you see people diving headfirst into anything?

Too seldom, right? But when we do . . . when we see a gutsy human throwing caution to the wind and taking a few risks . . . ah, now that's a person worthy of a pat on the . . . back.

So here's to all the Steve Lyons of the world.

Here's to the Miracles, a choral group out of Memphis, Tennessee, made up of the mentally retarded and the stouthearted. Just see if you can listen to them and still feel sorry for yourself.

Here's to the hero of the San Francisco marathon who crossed the finish line without seeing it. (He was blind.)

Here's to the woman whose husband left her with a nest of kids to raise and bills to pay, but who somehow tells me every Sunday that God has never been closer.

Here's to the single father of two girls who learned to braid their hair.

Here's to the grandparents who came out of retirement to raise the children their children couldn't raise.

Here's to the foster parents who took in a child long enough for that child to take their hearts—then gave the child up again.

Here's to the girl, told by everyone to abort the baby, who chose to keep the baby.

Here's to the doctor who treats more than half of his patients for free.

Here's to the heroin-addict-turned-missionary.

Here's to the executive who every Tuesday hosts a 5:30 AM meeting for Bible study and prayer.

Here's to all of you reckless lovers of life and God, who stand on first base because you paid a price to get there.

So what if you forget about pleasing the crowd and get caught with your pants down? At least you're playing ball in the pros.

Most of us aren't even in your league.

28

LEMONADE AND GRACE

*L*EMONADE, *5¢"*
The *e* is larger than the *L*. The *m* is upper cased; all the other letters are lowered. The last two letters, *de,* curve downward because the artist ran out of room on the poster board.

Norman Rockwell would have loved it.

Two girls sit on the sidewalk in little chairs behind a little table. The six-year-old is the cashier. She monitors a plastic bowl of change. The four-year-old is the waitress. She handles the ice. Pours the drinks. Stacks and restacks the paper cups.

Behind them, seated on the grass, is Dad. He leans against an oak tree and smiles as he witnesses his daughters' inauguration into capitalism.

Business has been steady. The Saturday-afternoon stream of patrons has nearly emptied the pitcher. The bottom of the cashier's bowl is covered with thirty-five cents of change. With the exception of a few spills, the service has been exceptional. No complaints. Many compliments.

Part of the success, though, has been due to the marketing strategy.

Our street doesn't get much traffic, so we did a little advertising. As my daughters painted the sign, I called several families in the neighborhood and invited them to the grand opening of our lemonade stand. So all of our clients, thus far, had been partial.

I was proud of myself. I leaned back against the tree. Closed my eyes. Turned up the radio I had brought. And listened to the baseball game.

Then I heard an unfamiliar voice.

"I'll have a cup of lemonade, please."

I opened my eyes. It was a customer. A real customer. An unsolicited neighbor who had driven by, seen the sign, stopped, and ordered a drink.

Uh-oh, I thought. Our service was about to be tested.

Andrea, the four-year-old, grabbed a cup that had already been used.

"Get a clean cup," I whispered.

"Oh," she giggled, and got a clean cup.

She opened the ice bucket, looked in, and then looked back at me. "Daddy, we are out of ice."

The patron overheard her. "That's OK. I'll take it warm."

She picked up the pitcher and poured. Syrupy sugar oozed out of the pitcher. "Daddy, there's just a little bit."

Our customer spoke again. "That's fine. I don't want much."

"I hope you like it sweet," I said under my breath.

She handed the cup to the man and he handed her a dollar. She gave it to Jenna.

Jenna turned to me. "Daddy, what do I do?" (We weren't used to such big bills.)

I stuck my hands in my pockets; they were empty.

"Uh, we don't have any . . ." I began.

"No problem," he said, smiling. "Just keep the change."

I smiled sheepishly. He thanked the girls. Told them they were doing a great job. Climbed back into his car. And drove off.

Quite a transaction, I thought. *We give him a warm, partially filled cup of lemonade syrup, and he gives us a compliment and a payment twenty times too much.*

I had set out to teach the girls about free enterprise. They ended up with a lesson on grace.

And so had I. For all the theologizing we preachers do about God's grace, the kind stranger modeled it better than the best of sermons state it.

Perhaps the story of the stranger who brought grace to our street is a good place for us to wrap up this book. For this story is the story of each of us.

Each of us has seen our ice melt in the July sun of stress. Who hasn't attempted to serve the best, only to find that the best has already been served and that the pitcher needs to be refilled? And there's not a person alive who hasn't wondered what God does when what we promise and what we produce aren't even close to being the same.

Lemonade stands and living life would be high-risk endeavors were it not for the appearance of gentle strangers on our streets. But, thank God, they come.

And, thank God, He came.

For isn't God the stranger who became our friend after looking past the dregs and into our hearts?

And aren't we not much more than surprised children, amazed that what we receive is twenty times, yea, verily a million times, more than what we ask for?

The next time your calm becomes chaos, think of that. The next time you find yourself in a storm and can't see God on the horizon, reflect on the lemonade stand. And if your walking on the water becomes floundering in the deep like Peter's did, lift your eyes and look . . .

A Gentle Stranger may be bringing grace to your street . . . to your life.

CONCLUSION

I JUST DID WHAT YOU JUST DID. I just read this book. It goes in the mail tomorrow. The overnight-express package is on my desk, and the label is typed. The editors and their red pens are waiting. The printers and their presses are expectant. But I wasn't ready to send it off yet. So I sat on the couch with coffee, and highlighter and sipped and read and . . . gratefully. . . smiled.

I liked it. You might find that surprising. You might assume that every writer likes what he or she writes. They should and normally do, I suppose. But I always have that lingering fear that with all the work done, I might sit down to read what I wrote . . . and gag.

But I didn't. I was pleased.

I smiled at the right spots and was warmed at others. It was good to visit the seashore again and see the patient Master touching the people. It was fun to read about the woman who called my bluff on the plane. It did me good to read about the lost contact lens and the recovered vision, Rickenbacker's lost crew and the mysterious sea gull, the impossible stairway and the nameless carpenter.

It was good to be reminded again that this journey is a brief one. That Jesus knows how I feel and that he'd scramble off a mountain and walk through a storm to convince me of that.

It was good to hear God's gentle thunder. I hope it has been good for you. Thanks for reading my book. I realize that it took your time and money. I hope it has been worth both.

And I hope you never forget the last Lighthouse Law: Approach life like a voyage on a schooner. Enjoy the view. Explore the vessel. Make friends with the captain. Fish a little. And then get off when you get home.

Good sailing!

NOTES

Chapter 2 • God Under Pressure

1. Matthew 14:1–13.
2. Luke 9:9.
3. The wording of Matthew 14:1–13 has given rise to some discussion. At the beginning of the passage, it is clear that John the Baptist is already dead because Herod is concerned that Jesus might be "John the Baptist . . . risen from the dead." Jesus withdraws when he "heard what had happened." A fair question is, what news did Jesus hear? Did he hear that John had been killed? Or did he hear that Herod might be after him? Or a combination of both? Those scholars who argue that Jesus retreated solely out of sorrow over the death of John the Baptist suggest that Matthew simply forgot how he began the chapter with a reference to Herod. "[Matthew] . . . has forgotten the parenthetic nature of the story of John the Baptist" (R. Bultmann, *The History of the Synoptic Translation,* ed. John Marsh [New York: Harper & Row, 1963], 48). Other scholars argue that it was the awareness that Herod was looking for him that spurred Jesus' withdrawal. Lamar Cope reasons that Jesus withdrew due to fear that Herod would pursue him next. He writes, "In unpunctuated Greek there were only limited ways to mark off sections of thought" (Lamar Cope, *Catholic Bible Quarterly,* 37:4 [1976]: 515–18). He explains that the Greek indicates that the John the Baptist story was an insert and that the phrase "when Jesus heard" directly refers to Herod's acquaintance with Jesus. Hence Jesus left in peril. Most scholars,

however, are in general agreement that the phrase, "When Jesus heard what had happened," refers to a combination of sorrow and caution. For references see: *A Commentary Critical, Experimental and Practical of the Old and New Testaments; Matthew-John,* ed. David Brown, vol. 5 (Grand Rapids, Mich.: Eerdmans, 1948), 159; J. S. Exell, ed., *The Biblical Illustrator: Matthew* (Grand Rapids, Mich.: Baker Book House, 1955), 267; J. W. McGarvey, ed., *New Testament Commentary: Matthew and Mark,* vol. 1 (Delight, Ark.: Gospel Light Publishing, 1900), 130; Alan Hugh McNeile, *The Gospel According to St. Matthew, Greek Text* (London: Macmillan & Co., 1952), 212; C. E. Montefiore, *Synoptic Gospels* (London: Macmillan & Co., 1909), 60; J. B. Orchard, *A Synopsis of the Four Gospels in Greek* (Macon, Ga.: Mercer University Press, 1983), 30; Adam Clarke, *Clark's Commentary: Matthew-Acts,* vol. 5 (Nashville, Tenn.: Abingdon Press, 1831, 1967), 157; Frederick Dale Bruner, *Matthew: The Churchbook,* vol. 2 (Dallas, Tex.: Word Publishing, 1990), 526, 527; William Barclay, *The Gospel of Matthew,* vol. 2 (Philadelphia, Pa.: Westminster Press, 1975), 98; *The Expositors Bible Commentary,* vol. 8 (Grand Rapids, Mich.: Zondervan Publishing House, 1984), 340, 341; see especially William Hendricksen, *The Gospel of Matthew* (Grand Rapids, Mich.: Baker Book House, 1973), 593, 594.

4. Mark 6:30.

5. Mark 6:12.

6. Matthew 14:21.

7. John MacArthur, *The MacArthur Commentary: Matthew 8–15* (Chicago, Ill.: Moody Press, 1987), 427.

8. Mark 6:31.

9. Ibid.

10. Luke 9:11.

11. Max Lucado, *God Came Near* (Portland, Oreg.: Multnomah Press, 1987), 26.

12. How divinity and humanity could coexist in the same body is not easy to comprehend. Indeed, the paradox of the Incarnation has been a source of tension for theologians throughout

Notes

history. Discomfort with the mystery has driven thinkers to relegate the doctrine into one of two extremes, each of which is equally dangerous. One line of reasoning, known as Ebionitism, denies the full divinity of Christ. Those who embrace this position reject the presence of God in Christ. He is presented as a religious genius, a spiritual master, a guru, but not God himself. He was the "perfect religious personality, a spiritual life completely filled by the realization of God who is love." (Walter Rausenbusch, *A Theology for the Social Gospel,* 154, 155, as quoted by Bloesch in *Essentials of Evangelical Theology,* 1:135.) The other approach to the incarnation of Jesus begins with the deity of Christ, but never arrives at his humanity. "Docetism," (which comes from the Greek word *dokeo,* which means "to seem, to have the appearance of"), rejects God as a touchable, reachable human and relegates Jesus to the metaphysical. See Stephen Neill, *Jesus Through Many Eyes* (Philadelphia, Pa.: Fortress Press, 1976), 139. This form of Gnosticism, although comfortable with the overarching pattern or truth that is exemplified in Christ, is unable to endorse the complete indwelling of God in the man, Jesus. Both approaches, Ebionitism and Docetism, strain to exalt one nature at the expense of the other. Both are equally heretical. One leaves you with a good teacher who deceived the world with falsehood and tricks. . . . The other offers a god who simply masked himself in humanity, but never experienced it. The apostles John and Paul have strong words for both. "Every spirit that acknowledges that Jesus Christ has come in the flesh is from God, but every spirit that does not acknowledge Jesus is not from God" (1 John 4:2–3). "For in Christ all the fullness of the Deity lives in bodily form" (Col. 2:9). "In the beginning was the Word, and the Word was with God, and the Word was God" (John 1:1). It was this Word [Jesus] who assumed the human state and "made his dwelling among us . . . full of grace and truth" (John 1:14). Other Scriptures join the chorus. Jesus was "born of a woman, born under law" (Gal. 4:4). He shared in "their humanity" (Heb. 2:14). He "offered up

prayers and petitions with loud cries and tears" (Heb. 5:7). He grew in "wisdom and stature" (Luke 2:40, KJV). Yet, although human, he was divine. He is called "our great God and Savior" (Titus 2:13). He forgave sins (Mark 2:5, 7, 10). He raised the dead; he gave and gives life (John 5:21). He defeated death (2 Tim. 2:8). How do we justify the paradox? How do we explain "the Lord humbled for communion with man and likewise the Servant exalted to communion with God?" (Karl Barth, *The Humanity of Gods,* trans. Thomas Wieser and John Newton Thomas [Richmond, Va.: John Knox Press, 1964], 64). How do we explain that God was equally human and divine? We don't. It is a secret beyond our reach and, consequentially, worthy of our worship. Hence Paul wrote: "Great beyond all question is the mystery of our religion: 'He who was manifested in the body, vindicated in the spirit, seen by angels; who was proclaimed among the nations, believed in throughout the world, glorified in high heaven'" (1 Tim. 3:16, NEB).
13. *More of Paul Harvey's The Rest of the Story,* ed. Paul Aurandt (New York: Bantam Books, 1980), 79, 80.

Chapter 3 • A Mother's Love—A Friend's Empathy

1. Matthew 14:14.
2. Mark 6:34.
3. Luke 9:11.
4. See John 6:15, 26.
5. Matthew 14:14.
6. Matthew 14:15.
7. Matthew 14:16.
8. Mark 6:37.
9. Ibid.
10. Mark 6:41.

Chapter 4 • When Fishermen Don't Fish

1. Mark 6:34.
2. Matthew 14:14.

3. Ibid.
4. Mark 6:34.

Chapter 7 • Thanks for the Bread

1. John 6:1–14.

Chapter 9 • Fending Off the Voices

1. Ann Trebbe and Valerie Helmbreck, "'Ideal' is body beautiful and 'clean cut,'" *USA Today,* 15 September 1989.
2. John 6:14.
3. John 6:15.
4. John 10:3.
5. Revelation 3:20.
6. Matthew 28:20.
7. Hebrews 13:5.
8. John 5:28–29.

Chapter 10 • The Photo and the File

1. Matthew 5:5.
2. Philippians 1:10.

Chapter 11 • Seeing God Through Shattered Glass

1. Matthew 14:22–24.
2. Mark 6:52.
3. Matthew 14:15.
4. Ibid.

Chapter 12 • Two Fathers, Two Feasts

1. 1 Thessalonians 5:9, NEB.
2. Isaiah 57:15.
3. Psalm 74:10; 89:46.
4. 1 Chronicles 29:15.

5. Psalm 39:5.
6. James 4:14.
7. Psalm 103:15, 16.
8. 2 Corinthians 4:16–18.
9. 2 Corinthians 11:23–27.

Chapter 14 • The Miracle of the Carpenter

1. Matthew 14:23.

Chapter 15 • The Woodcutter's Wisdom

1. Ecclesiastes 7:8.
2. Romans 12:12.
3. Matthew 6:34.

Chapter 16 • Laws of the Lighthouse

1. As quoted by Stephen R. Covey, *The Seven Habits of Highly Effective People* (New York: Fireside—Simon & Schuster, 1989), 33.

Chapter 17 • He Speaks Through the Storm

1. Job 42:5, TLB.
2. Job 13:4, 5, TLB.
3. Job 33:29.
4. Job 38:2.
5. Job 38:3.
6. Job 38:4, TLB.
7. Job 38:5–7, TLB.
8. Job 38:12, 13, TLB.
9. Job 38:17–21, TLB.
10. Job 40:4, 5, TLB.
11. Job 41:11, TLB.
12. Job 42:5, TLB.

Chapter 18 • Pilgrim Ponderings

1. Matthew 17:1–5.
2. Luke 9:29.
3. Matthew 17:5.

Chapter 19 • Our Storm Was His Path

1. Matthew 14:27.
2. Matthew 14:28.

Chapter 20 • They'd Do It Again

1. Matthew 14:33.

Chapter 21 • Castles of Sorrow

1. 2 Corinthians 7:10.

Chapter 22 • Fear That Becomes Faith

1. John 6:19.
2. Proverbs 9:10.
3. Exodus 14:15, 16.
4. 2 Kings 5:13, 14.
5. Romans 3.
6. Acts 12:6–17.
7. Matthew 14:28.
8. Ephesians 2:8, 9.
9. "Rock of Ages, Cleft for Me," by Augustus M. Toplady.
10. "The Solid Rock," by Edward Mote.
11. "Amazing Grace," by John Newton.
12. Matthew 14:30.
13. Ibid.
14. Matthew 14:31.
15. "Amazing Grace," by John Newton.

Chapter 23 • Why God Smiles

1. Matthew 15:28.
2. Matthew 15:22.
3. Matthew 15:24.
4. Matthew 15:25.
5. Matthew 15:26.
6. Matthew 15:27.
7. Paul Lee Tan, *Encyclopedia of 7700 Illustrations,* Rockville, MD: Assurance Publishers, 1979, p. 509.
8. Daniel 9:18.

Chapter 24 • The Sacrificial Visitor

1. Matthew 15:29–32.

Chapter 25 • Holiness in a Bathrobe

1. 1 Peter 4:8.
2. Hebrews 10:14.
3. Galatians 3:27.
4. Colossians 3:3.
5. 2 Corinthians 5:21.

Chapter 26 • The Choice

1. Genesis 1:1.
2. Genesis 1:31.
3. Mark 15:34.

Chapter 27 • Caught with Your Pants Down, But Your Head Up

1. "Moon Man," *Sports Illustrated,* 13 August 1990, 58–63.

STUDY
GUIDE

It is my hope that this book has given you encouragement to not only face and survive, but to grow through the storms of life. I hope it has given you encouragement to see Christ standing tall amidst the towering waves and step out toward his holy, helping hand.

This study guide is designed to help you move from encouraging thoughts to daring living in the eye of the storm. If you are reading through this book with a group, you might try to work through one study session a week. (Group leaders, please be sensitive to the personal nature of some of the questions in this guide. Sharing answers with the group should always be optional.)

Whether you use this study guide alone or with a group, I suggest that you have your Bible and notebook close at hand. Write down your thoughts and discoveries. Pray earnestly about how God would have you respond to his promises! Use this guide not as an end unto itself, but as a catalyst for further study—as a tool to further strengthen your faith against the fury of the storm.

SESSION 1 ————————————————

Chapter 1 *From Calm to Chaos*

1. Describe a moment when your life went from calm to chaos. When did it happen? What were the circumstances? Who was involved?

2. Afterwards, how did you feel about that sudden switch from calm to chaos? Did you recover quickly, or do you still bear scars from the trauma?

3. Think about the internal codes you might have used to deal with the chaos. Did you have the right ones? Did you know how to use them? What codes do you need to learn in order to keep cool in the pressure cooker?

Chapter 2 *God Under Pressure*

1. After learning about John the Baptist's murder and Herod's threat, and seeing how tired the disciples were, Jesus called a "time out." He and the disciples "withdrew by boat privately to a solitary place" (Luke 9:9).

   When you are dealing with a difficult situation—when you reach your limit of stress, pain, rejection, loneliness— how do you take "time out"? Where do you go? What do you do?

2. The following passages describe some of God's promises that we can hold onto during times of stress: Psalm 33:20; 34:7; 145:18; Proverbs 30:5; Isaiah 41:10; 43:2; Matthew 28:20; John 16:33; Romans 8:17; Ephesians 6:10–17; Hebrews 13:6; 1 Peter 5:10. Select one that is most meaningful

to you and write it down or memorize it so that it will comfort you the next time your world goes from calm to chaos.

3. While Jesus and the disciples were in the boat, peace reigned. Suddenly, when they reached land, the crowd converged on them again and dashed their hopes of having a few hours alone.

Can you relate? Describe a time when what you *sought* and what you *got* were completely different. How did you feel at the time? How did you respond?

4. Read Hebrews 4:15. What is your initial response to the statement, "Jesus knows how you feel"? Is there even the slightest temptation to think, "He knows how I feel most of the time, but he doesn't *really* know what *this* feels like"?

As you review the experiences in your life, is it hard for you to believe that Jesus has fully experienced them? Which ones do you think Jesus may not have fully experienced?

Why do you think it is so hard to truly believe that Jesus knows how we feel? What difference does it make that Jesus shared fully in our experience of temptation—but never sinned?

What experiences and hurts do you need to take to Jesus—your understanding Father and Physician—so that he may heal you?

5. Write down or discuss what the following references tell us about Jesus: Mark 2:5, 7, 10; Luke 2:40; John 1:1, 14; John 5:21; Colossians 2:9; Titus 2:13; Hebrews 2:14a; Hebrews 5:7; 1 John 4:2b, 3a.

SESSION 2

Chapter 3 *A Mother's Love—A Friend's Empathy*

1. Consider this: "Jesus knew the value of people. He knew that each human being is a treasure. And because he did, people were not a source of stress, but a source of joy."

   Could someone make the same statement about you? What do you think makes the difference between seeing people as a source of stress or a source of joy?

2. Try to place yourself in Jesus' position as the crowds surrounded him. Would you have healed all the sick that day, or only certain ones? By what criteria would you have made your decisions?

3. In your daily life, what criteria do you use to determine whether or not you will help someone? How does God's example of helping and healing out of his abundant goodness affect your decisions to help others? Under what conditions are you willing to help people who "have no desire to become Christians?"

4. If you had to list three areas of your life that God "overlooks" when he bestows his love on you, what would you list?

5. Irritated by the crowd, the disciples demanded that Jesus "send them away" (Matthew 14:15). Who in your life have you sent away when you could have meet the need in love?

6. How do you respond to the demands that people make on you? What has God asked you to do that left you

openmouthed and wondering whether or not he was kidding? Why do you think you assumed that God had asked you to do the impossible? Read Hebrews 11:1 and Romans 10:17. What is faith and where does it come from?

7. What has Jesus given you that could enable you to understand how another person feels? Is there someone in your life right now to whom you could reach out with Christ's love?

8. List three areas of your life in which you could use more peace and less chaos. How might the two inner codes—"Jesus knows how you feel" and "people are precious"—change how you handle the chaos?

SESSION 3

Chapter 4   *When Fishermen Don't Fish*

1. *Compassion* means to feel deep sorrow for a person who suffers misfortune and to desire to alleviate the suffering. Matthew 14:14 says that Jesus had compassion on the people, so he changed his agenda from that of quiet rest to offering healing for body and soul.

Has anyone ever shown this depth of compassion for you? If so, what was it like to be blessed by the compassion of another person?

When have you felt compassion for another person or group of people? What action did compassion prompt you to take?

2. When has God brought hurting people into your world to break the solitude and press you into service? Explain

how you did or did not find perspective when that occurred. Describe the balance between service and solitude that fosters a godly perspective in your life.

3. Read Mark 6:7–12, 30, 31. The disciples flourished when they went fishing, didn't they? They were so excited that the pressing crowd didn't dim their enthusiasm.

When do you flourish? What "miracles" do you do in Jesus' name that get you so excited that crowds don't bother you and you forget to eat?

4. Jesus' words in Luke 6:41–42 illustrate what happens when people stop fishing and flourishing and start fighting.

In practical terms, what steps can you take to focus more of your energy on fishing and flourishing? In what ways do you tend to complain about your friends' stinky socks in the camper?

Chapter 5   *The Joy in the Journey*

1. It's easy to judge people, isn't it? Read the following verses: Leviticus 19:15; Proverbs 24:23; Acts 10:34; Romans 10:12; Galatians 2:6.

When have you made judgments that you shouldn't have made about others and missed what you could have learned from them?

2. When has your journey been interrupted by a lesson you needed to learn? What lesson did you learn? Was it a lesson that you need to be reminded of frequently?

3. How might Jesus' words about an abundant life (John 10:10b) relate to your lifestyle? If you could do three

activities this week just for fun, what would they be? In what ways could you add joy to the routine activities in your life?

SESSION 4

Chapter 6   *Remarkable*

1. After reading this chapter, and its list of "remarkable" things, what remarkable aspects of your life do you tend to overlook? How might your life be different if you recognized more of the remarkable occurrences of everyday life?

2. Read Job 38:4–39:30; 40:9–41:11. How do these images expand your view of the remarkable?

3. Think back to the events surrounding the second most stressful day in Jesus' life (Matthew 14:1–21; Mark 6:7–44; Luke 9:1–17).

What remarkable things do you think the disciples could easily have overlooked on that day? If they had seen those things as truly remarkable, how might their responses have been different?

As you observe these events and the disciples' responses, what parallels do you see in your own life?

4. Read 1 Thessalonians 5:18. For what remarkable things can you now give thanks?

Chapter 7   *Thanks for the Bread*

1. This chapter shares the story of an engineer who took a risk that paid off. When has your life been touched by a person who took the risk to reach out to you?

2. Read John 6:1–14.

Have you, like the little boy, ever stood up and done something that might cause others to laugh at you? If so, how did you feel? What motivated you to do it, despite the risks?

What were the results of your action? If you don't know the results, what do you hope they were?

3. Jesus multiplied the little boy's lunch so that twelve baskets of food were left over. How might this illustration relate to your gifts? Do you believe that God can use you to accomplish great things for him? Why or why not?

4. People often say, "What you believe is fine for you, and what I believe is fine for me. So don't push what you believe on me." What does this chapter say about how God might have us take risks and share our faith with others?

5. Who in your life do you need to thank for taking a risk with you?

SESSION 5 ————————————————————————

Chapter 8 *Musings in Minnesota*

1. Who do you call when you "call home" as the author did in chapter eight? What makes calling home so special for you?

2. What do each of the following verses say about Jesus' willingness to listen and answer when we call? Psalm 91:15; Isaiah 55:6; 58:9; 65:24; Jeremiah 33:3; Luke 11:9.

3. When you, like Jesus in Matthew 14:19, face incredible pressure, how do you respond? Get angry? Shoo the crowds away? Take a moment to ask God for help?

Right now, close your eyes and—like Jesus—listen for the familiar, comforting sounds of heaven. Think about what you hear.

How might those sounds change the way you handle things if you were to stop and listen to them the next time the pressure builds?

Chapter 9 *Fending Off the Voices*

1. Tempting voices call out in hotel rooms, from the television, at the office . . . everywhere. Which voices clamor for your attention? What messages do they shout out to you?

2. Note how Jesus responded to the crowd's applause (John 6:14–15). List two temptations you face that on the surface seem positive and uplifting, but that really will lead you toward sin. How do you respond to the clamoring voices and temptations in your life?

3. In John 10:1–5, Jesus talks about how sheep listen to their shepherd's voice. In verses 7–17, he says that he is the Good Shepherd and that his sheep respond to his voice.

What does the voice of Jesus sound like to you? Can you always hear his voice? How can you seek his voice more intently so that you can be led by him?

4. Look up John 5:28, 29. When everyone hears God's voice, what will happen?

Chapter 10   *The Photo and the File*

1. Take a look at the activities you have planned for the coming weeks and months. What do they say about your priorities?

2. If you could make four things in your life a priority, what would you pick?

Now compare these four things to your calendar of events. What does the picture look like? Are your priorities and calendar in balance? What changes would bring your priorities and activities into better balance?

3. Read Philippians 1:9–11. How might these words help you set priorities in your life?

4. When people ask you to do certain things for them— things you are not really sure you should do—how do you typically respond?

Describe the last time someone used guilt and/or pride to try to entice you into making a wrong choice.

Read Matthew 14:22. Have you ever "dismissed the crowd" or said "no" in order to seek God? What did it feel like to make that decision?

5. Who in your life loves you for who you are rather than for what you can do? How does that person (or persons) fit into your priorities?

6. Did the story of the two paddleboats hit close to home? Have you ever won the race but burned the cargo? If so, describe that time.

SESSION 6

Chapter 11   *Seeing God Through Shattered Glass*

1. Can you remember a time when pain shattered your expectations of God, when he did something that didn't seem right to you or gave you the opposite of what you thought you should receive? If so, how did that experience affect your view of God?

2. Do you have a phrase (or even several) that is always ready to complete this sentence: "If God is God, then . . ."? What is it? How did that phrase develop in your thinking?

3. Read Matthew 14:22–24. Describe a time when you felt alone in the storm—abandoned by God's protection and care. Did you become weary, even exhausted?

   How did you feel about God during that time? In what ways was your heart, like the hearts of the disciples, hardened against him? (See Mark 6:52.)

4. Has God ever used an exhausting, painful, or seemingly impossible circumstance to teach you something about himself or your relationship with him? If so, describe the circumstance and the lesson.

5. In what areas of your life could you trust God more, rather than questioning how he seems to be working?

   When the next storm in your life appears, how can you be better prepared to see Jesus at work in the midst of the storm?

Chapter 12   *Two Fathers, Two Feasts*

1. According to 1 Thessalonians 5:9, what is God's ultimate destiny for your life? In what ways do you prefer to "rest rather than ride" toward the destiny God has for you?

2. When have you found yourself in an unlikely classroom, or on a "decision collision" with God regarding what stops should be made or which way to turn on your journey? Whose itinerary won out?

3. What requests has God said "no" to during your life's journey? Which "nos" were easier or more difficult to take? Why?

4. Reread 1 Chronicles 29:15, Psalm 39:5, James 4:14, and Psalm 103:15, 16. What do these verses say about our journey? About what should be important?

5. What will the eternal rewards be if you allow God to plan your earthly trip? What does "being renewed day by day" really mean? (See 2 Corinthians 4:16–18.)

What makes life's journey worth the hassles? Do you believe that God "will do what is right . . . and best" in your life? Why or why not?

6. As you anticipate the coming weeks, how do you feel? Tired? Strained? Angry? Joyful? Encouraged? What "light and momentary troubles" are you facing right now? In what ways might they be "achieving for you an eternal glory"? (See 2 Corinthians 4:16–18.)

7. Write down three requests that you wish God would honor this next week. Then pray honestly for the strength to follow the destiny he has chosen for you.

SESSION 7

Chapter 13   *Doubtstorms*

1. Jesus' disciples weren't the only ones in the Bible to have doubtstorms. Moses seemed to be plagued with them (see Exodus 3:7–4:17; 5:20–6:12; 6:28–7:6; 17:1–7—just to name a few). The entire book of Job is a doubtstorm. Some of Jesus' disciples faced doubtstorms after he died (Luke 24:13–32).

Can you envision the intensity of these doubtstorms? In what ways did God show his light? Do you think those glimmers of light were expected? Why or why not?

2. Describe your blackest doubtstorms. In what unexpected ways has God shown his light to you in the midst of those storms?

3. What gentle light from God have you seen recently? Did it appear in a way that you expected?

4. Have you ever missed—or almost missed—seeing God's gentle light in the midst of your doubtstorms? How can you train your heart to see his gentle light more clearly?

Chapter 14   *The Miracle of the Carpenter*

1. Write down or share a time when, like the Sisters of Loretto, you or someone close to you faced what seemed like an impossible situation and "ascended the mountain of prayer." Who, or what, did God bring into your life to meet the need?

2. When Jesus faced an impossible day, he took time out to pray. When times get tough for you, what do you do? Do you work harder or pray? Do you get angry or pray? What does it take for you to choose to pray when things get tough?

3. What are the impossible gulfs in your life that you cannot cross alone? Do you believe that Jesus came to span the gap between where you are and where you long to be? If so, write down how you plan to seek God's guidance and power in crossing the gulfs.

Chapter 15   *The Woodcutter's Wisdom*

1. Think about the woodcutter's story for a minute. How would you have responded to the events of the woodcutter's life? Would you have been quick to draw conclusions or content to see what unfolded?

Now consider the ways in which you pass judgment on the storms that blow into your own life. Could you benefit from adopting a perspective more like that of the woodcutter than that of the villagers? Explain your answer.

2. Why do you think it is so easy to pass judgment on life "with only one day's evidence"? What are the dangers of passing judgment too quickly?

3. Describe a time when you made judgments about a specific circumstance without realizing how limited your perspective really was. What was the result of your judgments? Did your judgments stand the test of time, or prove to be only fragments?

4. Read Matthew 6:33–34. What do you think Jesus was trying to communicate to his followers through those

words? How do those words provide perspective for your life?

SESSION 8

Chapter 16   *Laws of the Lighthouse*

1. Building on the Laws of the Lighthouse concept, where do most of your signals come from? Other ships on the sea? Friends on your ship? Lighthouses that shift position with the whims of culture? The time-tested lighthouse of God's Word?

2. Review the list of lights that the author looks for and the signals he heeds. Which ones stand out to you? Why?

Now make your own list. Write down the lights and signals that you believe are vital.

3. How carefully are you heeding the warnings of your lighthouse laws? In practical terms, what can you do to pay more attention to the Laws of the Lighthouse?

Chapter 17   *He Speaks Through the Storm*

1. Describe the most difficult circumstance you've ever faced. Who was involved? What happened? How long did it last?

Did you question or lash out at God during that time? What was the result?

What did you learn through that experience? How did it affect your view of yourself? Of God? Of others?

2. Think about friends who "advised" you during a difficult time. What type of wisdom did they give you? What kind of

advice have you given to others who have faced difficult times?

3. Do you sometimes receive God's unending love with mistrust? Name a situation in which you believed that God's love wasn't in your best interest. What was the outcome?

4. Read Job 1:8–12; 2:3–7. Why did God allow Job's difficult circumstances to occur? How does that knowledge add perspective to what happened to Job? Does that knowledge shed any light on the suffering in your life or in the life of someone you know? If so, explain.

5. The author writes that God is "best heard in the storm." Do you agree? Why or why not?

6. Read Job 38–41. What is God's message to you in his answer to Job's questions?

7. When God finished speaking, Job said, "I had heard about you before, but now I have seen you" (Job 42:5, TLB). What did Job gain as a result of seeing God?

Chapter 18 *Pilgrim Ponderings*

1. Why do you think God the Father spoke to Jesus on the mountain? (See Matthew 17:1–5.)

2. What kinds of experiences make you unbearably weary, leaving you sitting on the mountainside with your face in your hands? What does it take to encourage you during those times?

3. Describe a time when God transformed your desolation and met your need in a specific way.

SESSION 9 ——————————————————————————————

Chapter 19 *Our Storm Was His Path*

1. Has God ever used a storm "as his path to come to you"? What were the circumstances? What was the result in your life? In the lives of others around you?

2. What is your usual response when a storm lifts you up and then plunges you into a valley? Do you find it easier to sit in a tossing boat than to step out onto the water and walk toward Jesus? Why or why not?

3. When you have been desperately afraid in your life, and have seen an image coming toward you, have you ever cried out, "Lord, is it you?" If so, what was the answer? Was it as comforting as Jesus' response in Matthew 14:27?

4. Have you ever stepped out in faith like Peter did? (See Matthew 14:28—29.) Why did you do it? What was the result?

5. Write down a time in your life when God responded to your need in a special way and you knew you'd never be the same again. What did you discover about God in that situation that you had never seen before?

6. Most of us tend to look down on Peter's ill-fated walk on the water because he sank at the end. But at least he got out of the boat! In what ways can you take steps of faith and get out of the boat this week?

Chapter 20 *They'd Do It Again*

1. Have you, like the disciples, ever really worshiped God for who he is and for what he has done for you? If so, when? If not, why not?

2. What has Christ done that has touched you so deeply that your response could only be that of worship?

3. What kinds of "crutches" do you turn to when a raging storm erupts? How do they compare with God's strength?

4. At which times in your life have you found it easiest to turn to God when storms hit? Has it ever been difficult for you to worship God even after he has stilled a storm in your life? Explain your answer.

5. What price are you willing to pay for a clear view of God?

SESSION 10 ───────────────────────────────

Chapter 21 *Castles of Sorrow*

1. Which of your yesterdays imprisons your todays? What "haunting rooms in your castle" need to be opened to the light of day? What fears, failures, feelings of guilt, or dashed hopes need to be surrendered to God? You may need to work this answer out before the Lord during a special time with him.

2. Contrast the two types of sorrow mentioned in 2 Corinthians 7:10. What are the results of each kind of sorrow? Which kind of sorrow plays the greatest role in your life?

3. What kind of facades do you put up to hide your guilt, failures, or feelings of inadequacy? What hope does the story of Peter's encounter with Jesus on the water (Matthew 14:28–32) offer to you?

4. Read Psalm 1:1–2; Colossians 3:16; Ephesians 1:7; 2:8–9; James 1:22–25; 1 John 1:9; 2:12, 14. What is the foundation of your spiritual house? What can you do to strengthen it?

Chapter 22 *Fear That Becomes Faith*

1. How do you respond when you are backed into a corner? Does your faith flourish or flicker? Do you cling to God or your own self-sufficiency?

2. Would you agree that "faith is often the child of fear"? Why or why not?

What circumstances have produced greater faith in your life?

3. How would you define faith as it is portrayed in this chapter? Compare your answer to the description of faith in Hebrews 11:1, 6.

4. Matthew 14:28–31 tells about Peter's adventure on the water. What parallels do you see between this passage and aspects of your life? Describe a time when you took a small step of faith and were surprised by the way God met your need.

5. Read Matthew 21:21–22; Romans 1:17; 5:1, 2; Galatians 2:16; Ephesians 2:8. When we step out in faith, how does Jesus respond?

Write down three specific ways in which you will practice faith this week—at home, at work, with friends. Share your "faith steps" with a friend or family member.

SESSION 11 ——————————————————————

Chapter 23 *Why God Smiles*

1. How do you feel about a laughing Jesus? A smiling God? Do you feel comfortable with the idea? Is it difficult for you to imagine a Jesus who is that real? Explain your answers.

2. Think about the events in Jesus' life. In which ones can you imagine him flashing a smile or chuckling with a twinkle in his eye?

3. Jesus said that the woman mentioned in Matthew 15:21–28 had great faith. What, in your opinion, did he find so impressive about her faith? Is it what you would have expected him to be impressed with? Why or why not?

Read Hebrews 11:4–32. Make a list of other people in the Bible who impressed God by their faith. Is there a person you know whose faith impresses you? If so, what do you notice?

4. Read Matthew 14:23. How did the disciples feel toward the woman? How do you think they felt after Jesus spoke with her and honored her request?

Why, in our fast-paced culture, is it easy to respond to people the way the disciples did? In light of this biblical example, how might you change your responses to people?

5. Do you find that you prefer to get salvation the old-fashioned way, by earning it? If yes, list the ways in which you have tried to impress God. If not, describe the ways in which God has mercifully chosen to bless you.

Chapter 24   *The Sacrificial Visitor*

1. Matthew 15:29–32 records Jesus' healing of many people and their praise for the "God of Israel." But Jesus didn't preach at them; he just reached out to help them. What does this teach you about what sharing Christ with a hurting world really means?

2. Read Luke's version of this event (Luke 8:1–10). How do Matthew's and Luke's versions differ? In which aspects are they similar? What does Luke's account reveal about the disciples' faith?

3. Read John 3:16; Matthew 1:21; John 10:9; John 1:29; Revelation 5:12; Hebrews 7:26, 27. In what ways have you been saved by a Sacrificial Visitor—Jesus Christ?

4. A miracle occurred in Rickenbacker's life that kept him alive. What miracle has God done in your life or in the life of someone you know?

   Rickenbacker gives buckets of shrimp to sea gulls to show his gratitude. What can you give to God to say "thank you"?

5. The crowds were amazed when they saw what Jesus had done (Matthew 15:31). How do you respond when God does something special in your life? Write down four things for which you can praise—or worship—God today.

Chapter 25   *Holiness in a Bathrobe*

1. Were you surprised by what the "holy moment" was? Why or why not?

2. As you read this chapter, did you gain a new understanding of the relationship between *honesty* and *holiness*, the difference between *perfection earned* and *perfection paid*? (See also, Colossians 1:22 and 1 Corinthians 1:8.) Explain your answer.

3. Are you ready to take an honest look in the mirror? If so, what have you been trying to do to make yourself more presentable to God?

Read Hebrews 10:14. How has God made you perfect?

What effect does his love and your perfection in his eyes have on the way you feel about yourself? On the way you relate to others? On how you relate to him?

SESSION 12 ─────────────────────────────

Chapter 26 *The Choice*

1. Read Genesis 1:1–26. When was the last time you took time to appreciate God's creation? Which of God's creations amaze you? What do they communicate about the character of God? How does it feel to be the creation that made all of God's creation complete?

2. Why is it so important that God gave Adam and Eve the opportunity to choose? (See Genesis 2:15–17; 3:1–13.) If God hadn't given us a choice, how would that have influenced our relationship with him? Why is our choice as to whether or not we'll love God so important?

What were the consequences of Adam's and Eve's choice? (See Genesis 3:14–19.)

3. What choice did Jesus make to deal with the sins of all mankind?

4. What choice is the author referring to when he writes, "Now it's our choice"?

Chapter 27 *Caught with Your Pants Down, But Your Head Up*

1. How do you think people will remember you? As a person who dove headfirst into life—and perhaps made some memorable mistakes? As a person who cheered from the sidelines? As a person who half-heartedly listened to the game on the radio? Be honest!

2. Read Jeremiah 29:11; Matthew 14:30–31; John 14:12; Romans 10:11. What effect should God's promises have on those of us who are afraid to risk?

3. Have you ever paid a price to "stand on first base"? If so, write down the experience. (If you're meeting with a group, share it with them.)

Would you do it again? Why or why not? How does a person's view of God determine the type of risks he or she will take?

4. Make a list of headlong heroes—those who haven't been afraid to go all-out for what was important to them. How do your heroes inspire you to "get in the game"?

Chapter 28 *Lemonade and Grace*

1. Did the lemonade story remind you of a time in your life when God's grace overlooked your flawed accomplishments? If so, describe what happened.

2. How does God respond to us, even though he knows that what we offer him may turn out to be a gooey mess? (See Romans 8:32, 35; Ephesians 2:4, 5; Hebrews 4:16.)

3. Is it possible, as the author writes, "that a Gentle Stranger may be bringing grace to your street . . . to your life"? In what ways?

THE
APPLAUSE
OF
HEAVEN

To Stanley Shipp,
my father in the faith

Contents

Publisher's Preface

Since *The Applause of Heaven* first appeared in the fall of 1990, Max Lucado has truly become a household name in Christian America. Over the years his books have touched the hearts of millions of men and women around the world. Enthusiastic response to this book—including reviews in many periodicals—makes it clear that the work has become a modern classic. It is a book that will be treasured for generations to come.

What readers find in these pages is a series of soul-stirring insights into some of Christ's most provocative teachings in the New Testament. It is not a theological treatise, however, but a heart-to-heart conversation. By offering a fresh look at the Beatitudes—as they appear in the Gospel of Matthew—Lucado's narrative opens our eyes to old truths in compelling new ways. It allows us to see ideas and images we may have missed, no matter how many times we have read them before.

In the hands of this gifted writer, words and phrases become instruments of wonder and imagination. Max Lucado's personal examples and his stories from real life reveal the sparkling facets of the biblical text in a penetrating and colorful light. Every page offers new treasures and new

287

moments of joy. The work, as a whole, is a re-examination of heaven's value system. No wonder *The Applause of Heaven* has become one of the most successful Christian books of our time.

To add to the overall enjoyment of this edition, we have chosen eighteen dramatic illustrations by several great masters, each one representing in some way the theme or message of the accompanying chapter. We hope you agree that these pictures, in a variety of styles and media, are a natural complement to the remarkable breadth and versatility of Max Lucado's poetic vision.

Max Lucado reminds us that "Matthew, chapter five is not a list of proverbs or a compilation of independent sayings, but rather a step-by-step description of how God rebuilds the believer's heart." In the Beatitudes, Jesus promises "blessings" to all who come after him—to all who decide to live their lives each day by his example. This edition of *The Applause of Heaven* shows us how to have that kind of life, and how to live it more abundantly.

THE PUBLISHER

Foreword

God says all the big words in our lives. Still, it is ofttimes the little words that make the Big Word sing. Max Lucado is a rare and welcome talent who is dedicated to the Word made flesh, but is also a spellbinding spinner of such smaller words as may ornament God's Word.

I first discovered Lucado when I casually took *No Wonder They Call Him the Savior* off a bookstore shelf. Nothing was casual after his first line hooked my eye. Lucado has become popular for two reasons: He reveres Christ, and he loves the world around him. This double love binds our minds and beckons us to follow closely to see where his paragraphs may lead.

It is because Max Lucado loves his Lord that he turns from the muddlesome and thumbworn language so common in the church. To Lucado, Jesus is no ordinary noun to be theologized into dullness. Rather, all holy relationships are glorious, and only the best, most creative English is worthy. So he weaves anew the Shroud of Turin, leaving us no doubt that this splendid cloth has touched the body of our Lord and been forever marked by the imprimatur of Lucado's reverence. Where no ordinary words will serve, here's how he bids us know the Christ:

"Sacred delight derives from stubborn joy," he exults.

"If you have time to read this chapter, you probably don't need to," he calls to those who think they're too busy for the spiritual disciplines.

On and on his wisdom flows: "Show a man his failures without Jesus, and the result will be found in the roadside gutter. Give a man religion without reminding him of his filth, and the result will be arrogance in a three-piece suit."

He counsels the arrogant that facing Christ is like entering the church of the nativity: "The door is so low, you can't go in standing up."

He rebukes the bitter: "Hatred is the rabid dog that turns on its owner.... The very word grudge starts with ... GRRR ... a growl!"

This book introduces the Beatitudes, which introduce the Sermon on the Mount. The Beatitudes fly at us, but in the simple metaphors of ordinary life. So you'll meet Christ even as you meet the *Exxon Valdez* that dark March night in 1989, when she spilled her crude venom on Bligh Reef in Alaska. The Christ of communion will come to you as you meet Gayaney Petroysan, an Armenian four years old who begged her mother's blood to live. And any number of great Bible heroes come and go in this book to make real the introduction to Jesus' great Sermon on the Mount.

Max and I are friends. I may have overpressed him to be my friend, and I will admit the friendship was originally my idea. But, I confess, I wanted to know Christ as Max does. I wanted to feel the April wind that breathed upon the cross, as he does. I wanted to fall like Thomas before Christ and cry, "My Lord and my God!" as he does. I needed Max to give me lessons on obedience and spiritual need.

Read this book in a quiet place and you may feel a wounded hand fall lightly on your shoulder. Be not afraid of the nearness you will feel to Christ, but go on and walk his paragraphs. Then you will know by experience that Lucado travels the high country of the Galilee of the heart.

CALVIN MILLER

Before You Begin

This book was almost as difficult to title as it was to write. We went through list after list of options. Dozens of titles were suggested and dozens were discarded. Carol Bartley, Dave Moberg, the late Kip Jordan, and others at Word Publishing spent hours searching for the appropriate phrase that would describe the heart of the book.

In my mind, the scales were tipped in favor of *The Applause of Heaven* when my editor, Carol, read part of the manuscript to some of the Word executives. She read a portion of the book that describes our final journey into the city of God. She read some thoughts I wrote about God's hunger to have his children home, about how he longs to welcome us and may even applaud when we enter the gates.

After Carol read this section, she noticed one of the men was brushing away a tear. He explained his emotion by saying, "It's hard for me to imagine God applauding for me."

Can you relate?

I can. Certain things about God are easy to imagine. I can

293

imagine him creating the world and suspending the stars. I can envision him as almighty, all-powerful, and in control. I can fathom a God who knows me, who made me, and I can even fathom a God who hears me. But a God who is in love with me? A God who is crazy for me? A God who cheers for me?

But that is the message of the Bible. Our Father is relentlessly in pursuit of his children. He has called us home with his word, paved the path with his blood, and is longing for our arrival.

God's love for his children is the message of the Bible. And that is the message of this book.

Indulge me as I say thank-you to some dear friends who made this project possible.

First, to Calvin Miller. In 1977, a dear friend gave me a rectangular-shaped book called *The Singer* and urged me to read it. I did . . . several times. I was amazed. Never had I seen such word crafting. Never had I seen such passion. I still have the book on my shelf. It is dog-eared, weatherworn, and coffee stained.

But I will never discard it. For through it, Calvin Miller introduced me to a new caliber of writing—a fruitful hybrid of faith and creativity.

Thank you, Calvin, for what you've meant to thousands of readers over the last two decades. Thank you for sitting patiently until God gave you a fresh way to tell the ancient tale. And thank you for ushering this writer into a new palace of possibilities.

Thanks, also:

To Kip Jordon and Byron Williamson, two dear brothers who helped Word Publishing to be a ministry as well as a business.

To Ernie Owen, a Christian sage with one eye on him and the other on his children. Thanks for the counsel.

To Carol Bartley and Anne Christian Buchanan. Thanks for editing and editing and editing and editing and . . . You did a great job. (All my mistakes are our little secret, OK?)

To Mary Stain. Because of your secretarial skills and remarkable flexibility, another manuscript is completed. I'm grateful.

To the rest of the Oak Hills Church staff. What would I do without friends like you? Thank you so much.

To Tim Kimmel and John Trent. One conversation with you guys gives me enough encouragement for a whole month.

To the Oak Hills elders and church. I never dreamed I would have the privilege of serving with such a faithful family. I thank God for what he is doing.

To Dave Moberg, Nancy Guthrie, and David Edmonson, for making me look better than I really do.

To Michael Card, a troubadour of truth whose heart touches mine.

And lastly, two special people.

To my wife, Denalyn. Thank you for making coming home the highlight of my day.

And thanks to you, the reader, for spending your time and money in hopes of seeing Jesus. May he honor the desire of your heart.

Now when he saw the crowds, he went up on a mountainside and sat down. His disciples came to him, and he began to teach them, saying:

> *Blessed are the poor in spirit,*
> *   for theirs is the kingdom of heaven.*
> *Blessed are those who mourn,*
> *   for they will be comforted.*
> *Blessed are the meek,*
> *   for they will inherit the earth.*
> *Blessed are those who hunger and thirst for righteousness,*
> *   for they will be filled.*
> *Blessed are the merciful,*
> *   for they will be shown mercy.*
> *Blessed are the pure in heart,*
> *   for they will see God.*
> *Blessed are the peacemakers,*
> *   for they will be called sons of God.*
> *Blessed are those who are persecuted because of righteousness,*
> *   for theirs is the kingdom of heaven.*

Matthew 5:1–10

$\mathcal{B}$lessed . . .

CHAPTER I

Sacred Delight

She has every reason to be bitter. Though talented, she went unrecognized for years. Prestigious opera circles closed their ranks when she tried to enter. American critics ignored her compelling voice. She was repeatedly rejected for parts for which she easily qualified. It was only after she went to Europe and won the hearts of tough-to-please European audiences that stateside opinion leaders acknowledged her talent.

Not only has her professional life been a battle, her personal life has been marked by challenge. She is the mother of two handicapped children, one of whom is severely retarded. Years ago, in order to escape the pace of New York City, she purchased a home on Martha's Vineyard.

It burned to the ground two days before she was to move in.

Professional rejection. Personal setbacks. Perfect soil for the seeds of bitterness. A receptive field for the roots of resentment. But in this case, anger found no home.

Her friends don't call her bitter; they call her "Bubbles."

Beverly Sills. Internationally acclaimed opera singer. Retired director of the New York City Opera.

Her phrases are sugared with laughter. Her face is softened with serenity. Upon interviewing her, Mike Wallace stated that "she is one of the most impressive—if not *the* most impressive—ladies I've ever interviewed."

How can a person handle such professional rejection and personal trauma and still be known as Bubbles? "I choose to be cheerful," she says. "Years ago I knew I had little or no choice about success, circumstances or even happiness; but I knew I could choose to be cheerful."

"We have prayed for healing. God has not given it. But he has blessed us."

Glyn spoke slowly. Partly because of her conviction. Partly because of her disease. Her husband, Don, sat in the chair next to her. The three of us had come together to plan a funeral—hers. And now, with that task done, with the hymns selected and the directions given, Glyn spoke.

"He has given us strength we did not know.

"He gave it when we needed it and not before." Her words were slurred, but clear. Her eyes were moist, but confident.

I wondered what it would be like to have my life taken from me at age forty-five. I wondered what it would be like to say good-bye to my children and spouse. I wondered what it would be like to be a witness to my own death.

"God has given us peace in our pain. He covers us all the time. Even when we are out of control, he is still there."

It had been a year since Glyn and Don had learned of Glyn's condition—amyotrophic lateral sclerosis (Lou Gehrig's disease). The cause and the cure remain a mystery. But the result doesn't. Muscle strength and mobility steadily deteriorate, leaving only the mind and the faith.

And it was the coming together of Glyn's mind and faith that caused me to realize I was doing more than planning a funeral. I was beholding holy jewels she had quarried out of the mine of despair.

"We can use any tragedy as a stumbling block or a stepping stone. . . .

"I hope this will not cause my family to be bitter. I hope I can be an example that God is wanting us to trust in the good times and the bad. For if we don't trust when times are tough, we don't trust at all."

Don held her hand. He wiped her tears. He wiped his own.

"Who are these two?" I asked myself as I watched him touch a tissue to her cheek. "Who are these, who, on the edge of life's river, can look across with such faith?"

The moment was solemn and sweet. I said little. One is not bold in the presence of the sacred.

✳

"I have everything I need for joy!" Robert Reed said. "Amazing!" I thought.

His hands are twisted and his feet are useless. He can't bathe himself. He can't feed himself. He can't brush his teeth, comb his hair, or put on his underwear. His shirts are held together by strips of Velcro. His speech drags like a worn-out audio cassette.

Robert has cerebral palsy.

The disease keeps him from driving a car, riding a bike, and going for a walk. But it didn't keep him from graduating from high school or attending Abilene Christian University, from which he graduated with a degree in Latin. Having cerebral palsy didn't keep him from teaching at a St. Louis junior college or from venturing overseas on five mission trips.

And Robert's disease didn't prevent him from becoming a missionary in Portugal.

He moved to Lisbon, alone, in 1972. There he rented a hotel room and began studying Portuguese. He found a restaurant owner who would feed him after the rush hour and a tutor who would instruct him in the language.

Then he stationed himself daily in a park, where he distributed brochures about Christ. Within six years he led seventy people to the Lord, one of whom became his wife, Rosa.

I heard Robert speak recently. I watched other men carry him in his wheelchair onto the platform. I watched them lay a Bible in his lap. I watched his stiff fingers force open the pages. And I watched people in the audience wipe away tears of admiration from their faces. Robert could have asked for sympathy or pity, but he did just the opposite. He held his bent hand up in the air and boasted, "I have everything I need for joy."

His shirts are held together by Velcro, but his life is held together by joy.

No man had more reason to be miserable than this one—yet no man was more joyful.

His first home was a palace. Servants were at his fingertips. The snap of his fingers changed the course of history. His name was known and loved. He had everything—wealth, power, respect.

And then he had nothing.

Students of the event still ponder it. Historians stumble as they attempt to explain it. How could a king lose everything in one instant?

One moment he was royalty; the next he was in poverty.

His bed became, at best, a borrowed pallet—and usually the hard earth. He never owned even the most basic mode of transportation and was dependent upon handouts for his income. He was sometimes so hungry he would eat raw grain or pick fruit off a tree. He knew what it was like to be rained on, to be cold. He knew what it meant to have no home.

His palace grounds had been spotless; now he was exposed to filth. He had never known disease, but was now surrounded by illness.

In his kingdom he had been revered; now he was ridiculed. His neighbors tried to lynch him. Some called him a lunatic. His family tried to confine him to their house.

Those who didn't ridicule him tried to use him. They wanted favors. They wanted tricks. He was a novelty. They wanted to be seen with him—that is, until being with him was out of fashion. Then they wanted to kill him.

He was accused of a crime he never committed. Witnesses were hired to lie. The jury was rigged. No lawyer was assigned to his defense. A judge swayed by politics handed down the death penalty.

They killed him.

He left as he came—penniless. He was buried in a borrowed grave, his funeral financed by compassionate friends. Though he once had everything, he died with nothing.

He should have been miserable. He should have been bitter. He had every right to be a pot of boiling anger. But he wasn't.

He was joyful.

Sourpusses don't attract a following. People followed him wherever he went.

Children avoid soreheads. Children scampered after this man.

Crowds don't gather to listen to the woeful. Crowds clamored to hear him.

Why? He was joyful. He was joyful when he was poor. He was joyful when he was abandoned. He was joyful when he was betrayed. He was even joyful as he hung on a tool of torture, his hands pierced with six-inch Roman spikes.

Jesus embodied a stubborn joy. A joy that refused to bend in the wind of hard times. A joy that held its ground against pain. A joy whose roots extended deep into the bedrock of eternity.

Perhaps that's where Beverly Sills learned it. Without doubt, that is where Glyn Johnson and Robert Reed learned it. And that is where we can learn it.

What type of joy is this? What is this cheerfulness that dares to wink at adversity? What is this bird that sings while it is still dark? What is the source of this peace that defies pain?

I call it sacred delight.

It is sacred because it is not of the earth. What is sacred is God's. And this joy is God's.

It is delight because delight can both satisfy and surprise.

Delight is the Bethlehem shepherds dancing a jig outside a cave. Delight is Mary watching God sleep in a feed trough. Delight is white-haired Simeon praising God, who is about to be circumcised. Delight is Joseph teaching the Creator of the world how to hold a hammer.

Delight is the look on Andrew's face at the lunch pail that

never came up empty. Delight is the dozing wedding guests who drank the wine that had been water. Delight is Jesus walking through waves as casually as you walk through curtains. Delight is a leper seeing a finger where there had been only a nub . . . a widow hosting a party with food made for a funeral . . . a paraplegic doing somersaults. Delight is Jesus doing impossible things in crazy ways: healing the blind with spit, paying taxes with a coin found in a fish's mouth, and coming back from the dead disguised as a gardener.

What is sacred delight? It is God doing what gods would be doing only in your wildest dreams—wearing diapers, riding donkeys, washing feet, dozing in storms. Delight is the day they accused God of having too much fun, attending too many parties, and spending too much time with the Happy Hour crowd.

Delight is the day's wage paid to workers who had worked only one hour . . . the father scrubbing the pig smell off his son's back . . . the shepherd throwing a party because the sheep was found. Delight is a discovered pearl, a multiplied talent, a heaven-bound beggar, a criminal in the kingdom. Delight is the surprise on the faces of street folks who have been invited to a king's banquet.

Delight is the Samaritan woman big-eyed and speechless, the adulteress walking out of the stone-cluttered courtyard, and a skivvy-clad Peter plunging into cold waters to get close to the one he'd cursed.

Sacred delight is good news coming through the back door of your heart. It's what you'd always dreamed but never expected. It's the too-good-to-be-true coming true. It's having God as your pinch-hitter, your lawyer, your dad, your biggest fan, and your best friend. God on your side, in your heart, out in front, and protecting your back. It's hope where you least expected it: a flower in life's sidewalk.

It is *sacred* because only God can grant it. It is a *delight* because it thrills. Since it is sacred, it can't be stolen. And since it is delightful, it can't be predicted.

It was this gladness that danced through the Red Sea. It was this joy that blew the trumpet at Jericho. It was this secret that made Mary sing. It was this surprise that put the springtime into Easter morning.

It is God's gladness. It's sacred delight.

And it is this sacred delight that Jesus promises in the Sermon on the Mount.

Nine times he promises it. And he promises it to an unlikely crowd:

- *"The poor in spirit."* Beggars in God's soup kitchen.

- *"Those who mourn."* Sinners Anonymous bound together by the truth of their introduction: "Hi, I am me. I'm a sinner."

- *"The meek."* Pawnshop pianos played by Van Cliburn. (He's so good no one notices the missing *keys*.)

- *"Those who hunger and thirst."* Famished orphans who know the difference between a TV dinner and a Thanksgiving feast.

- *"The merciful."* Winners of the million-dollar lottery who share the prize with their enemies.

- *"The pure in heart."* Physicians who love lepers and escape infection.
- *"The peacemakers."* Architects who build bridges with wood from a Roman cross.
- *"The persecuted."* Those who manage to keep an eye on heaven while walking through hell on earth.

It is to this band of pilgrims that God promises a special blessing. A heavenly joy. A sacred delight.

But this joy is not cheap. What Jesus promises is not a gimmick to give you goose bumps nor a mental attitude that has to be pumped up at pep rallies. No, Matthew 5 describes God's radical reconstruction of the heart.

Observe the sequence. First, we recognize we are in need (we're poor in spirit). Next, we repent of our self-sufficiency (we mourn). We quit calling the shots and surrender control to God (we're meek). So grateful are we for his presence that we yearn for more of him (we hunger and thirst). As we grow closer to him, we become more like him. We forgive others (we're merciful). We change our outlook (we're pure in heart). We love others (we're peacemakers). We endure injustice (we're persecuted).

It's no casual shift of attitude. It is a demolition of the old structure and a creation of the new. The more radical the change, the greater the joy. And it's worth every effort, for this is the joy of God.

It's no accident that the same word used by Jesus to promise sacred delight is the word used by Paul to describe God:

"The blessed God . . ." [1]
"God, the blessed and only Ruler . . ." [2]

Think about God's joy. What can cloud it? What can quench it? What can kill it? Is God ever in a bad mood because of bad weather? Does God get ruffled over long lines or traffic jams? Does God ever refuse to rotate the earth because his feelings are hurt?

No. His is a joy which consequences cannot quench. His is a peace which circumstances cannot steal.

There is a delicious gladness that comes from God. A holy joy. A sacred delight.

And it is within your reach. You are one decision away from Joy.

Now when he saw the crowds, he went
up on a mountainside and sat down.

CHAPTER 2

His Summit

*I*f you have time to read this chapter, you probably don't need to.

If you are reading slowly in order to have something to occupy your time . . . if your reading hour is leisurely sandwiched between a long stroll and a good nap . . . if your list of things to do today was done an hour after you got up . . . then you might want to skip over to the next chapter. You probably have mastered the message of the next few pages.

If, however, you are reading in your car with one eye on the stoplight . . . or in the airport with one ear listening for your flight . . . or in the baby's room with one hand rocking the crib . . . or in bed late at night, knowing you have to get up early in the morning . . . then read on, friend. This chapter is for you.

You are in a hurry. America is in a hurry. Time has sky-rocketed in value. The value of any commodity depends on its scarcity. And time that once was abundant now is going to the highest bidder.

A man in Florida bills his ophthalmologist ninety dollars for keeping him waiting one hour.

A woman in California hires someone to do her shopping for her—out of a catalog.

Twenty bucks will pay someone to pick up your cleaning.

Fifteen hundred bucks will buy a fax machine . . . for your car.

Greeting cards can be purchased to express to your children things you want to say, but don't have time to: "Have a great day at school" or "I wish I were there to tuck you in."

America—the country of shortcuts and fast lanes. (We're the only nation on earth with a mountain called "Rushmore.")

"Time," according to pollster Louis Harris, "may have become the most precious commodity in the land."

Do we really have less time? Or is it just our imagination?

In 1965 a testimony before a Senate subcommittee claimed the future looked bright for free time in America. By 1985, predicted the report, Americans would be working twenty-two hours a week and would be able to retire at age thirty-eight.

The reason? The computer age would usher in a gleaming array of advances that would do our work for us while stabilizing our economy.

Take the household, they cited. Microwaves, quickfix

foods, and food processors will pave the way into the care-free future. And the office? Well, you know that old stencil machine? It'll be replaced by a copier. And the files? Computers are the files of the future. And that electric type-writer? Don't get too attached to it; a computer will do its work, too.

And now, years later, we have everything the report promised. The computers are byting, the VCRs are recording, the fax machines are faxing. Yet the clocks are still ticking, and people are still running. The truth is, the average amount of leisure time has shrunk 37 percent since 1973. The average work week has increased from forty-one to forty-seven hours. (And, for many of you, forty-seven hours would be a calm week.)[1]

Why didn't the forecast come true? What did the com-mittee overlook? They misjudged the appetite of the con-sumer. As the individualism of the sixties led to the materialism of the eighties, the free time gained for us by technology didn't make us relax; it made us run. Gadgets provided more time . . . more time meant more potential money . . . more potential money meant more time needed . . . and round and round it went. Lives grew louder as demands became greater. And as demands became greater, lives grew emptier.

"I've got so many irons in the fire, I can't keep any of them hot," complained one young father.

Can you relate?

When I was ten years old, my mother enrolled me in piano lessons. Now, many youngsters excel at the keyboard. Not me. Spending thirty minutes every afternoon tethered to a piano bench was a torture just one level away from swallowing broken glass. The metronome inspected each second with glacial slowness before it was allowed to pass.

Some of the music, though, I learned to enjoy. I hammered the staccatos. I belabored the crescendos.

The thundering finishes I kettle-drummed. But there was one instruction in the music I could never obey to my teacher's satisfaction. The rest. The zigzagged command to do nothing. Nothing! What sense does that make? Why sit at the piano and pause when you can pound?

"Because," my teacher patiently explained, "music is always sweeter after a rest."

It didn't make sense to me at age ten. But now, a few decades later, the words ring with wisdom—divine wisdom. In fact, the words of my teacher remind me of the convictions of another Teacher.

"When he saw the crowds, he went up on a mountainside. . . ."

Don't read the sentence so fast you miss the surprise. Matthew didn't write what you would expect him to. The verse doesn't read, "When he saw the crowds, he went into their midst." Or "When he saw the crowds, he healed their hurts." Or "When he saw the crowds, he seated them and began to teach them." On other occasions he did that . . . but not this time.

Before he went to the masses, he went to the mountain. Before the disciples encountered the crowds, they encountered the Christ. And before they faced the people, they were reminded of the sacred.

I often write late at night. Not necessarily because I want to, but because sanity only comes to our house after the ten o'clock news.

From the moment I get home in the afternoon to the minute I sit down at this computer some five hours later, the motion is nonstop. Within thirty seconds of my entering the door, both of my knees are attacked by two squealing girls. A fuzzy-headed infant is placed in my arms and a welcome-home kiss is placed on my lips.

"The cavalry is here," I announce.

"And none too soon," my wife, Denalyn, replies with a grateful smile.

The next few hours bring a chorus of family noises: giggles, clanging dishes, rumbles on the floor, screams of agony over stumped toes, splashes in the bath, and thuds from toys tossed in the basket. The conversation is as continuous as it is predictable.

"Can I have more pie?"

"Jenna has my doll!"

"Can I hold the baby?"

"Honey, where is the pacifier?"

"Are there any clean gowns in the dryer?"

"Girls, it's time to go to bed.

"One more song?"

Then, eventually, the nightly hurricane passes, and the roar subsides. Mom looks at Dad. The day's damage is surveyed and cleaned up. Mom goes to bed, and Dad goes into the playroom to write.

That's where I am now. I sit in the stillness accompanied by the tap of a computer keyboard, the aroma of coffee, and the rhythm of the dishwasher. What was a playroom thirty minutes ago is now a study. And what is a study now may—just may—become a sanctuary. For what may happen in the next few minutes borders on the holy.

The quietness will slow my pulse, the silence will open my ears, and something sacred will happen. The soft slap of sandaled feet will break the stillness, a pierced hand will extend a quiet invitation, and I will follow.

I wish I could say it happens every night; it doesn't. Some nights he asks and I don't listen. Other nights he asks and I just don't go. But some nights I hear his poetic whisper, "Come to me, all you who are weary and burdened . . ."[2] and I follow. I leave behind the budgets, bills, and deadlines and walk the narrow trail up the mountain with him.

You've been there. You've escaped the sandy foundations of the valley and ascended his grand outcropping of granite. You've turned your back on the noise and sought his voice. You've stepped away from the masses and followed the Master as he led you up the winding path to the summit.

His summit. Clean air. Clear view. Crisp breeze. The roar of the marketplace is down there, and the perspective of the peak is up here.

Gently your guide invites you to sit on the rock above the tree line and look out with him at the ancient peaks that will never erode. "What is necessary is still what is sure," he confides. "just remember:

"You'll go nowhere tomorrow that I haven't already been.

"Truth will still triumph.

"Death will still die.

"The victory is yours.

"And delight is one decision away—seize it."

The sacred summit. A place of permanence in a world of transition.

Think about the people in your world. Can't you tell the ones who have been to his mountain? Oh, their problems aren't any different. And their challenges are just as severe. But there is a stubborn peace that enshrines them. A confidence that life isn't toppled by unmet budgets or rerouted airplanes. A serenity that softens the corners of their lips. A contagious delight sparkling in their eyes.

And in their hearts reigns a fortresslike confidence that the valley can be endured, even enjoyed, because the mountain is only a decision away.

I read recently about a man who had breathed the summit air. His trips up the trail began early in his life and sustained him to the end. A few days before he died, a priest went to visit him in the hospital. As the priest entered the room, he noticed an empty chair beside the man's bed. The priest asked him if someone had been by to visit. The old man smiled, "I place Jesus on that chair, and I talk to him."

The priest was puzzled, so the man explained. "Years ago a friend told me that prayer was as simple as talking to a good friend. So every day I pull up a chair, invite Jesus to sit, and we have a good talk."

Some days later, the daughter of this man came to the parish house to inform the priest that her father had just died. "Because he seemed so content," she said, "I left him in his room alone for a couple of hours. When I got back to the room, I found him dead. I noticed a strange thing, though: His head was resting, not on the pillow, but on an empty chair that was beside his bed."[3]

Learn a lesson from the man with the chair. Make note of the music teacher and the rest. Take a trip with the King to the mountain peak. It's pristine, uncrowded, and on top of the world. Stubborn joy begins by breathing deep up there before you go crazy down here.

Oops, I think I hear someone calling your flight. . . .

Blessed are the poor in spirit . . .

CHAPTER 3

The Affluent Poor

$\mathcal{W}$e could begin with Sarai laughing. Her wrinkled face buried in bony hands. Her shoulders shaking. Her lungs wheezing. She knows she shouldn't laugh; it's not kosher to laugh at what God says. But just as she catches her breath and wipes away the tears, she thinks about it again—and a fresh wave of hilarity doubles her over.

We could begin with Peter staring. It's a stunned stare. His eyes are the size of grapefruits. He's oblivious to the fish piled to his knees and to the water lapping over the edge of the boat. He's deaf to the demands that he snap out of it and help. Peter is numb, absorbed in one thought—a thought too zany to say aloud.

The Applause of Heaven

We could begin with Paul resting. For three days he has wrestled; now he rests. He sits on the floor, in the corner. His face is haggard. His stomach is empty.

His lips are parched. Bags droop beneath the blinded eyes. But there is a slight smile on his lips. A fresh stream is flowing into a stagnant pool, and the water is sweet.

But let's not begin with these. Let's begin elsewhere.

Let's begin with the New Testament yuppie negotiating.

He's rich. Italian shoes. Tailored suit. His money is invested. His plastic is golden. He lives like he flies—first class.

He's young. He pumps away fatigue at the gym and slam-dunks old age on the court. His belly is flat, his eyes sharp. Energy is his trademark, and death is an eternity away.

He's powerful. If you don't think so, just ask him. You got questions? He's got answers. You got problems? He's got solutions. You got dilemmas? He's got opinions. He knows where he's going, and he'll be there tomorrow. He's the new generation. So the old had better pick up the pace or pack their bags.

He has mastered the three "Ps" of yuppiedom. Prosperity. Posterity. Power. He's the rich . . . young . . . ruler.[1]

Till today, life for him has been a smooth cruise down a neon avenue. But today he has a question. A casual concern or a genuine fear? We don't know. We do know he has come for some advice.

324

For one so used to calling the shots, calling on this carpenter's son for help must be awkward. For a man of his pedigree to seek the counsel of a country rube is not standard procedure. But this is no standard question.

"Teacher," he asks, "what good thing must I do to get eternal life?" The wording of his question betrays his misunderstanding. He thinks he can get eternal life as he gets everything else—by his own strength.

"What must I do?"

What are the requirements, Jesus? What's the break-even point? No need for chitchat; go straight to the bottom line. How much do I need to invest to be certain of my return?

Jesus' answer is intended to make him wince. "If you want to enter life, obey the commandments."

A man with half a conscience would have thrown up his hands at that point. "Keep the commandments? Keep the commandments! Do you know how many commandments there are? Have you read the Law lately? I've tried—honestly, I've tried—but I can't."

That is what the ruler should say, but confession is the farthest thing from his mind. Instead of asking for help, he grabs a pencil and paper and asks for the list.

"Which ones?" He licks his pencil and arches an eyebrow.

Jesus indulges him. "Do not murder, do not commit adultery, do not steal, do not give false testimony, honor your father and mother, and love your neighbor as yourself."

"Great!" thinks the yuppie as he finishes the notes. "Now I've got the quiz. Let's see if I pass.

"Murder? Of course not. Adultery? Well, nothing any red-blooded boy wouldn't do. Stealing? A little extortion, but all justifiable. False testimony? Hmmmm . . . let's move on. Honor your father and mother? Sure, I see them on holidays. Love your neighbor as yourself . . . ?

"Hey," he grins, "a piece of cake. I've done all of these. In fact, I've done them since I was a kid." He swaggers a bit and hooks a thumb in his belt. "Got any other commandments you want to run past me?"

How Jesus keeps from laughing—or crying—is beyond me. The question that was intended to show the ruler how he falls short only convinces him that he stands tall. He's a child dripping water on the floor while telling his mom he hasn't been in the rain.

Jesus gets to the point. "If you want to be perfect, then go sell your possessions and give to the poor, and you will have treasure in heaven."

The statement leaves the young man distraught and the disciples bewildered.

Their question could be ours: "Who then can be saved?"

Jesus' answer shell-shocks the listeners, "With man this is impossible. . . ."

Impossible.

He doesn't say improbable. He doesn't say unlikely. He doesn't even say it will be tough. He says it is "impossible." No chance. No way. No loopholes. No hope. Impossible. It's impossible to swim the Pacific. It's impossible to go to the moon on the tail of a kite. You can't climb Mount Everest with a picnic basket and a walking stick. And unless somebody does something, you don't have a chance of going to heaven.

Does that strike you as cold? All your life you've been rewarded according to your performance. You get grades according to your study. You get commendations according to your success. You get money in response to your work.

That's why the rich young ruler thought heaven was just a payment away. It only made sense. You work hard, you pay your dues, and "zap"—your account is credited as paid in full. Jesus says, "No way." What you want costs far more than what you can pay. You don't need a system, you need a Savior. You don't need a resume, you need a Redeemer. For "what is impossible with men is possible with God." [2]

Don't miss the thrust of this verse: You cannot save yourself. Not through the right rituals. Not through the right doctrine. Not through the right devotion. Not through the right goose bumps. Jesus' point is crystal clear. It is impossible for human beings to save themselves.

You see, it wasn't the money that hindered the rich man; it was the self-sufficiency. It wasn't the possessions; it was the pomp. It wasn't the big bucks; it was the big head. "How hard it is for the rich to enter the kingdom of God!" [3] It's not just the rich who have difficulty. So do the educated, the strong, the good-looking, the popular, the religious. So do you if you think your piety or power qualifies you as a kingdom candidate.

And if you have trouble digesting what Jesus said to the rich young ruler, then his description of the judgment day will stick in your throat.

It's a prophetic picture of the final day: "Many will say to me on that day, 'Lord, Lord, did we not prophesy in your name, and in your name drive out demons and perform many miracles?'"[4]

Astounding. These people are standing before the throne of God and bragging about themselves. The great trumpet has sounded, and they are still tooting their own horns. Rather than sing his praises, they sing their own. Rather than worship God, they read their résumés. When they should be speechless, they speak. In the very aura of the King they boast of self. What is worse—their arrogance or their blindness?

You don't impress the officials at NASA with a paper airplane. You don't boast about your crayon sketches in the presence of Picasso. You don't claim equality with Einstein because you can write "H2O."

And you don't boast about your goodness in the presence of the Perfect.

"Then I will tell them plainly, 'I never knew you. Away from me, you evildoers.'"[5]

Mark it down. God does not save us because of what we've done. Only a puny god could be bought with tithes. Only an egotistical god would be impressed with our pain. Only a temperamental god could be satisfied by sacrifices. Only a heartless god would sell salvation to the highest bidders.

And only a great God does for his children what they can't do for themselves.

That is the message of Paul: "For what the law was powerless to do . . . God did."[6]

And that is the message of the first beatitude.

"Blessed are the poor in spirit. . . ."

The jewel of joy is given to the impoverished spirits, not the affluent.[7] God's delight is received upon surrender, not awarded upon conquest. The first step to joy is a plea for help, an acknowledgment of moral destitution, an admission of inward paucity. Those who taste God's presence have declared spiritual bankruptcy and are aware of their spiritual crisis. Their cupboards are bare. Their pockets are empty. Their options are gone. They have long since stopped demanding justice; they are pleading for mercy.[8]

They don't brag; they beg.

They ask God to do for them what they can't do without him. They have seen how holy God is and how sinful they are and have agreed with Jesus' statement, "Salvation is impossible."

Oh, the irony of God's delight—born in the parched soil of destitution rather than the fertile ground of achievement.

It's a different path, a path we're not accustomed to taking. We don't often declare our impotence. Admission of failure is not usually admission into joy. Complete confession is not commonly followed by total pardon. But then again, God has never been governed by what is common.

. . . for theirs is the kingdom of heaven.

CHAPTER 4

The Kingdom of the Absurd

𝒯he kingdom of heaven. Its citizens are drunk on wonder.

Consider the case of Sarai.[1] She is in her golden years, but God promises her a son. She gets excited. She visits the maternity shop and buys a few dresses. She plans her shower and remodels her tent . . . but no son. She eats a few birthday cakes and blows out a lot of candles . . . still no son. She goes through a decade of wall calendars . . . still no son.

So Sarai decides to take matters into her own hands. ("Maybe God needs me to take care of this one.")

She convinces Abram that time is running out. ("Face it, Abe, you ain't getting any younger, either.") She commands her maid, Hagar, to go into Abram's tent and see if he needs anything. ("And I mean 'anything'!") Hagar goes in a maid. She comes out a mom. And the problems begin.

Hagar is haughty. Sarai is jealous. Abram is dizzy from the dilemma. And God calls the baby boy a "wild donkey"—an appropriate name for one born out of stubbornness and destined to kick his way into history.

It isn't the cozy family Sarai expected. And it isn't a topic Abram and Sarai bring up very often at dinner.

Finally, fourteen years later, when Abram is pushing a century of years and Sarai ninety . . . when Abram has stopped listening to Sarai's advice, and Sarai has stopped giving it . . . when the wallpaper in the nursery is faded and the baby furniture is several seasons out of date . . . when the topic of the promised child brings sighs and tears and long looks into a silent sky . . . God pays them a visit and tells them they had better select a name for their new son.

Abram and Sarai have the same response: laughter. They laugh partly because it is too good to happen and partly because it might. They laugh because they have given up hope, and hope born anew is always funny before it is real.

They laugh at the lunacy of it all.

Abram looks over at Sarai—toothless and snoring in her rocker, head back and mouth wide open, as fruitful as a pitted prune and just as wrinkled. And he cracks up. He tries to contain it, but he can't. He has always been a sucker for a good joke.

Sarai is just as amused. When she hears the news, a cackle escapes before she can contain it. She mumbles something about her husband's needing a lot more than what he's got and then laughs again.

They laugh because that is what you do when someone says he can do the impossible. They laugh a little *at* God, and a lot *with* God—for God is laughing, too. Then, with the smile still on his face, he gets busy doing what he does best—the unbelievable.

He changes a few things—beginning with their names. Abram, the father of one, will now be Abraham, the father of a multitude. Sarai, the barren one, will now be Sarah, the mother.

But their names aren't the only things God changes. He changes their minds. He changes their faith. He changes the number of their tax deductions. He changes the way they define the word *impossible.*

But most of all, he changes Sarah's attitude about trusting God. Were she to hear Jesus' statement about being poor in spirit, she could give a testimony: "He's right. I do things my way, I get a headache. I let God take over, I get a son. You try to figure that out. All I know is I am the first lady in town to pay her pediatrician with a Social Security check."

Two thousand years later, here's another testimony[2]:

"The last thing I wanted to do was fish. But that was

exactly what Jesus wanted to do. I had fished all night. My arms ached. My eyes burned. My neck was sore. All I wanted was to go home and let my wife rub the knots out of my back.

"It had been a long night. I don't know how many times we had thrown that net into the blackness and heard it slap against the sea. I don't know how many times we had held the twine rope as the net sank into the water. All night we had waited for that bump, that tug, that jerk that would clue us to haul in the catch . . . but it had never come. At day-break, I was ready to go home.

"Just as I was about to leave the beach, I noticed a crowd coming toward me. They were following a lanky fellow who walked with a broad swing and wide gait. He saw me and called my name. 'Morning, Jesus!' I called back. Though he was a hundred yards away, I could see his white smile. 'Quite a crowd, eh?' he yelled, motioning at the mass behind him. I nodded and sat down to watch.

"He stopped near the edge of the water and began to speak. Though I couldn't hear much, I could see a lot. I could see more and more people coming. With all the pressing and shoving, it's a wonder Jesus didn't get pushed down into the water. He was already knee-deep when he looked at me.

"I didn't have to think twice. He climbed into my boat, and John and I followed. We pushed out a bit. I leaned back against the bow, and Jesus began to teach.

"It seemed that half of Israel was on the beach. Men had left their work, women their household chores. I even recognized some priests. How they all listened! They scarcely moved, yet their eyes danced as if they were in some way seeing what they could be.

"When Jesus finished, he turned to me. I stood and had begun to pull anchor when he said, 'Push out into the deep, Peter. Let's fish.'

"I groaned. I looked at John. We were thinking the same thing. As long as he wanted to use the boat for a platform, that was fine. But to use it for a fishing boat—that was our territory. I started to tell this carpenter-teacher, 'You stick to preaching, and I'll stick to fishing.' But I was more polite: 'We worked all night. We didn't catch a thing.'

"He just looked at me. I looked at John. John was waiting for my cue . . .

"I wish I could say I did it because of love. I wish I could say I did it out of devotion. But I can't. All I can say is there is a time to question and a time to listen. So, as much with a grunt as with a prayer, we pushed out.

"With every stroke of the oar, I muttered. With every pull of the paddle, I grumbled. 'No way. No way. Impossible. I may not know much, but I know fishing. And all we're going to come back with are some wet nets.'

"The noise on the beach grew distant, and soon the only sound was the smack of the waves against the hull. Finally we cast anchor. I picked up the heavy netting, held it waist-high, and started to throw it. That's when I caught a glimpse of Jesus out of the corner of my eye. His expression stopped me in midmotion.

"He was leaning out over the edge of the boat, looking out into the water where I was about to throw the net. And, get this, he was smiling. A boyish grin pushed his cheeks high and turned his round eyes into half-moons—the kind of smile you see when a child gives a gift to a friend and watches as it is unwrapped.

"He noticed me looking at him, and he tried to hide the smile, but it persisted. It pushed at the corners of his mouth until a flash of teeth appeared. He had given me a gift and could scarcely contain himself as I opened it.

"'Boy, is he in for a disappointment,' I thought as I threw the net. It flew high, spreading itself against the blue sky and floating down until it flopped against the surface, then sank. I wrapped the rope once around my hand and sat back for the long wait.

"But there was no wait. The slack rope yanked taut and tried to pull me overboard. I set my feet against the side of the boat and yelled for help. John and Jesus sprang to my side.

"We got the net in just before it began to tear. I'd never seen such a catch. It was like plopping down a sack of rocks in the boat. We began to take in water. John screamed for the other boat to help us.

"It was quite a scene: four fishermen in two boats, knee-deep in fish, and one carpenter seated on our bow, relishing the pandemonium.

"That's when I realized who he was. And that's when I realized who I was: I was the one who told God what he couldn't do!

"'Go away from me, Lord; I'm a sinful man.' There wasn't anything else I could say.

"I don't know what he saw in me, but he didn't leave. Maybe he thought if I would let him tell me how to fish, I would let him tell me how to live.

"It was a scene I would see many times over the next couple of years—in cemeteries with the dead, on hillsides with the hungry, in storms with the frightened, on roadsides with the sick. The characters would change, but the theme wouldn't. When we would say, 'No way,' he would say, 'My way.' Then the ones who doubted would scramble to salvage the blessing. And the One who gave it would savor the surprise."

"My power shows up best in weak people."[3]

God said those words. Paul wrote them down. God said he was looking for empty vessels more than strong muscles. Paul proved it.

Before he encountered Christ, Paul had been somewhat of a hero among the Pharisees. You might say he was their Wyatt Earp. He kept the law and order—or, better said, revered the Law and gave the orders. Good Jewish moms held him up as an example of a good Jewish boy. He was given the seat of honor at the Jerusalem Lions' Club Wednesday luncheon. He had a "Who's Who in Judaism" paperweight on his desk and was selected "Most Likely to Succeed" by his graduating class. He was quickly establishing himself as the heir apparent to his teacher, Gamaliel.

If there is such a thing as a religious fortune, Paul had it. He was a spiritual billionaire, born with one foot in heaven, and he knew it:

> If anyone ever had reason to hope that he could save him-self, it would be I. If others could be saved by what they are, certainly I could! For I went through the Jewish initiation ceremony when I was eight days old, having been born into a pure-blooded Jewish home that was a branch of the old original Benjamin family. So I was a real Jew if there ever was one! What's more, I was a member of the Pharisees who demand the strictest obedience to every Jewish law and custom. And sincere? Yes, so much so that I greatly perse-cuted the Church; and I tried to obey every Jewish rule and regulation down to the very last point.[4]

Blue-blooded and wild-eyed, this young zealot was hell-bent on keeping the kingdom pure—and that meant keeping the Christians out. He marched through the countryside like a general demanding that backslidden Jews salute the flag of the motherland or kiss their family and hopes good-bye.

All this came to a halt, however, on the shoulder of a highway. Equipped with subpoenas, handcuffs, and a posse, Paul was on his way to do a little personal evangelism in Damascus. That's when someone slammed on the stadium lights, and he heard the voice.

When he found out whose voice it was, his jaw hit the ground, and his body followed. He braced himself for the worst. He knew it was all over. He felt the noose around his neck. He smelled the flowers in the hearse. He prayed that death would be quick and painless.

But all he got was silence and the first of a lifetime of surprises.

He ended up bewildered and befuddled in a borrowed bedroom. God left him there a few days with scales on his eyes so thick that the only direction he could look was inside himself. And he didn't like what he saw.

He saw himself for what he really was—to use his own words, the worst of sinners.[5] A legalist. A killjoy. A bumptious braggart who claimed to have mastered God's code. A dispenser of justice who weighed salvation on a panscale.

That's when Ananias found him. He wasn't much to look at—haggard and groggy after three days of turmoil. Sarai wasn't much to look at either, nor was Peter. But what the three have in common says more than a volume of systematic theology. For when they gave up, God stepped in, and the result was a rollercoaster ride straight into the kingdom.

Paul was a step ahead of the rich young ruler. He knew better than to strike a deal with God. He didn't make any excuses; he just pleaded for mercy. Alone in the room with his sins on his conscience and blood on his hands, he asked to be cleansed.

Ananias' instructions to Paul are worth reading: "What are you waiting for? Get up, be baptized and wash your sins away, calling on his name."[6]

He didn't have to be told twice. The legalist Saul was buried, and the liberator Paul was born. He was never the same afterwards. And neither was the world.

Stirring sermons, dedicated disciples, and six thousand miles of trails. If his sandals weren't slapping, his pen was writing. If he wasn't explaining the mystery of grace, he was articulating the theology that would determine the course of Western civilization.

All of his words could be reduced to one sentence. "We preach Christ crucified."[7] It wasn't that he lacked other sermon outlines; it was just that he couldn't exhaust the first one.

The absurdity of the whole thing kept him going. Jesus should have finished him on the road. He should have left him for the buzzards. He should have sent him to hell. But he didn't. He sent him to the lost.

Paul himself called it crazy. He described it with phrases like "stumbling block" and "foolishness," but chose in the end to call it "grace."[8]

And he defended his unquenchable loyalty by saying, "The love of Christ leaves [me] no choice."[9]

Paul never took a course in missions. He never sat in on a committee meeting. He never read a book on church growth. He was just inspired by the Holy Spirit and punch-drunk on the love that makes the impossible possible: salvation.

The message is gripping: Show a man his failures without Jesus, and the result will be found in the roadside gutter. Give a man religion without reminding him of his filth, and the result will be arrogance in a three-piece suit. But get the two in the same heart—get sin to meet Savior and Savior to meet sin—and the result just might be another Pharisee turned preacher who sets the world on fire.

The Kingdom of the Absurd

Four people: the rich young ruler, Sarah, Peter, Paul. A curious thread strings the four together—their names.

The final three had their names changed—Sarai to Sarah, Simon to Peter, Saul to Paul. But the first one, the young yuppie, is never mentioned by name.

Perhaps that's the clearest explanation of the first beatitude. The one who made a name for himself is nameless. But the ones who called on Jesus' name—and his name only —got new names and, even more, new life.

Blessed are those who mourn . . .

CHAPTER 5

The Prison of Pride

$\mathcal{A}$s Brazilian jail cells go this one wasn't too bad. There was a fan on the table. The twin beds each had a thin mattress and a pillow. There was a toilet and a sink.

No, it wasn't too bad. But, then again, I didn't have to stay. Anibal did. He was there to stay.

Even more striking than his name (pronounced "uh-nee-ball") was the man himself. The tattooed anchor on his forearm symbolized his personality—cast-iron. His broad chest stretched his shirt. The slightest movement of his arm bulged his biceps. His face was as leathery in texture as it was in color. His glare could blister a foe. His smile was an explosion of white teeth.

But today the glare was gone and the smile was forced. Anibal wasn't on the street where he was the boss; he was in a jail where he was the prisoner.

He'd killed a man—a "neighborhood punk," as Anibal called him, a restless teenager who sold marijuana to the kids on the street and made a nuisance of himself with his mouth. One night the drug dealer had used his mouth one time too many and Anibal had decided to silence it. He'd left the crowded bar where the two of them had been arguing, gone home, taken a pistol out of a drawer, and walked back to the bar. Anibal had entered and called the boy's name. The drug dealer had turned around in time to take a bullet in the heart.

Anibal was guilty. Period. His only hope was that the judge would agree that he had done society a favor by getting rid of a neighborhood problem. He would be sentenced within the month.

I came to know Anibal through a Christian friend, Daniel. Anibal had lifted weights at Daniel's gym. Daniel had given Anibal a Bible and had visited him several times. This time Daniel took me with him to tell Anibal about Jesus.

Our study centered on the cross. We talked about guilt. We talked about forgiveness. The eyes of the murderer softened at the thought that the one who knows him best loves him most. His heart was touched as we discussed heaven, a hope that no executioner could take from him.

But as we began to discuss conversion, Anibal's face began to harden. The head that had leaned toward me in interest now straightened in caution. Anibal didn't like my statement that the first step in coming to God is an admission of guilt. He was uneasy with words like "I've been wrong" and "forgive me." Saying "I'm sorry" was out of character for him. He had never backed down before any man, and he wasn't about to do it now—even if the man were God.

In one final effort to pierce his pride, I asked him, "Don't you want to go to heaven?"

"Sure," he grunted.

"Are you ready?"

Earlier he might have boasted yes, but now he'd heard too many verses from the Bible. He knew better.

He stared at the concrete floor for a long time, meditating on the question. For a moment I thought his stony heart was cracking. For a second, it appeared that burly Anibal would for the first time admit his failures.

But I was wrong. The eyes that lifted to meet mine weren't tear-filled; they were angry. They weren't the eyes of a repentant prodigal; they were the eyes of an angry prisoner.

"All right," he shrugged. "I'll become one of your Christians. But don't expect me to change the way I live."

The conditional answer left my mouth bitter. "You don't draw up the rules," I told him. "It's not a contract that you negotiate before you sign. It's a gift—an undeserved gift! But to receive it, you have to admit that you need it."

"OK." He ran his thick fingers through his hair and stood up. "But don't expect to see me at church on Sundays."

I sighed. How many knocks in the head does a guy need before he'll ask for help?

As I watched Anibal pace back and forth in the tiny cell, I

realized that his true prison was not made of bricks and mortar, but of pride. He was twice imprisoned. Once because of murder, and once because of stubbornness. Once by his country, and once by himself.

*

The prison of pride. For most of us it isn't as blatant as it was with Anibal, but the characteristics are the same. The upper lip is just as stiff. The chin ever protrudes upward, and the heart is just as hard.

A prison of pride is filled with self-made men and women determined to pull themselves up by their own bootstraps even if they land on their rear ends. It doesn't matter what they did or to whom they did it or where they will end up; it only matters that "I did it my way."

You've seen the prisoners. You've seen the alcoholic who won't admit his drinking problem. You've seen the woman who refuses to talk to anyone about her fears. You've seen the businessman who adamantly rejects help, even when his dreams are falling apart.

Perhaps to see such a prisoner all you have to do is look in the mirror.

"If we confess our sins, he is faithful and just . . ."[1] The biggest word in Scripture just might be that two-letter one, *if.* For confessing sins—admitting failure—is exactly what prisoners of pride refuse to do.

You know the lingo:

"Well, I may not be perfect, but I'm better than Hitler and certainly kinder than Idi Amin!"

"Me a sinner? Oh, sure, I get rowdy every so often, but I'm a pretty good ol' boy."

"Listen, I'm just as good as the next guy. I pay my taxes. I coach the Little League team. I even make donations to Red Cross. Why, God's probably proud to have somebody like me on his team."

Justification. Rationalization. Comparison. These are the tools of the jailbird. They sound good. They sound familiar. They even sound American. But in the kingdom, they sound hollow.

"Blessed are those who mourn . . ."

To mourn for your sins is a natural outflow of poverty of spirit. The second beatitude should follow the first. But that's not always the case. Many deny their weakness. Many know they are wrong, yet pretend they are right. As a result, they never taste the exquisite sorrow of repentance.

Of all the paths to joy, this one has to be the strangest. True blessedness, Jesus says, begins with deep sadness.

"Blessed are those who know they are in trouble and have enough sense to admit it."[2]

Joy through mourning? Freedom through surrender? Liberty through confession?

Want a model? Let me introduce you to one.

He was nitroglycerin; if you bumped him the wrong way, he blew up. He made a living with his hands and got in trouble with his mouth. In some ways, he had a lot in common with Anibal. If he had had a tattoo, it would have been a big, black anchor on his forearm. If they had had bumper stickers, his would have read, "I don't get mad; I get even."

He was a man among men on the Galilean sea. His family called him Simon, but his master called him "Rocky." You know him as Peter.

And though he might not have known everything about self-control, he knew one thing about being a fisherman. He knew better than to get caught in a storm. . . .

And this night, Peter knows he is in trouble.

The winds roar down onto the Sea of Galilee like a hawk on a rat. Lightning zigzags across the black sky. The clouds vibrate with thunder. The rain taps, then pops, then slaps against the deck of the boat until everyone aboard is soaked and shaking. Ten-foot waves pick them up and slam them down again with bonejarring force.

These drenched men don't look like a team of apostles who are only a decade away from changing the world. They don't look like an army that will march to the ends of the earth and reroute history. They don't look like a band of pioneers who will soon turn the world upside down. No, they look more like a handful of shivering sailors who are wondering if the next wave they ride will be their last.

And you can be sure of one thing. The one with the widest eyes is the one with the biggest biceps—Peter. He's seen these storms before. He's seen the wreckage and bloated bodies float to shore. He knows what the fury of wind and wave can do. And he knows that times like this are not times to make a name for yourself; they're times to get some help.

That is why, when he sees Jesus walking on the water toward the boat, he is the first to say, "Lord, if it's you . . . tell me to come to you on the water."³

Now, some say this statement is a simple request for veri-fication. Peter, they suggest, wants to prove that the one they see is really Jesus and not just anyone who might be on a stroll across a storm-tossed sea in the middle of the night. (You can't be too careful, you know.)

So, Peter consults his notes, removes his glasses, clears his throat, and asks a question any good attorney would. "Ahem, Jesus, if you would kindly demonstrate your power and prove your divinity by calling me out on the water with you, I would be most appreciative."

I don't buy that. I don't think Peter is seeking clarification; I think he's trying to save his neck. He is aware of two facts: He's going down, and Jesus is staying up. And it doesn't take him too long to decide where he would rather be.

Perhaps a better interpretation of his request would be, "Jeeeeeeeesus. If that is you, then get me out of here!"

"Come on" is the invitation.

And Peter doesn't have to be told twice. It's not every day that you walk on water through waves that are taller than you are. But when faced with the alternative of sure death or possible life, Peter knows which one he wants.

The first few steps go well. But a few strides out onto the

water, and he forgets to look to the One who got him there in the first place, and down he plunges.

At this point we see the major difference between Anibal and Peter—the difference between a man who hides his problem and one who admits it.

Anibal would be more concerned about his image than about his neck. He would prefer to go under rather than let his friends hear him ask for help. He would rather go down "his way" than get out "God's way."

Peter, on the other hand, knows better than to count the teeth in the mouth of a gift horse. He knows better than to bite the hand that can save him. His response may lack class —it probably wouldn't get him on the cover of *Gentleman's Quarterly* or even *Sports Illustrated*—but it gets him out of some deep water:

"Help me!"

And since Peter would rather swallow pride than water, a hand comes through the rain and pulls him up.

The message is clear.

As long as Jesus is one of many options, he is no option. As long as you can carry your burdens alone, you don't need a burden bearer. As long as your situation brings you no grief, you will receive no comfort. And as long as you can take him or leave him, you might as well leave him, because he won't be taken half-heartedly.

But when you mourn, when you get to the point of sorrow for your sins, when you admit that you have no other option but to cast all your cares on him, and when there is truly no other name that you can call, then cast all your cares on him, for he is waiting in the midst of the storm.

. . . *for they will be comforted.*

CHAPTER 6

Touches of Tenderness

$\mathcal{B}$eing a parent is better than a theology course.

Two ten-year-old boys walked up to my five-year-old daughter on the bus yesterday, scowled at her, and demanded that she scoot over.

When I came home from work, she told me about it. "I wanted to cry, but I didn't. I just sat there—afraid."

My immediate impulse was to find out the names of the boys and punch their dads in the nose. But I didn't. I did what was more important. I pulled my little girl up into my lap and let her get lost inside my arms and told her not to worry about those old bullies because her daddy was here, and I'd make sure if any thugs ever got close to my princess they'd be taking their lives in their own hands, yessir.

And that was enough for Jenna. She bounded down and ran outside.

She came back a few minutes later, crying. Her elbow was scraped.

I picked her up and carried her into the bathroom for first aid. She tried to tell me what happened.

"I"—sniff, sniff—"was turning in circles"—sniff, sniff—"like a helicopter"—sniff, sniff—"and then I fell doaaaaawwwn," she wailed.

"It's gonna be OK," I said as I set her on the bathroom counter.

"Can I have a Band-Aid?"

"Of course."

"A big one?"

"The biggest."

"Really?"

I stretched the adhesive bandage over the scrape and held her arm up in the mirror so she could see her badge of courage.

"Wow. Can I go show Mommy?"

"Sure." I smiled.

And that was enough for Jenna.

"Daddy."

The voice was coming from another world—the world

of the awake. I ignored it and stayed in the world of slumber.

"Daddy." The voice was insistent.

I opened one eye. Andrea, our three-year-old, was at the edge of my bed only a few inches from my face.

"Daddy, I'm scared."

I opened the other eye. It was three in the morning.

"What's wrong?"

"I need a fwashwight in my woom.

"What?"

"I need a fwashwight in my woom."

"Why?"

"'Cause it's dark."

I told her the lights were on. I told her the night light was on and the hall light was on.

"But Daddy," she objected, "what if I open my eyes and can't see anything?"

"Say that again."

"What if I open my eyes and can't see anything?"

Just as I was about to tell her that this was not the best time for questions on affliction, my wife interrupted. She explained to me that there was a power failure around midnight and Andrea must have awakened in the dark. No night light. No hall light. She had opened her eyes and had been unable to see anything. Just darkness.

Even the hardest of hearts would be touched by the thought of a child waking up in a darkness so black she couldn't find her way out of her room.

I climbed out of bed, picked Andrea up, got a flashlight

out of the utility room, and carried her to her bed. All the while, I told her that Mom and Dad were here and that she didn't need to be afraid. I tucked her in and gave her a kiss.

And that was enough for Andrea.

My child's feelings are hurt. I tell her she's special. My child is injured. I do whatever it takes to make her feel better.

My child is afraid. I won't go to sleep until she is secure.

I'm not a hero. I'm not a superstar. I'm not unusual. I'm a parent. When a child hurts, a parent does what comes naturally. He helps.

And after I help, I don't charge a fee. I don't ask for a favor in return. When my child cries, I don't tell her to buck up, act tough, and keep a stiff upper lip. Nor do I consult a list and ask her why she is still scraping the same elbow or waking me up again.

I'm not brilliant, but you don't have to be to remember that a child is not an adult. You don't have to be a child psychologist to know that kids are "under construction." You don't have to have the wisdom of Solomon to realize that they didn't ask to be here in the first place and that spilled milk can be wiped up and broken plates can be replaced.

I'm not a prophet, nor the son of one, but something tells me that in the whole scheme of things the tender moments described above are infinitely more valuable than anything I do in front of a computer screen or congregation. Something tells me that the moments of comfort I give my child are a small price to pay for the joy of someday seeing my daughter do for her daughter what her dad did for her.

Moments of comfort from a parent. As a father, I can tell you they are the sweetest moments in my day. They come naturally. They come willingly. They come joyfully.

If all of that is true, if I know that one of the privileges of fatherhood is to comfort a child, then why am I so reluctant to let my heavenly Father comfort me?

Why do I think he wouldn't want to hear about my problems? ("They are puny compared to people starving in India.")

Why do I think he is too busy for me? ("He's got a whole universe to worry about.")

Why do I think he's tired of hearing the same old stuff?

Why do I think he groans when he sees me coming?

Why do I think he consults his list when I ask for forgiveness and asks, "Don't you think you're going to the well a few too many times on this one?"

Why do I think I have to speak a holy language around him that I don't speak with anyone else?

Why do I think he won't do in a heartbeat to the Father of Lies what I thought about doing to the fathers of those bullies on the bus?

Do I think he was just being poetic when he asked me if the birds of the air and the grass of the field have a worry? (No sir.) And if they don't, why do I think I will? (Duh. . . .)[1]

Why do I not take him seriously when he questions, "If you, then, though you are evil, know how to give good gifts to your children, how much more will your Father in heaven give good gifts to those who ask him!"[2]

Why don't I let my Father do for me what I am more than willing to do for my own children?

I'm learning, though. Being a parent is better than a course on theology. Being a father is teaching me that when I am criticized, injured, or afraid, there is a Father who is ready to comfort me. There is a Father who will hold me until I'm better, help me until I can live with the hurt, and who won't go to sleep when I'm afraid of waking up and seeing the dark.

Ever.

And that's enough.

Blessed are the meek . . .

The Glory in the Ordinary

There is one word that describes the night he came—ordinary.

The sky was ordinary. An occasional gust stirred the leaves and chilled the air. The stars were diamonds sparkling on black velvet. Fleets of clouds floated in front of the moon.

It was a beautiful night—a night worth peeking out your bedroom window to admire—but not really an unusual one. No reason to expect a surprise. Nothing to keep a person awake. An ordinary night with an ordinary sky.

The sheep were ordinary. Some fat. Some scrawny. Some with barrel bellies. Some with twig legs. Common animals. No fleece made of gold. No history makers. No blue-ribbon winners. They were simply sheep—lumpy, sleeping silhouettes on a hillside.

And the shepherds. Peasants they were. Probably wearing all the clothes they owned. Smelling like sheep and looking just as woolly. They were conscientious, willing to spend the night with their flocks. But you won't find their staffs in a museum nor their writings in a library. No one asked their opinion on social justice or the application of the Torah. They were nameless and simple.

An ordinary night with ordinary sheep and ordinary shepherds. And were it not for a God who loves to hook an "extra" on the front of the ordinary, the night would have gone unnoticed. The sheep would have been forgotten, and the shepherds would have slept the night away.

But God dances amidst the common. And that night he did a waltz.

The black sky exploded with brightness. Trees that had been shadows jumped into clarity. Sheep that had been silent became a chorus of curiosity. One minute the shepherd was dead asleep, the next he was rubbing his eyes and staring into the face of an alien.

The night was ordinary no more.

The angel came in the night because that is when lights are best seen and that is when they are most needed. God comes into the common for the same reason.

His most powerful tools are the simplest.

Consider the rod of Moses.[1] By this time in his life, Moses had been a shepherd as long as he had been a prince, and he'd grown accustomed to it. Herding sheep wasn't as lively as living with Egyptian royalty, but it had its moments, especially the moment God spoke to him through a burning bush that didn't burn up. God announced that Moses was his man to deliver the Israelites. Moses wasn't convinced he was the one for the job. God said that who Moses was didn't matter; what mattered was who God was. And God set out to demonstrate.

"Moses," spoke the voice from the bush, "throw down your staff."

Moses, who had walked this mountain for forty years, was not comfortable with the command.

"God, you know a lot about a lot of things, but you may not know that out here, well, you just don't go around throwing down your staff. You never know when . . ."

"Throw it down, Moses."

Moses threw it down. The rod became a snake, and Moses began to run.

"Moses!"

The old shepherd stopped.

"Pick up the snake."

Moses peered over his shoulder, first at the snake and then the bush, and then he gave the most courageous response he could muster.

"What?"

"Pick up the snake . . . by the tail." (God had to be smiling at this point.)

"God, I don't mean to object. I mean, you know a lot of things, but out here in the desert, well, you don't pick up snakes too often, and you *never* pick up snakes by the tail."

"Moses!"

"Yessir."

Just as Moses' hand touched the squirmy scales of the snake, it hardened. And Moses lifted up the rod. The same rod he would lift up in Pharaoh's court. The same rod he would lift up to divide the water and guide two million people through a desert. The rod that would remind Moses that if God can make a stick become a snake, then become a stick again—then perhaps he can do something with stubborn hearts and a stiff-necked people.

Perhaps he can do something with the common.

Or consider another shepherd from Bethlehem.[2]

There are certain things anyone knows not to do. You don't try to lasso a tornado. You don't fight a lion with a toothpick. You don't sneeze into the wind. You don't go bear hunting with a cork gun. And you don't send a shepherd boy to battle a giant.

You don't, that is, unless you are out of options. Saul was. And it is when we are out of options that we are most ready for God's surprises.

Was Saul ever surprised!

The king tried to give David some equipment. "What do you want, boy? Shield? Sword? Grenades? Rifles? A helicopter? We'll make a Rambo out of you."

David had something else in mind. Five smooth stones and an ordinary leather sling.

The soldiers gasped. Saul sighed. Goliath jeered.

David swung. And God made his point. "Anyone who underestimates what God can do with the ordinary has rocks in his head."

Or what about the blind man Jesus and the disciples discovered?[3]

The followers thought he was a great theological case study.

"Why do you think he's blind?" one asked.

"He must have sinned."

"No, it's his folks' fault."

"Jesus, what do you think? Why is he blind?"

"He's blind to show what God can do."

The apostles knew what was coming; they had seen this look in Jesus' eyes before. They knew what he was going to do, but they didn't know how he was going to do it. "Lightning? Thunder? A shout? A clap of the hands?" They all watched.

Jesus began to work his mouth a little. The onlookers

stared. "What is he doing?" He moved his jaw as if he were chewing on something.

Some of the people began to get restless. Jesus just chewed. His jaw rotated around until he had what he wanted. Spit. Ordinary saliva.

If no one said it, somebody had to be thinking it: "Yuk!"

Jesus spat on the ground, stuck his finger into the puddle, and stirred. Soon it was a mud pie, and he smeared some of the mud across the blind man's eyes.

The same One who'd turned a stick into a scepter and a pebble into a missile now turned saliva and mud into a balm for the blind.

Once again, the mundane became majestic. Once again the dull became divine, the humdrum holy. Once again God's power was seen not through the ability of the instrument, but through its availability.

"Blessed are the meek," Jesus explained. Blessed are the available. Blessed are the conduits, the tunnels, the tools. Deliriously joyful are the ones who believe that if God has used sticks, rocks, and spit to do his will, then he can use us.

We would do well to learn a lesson from the rod, the rock, and the saliva. They didn't complain. They didn't question God's wisdom. They didn't suggest an alternative plan. Perhaps the reason the Father has used so many inanimate objects for his mission is that they don't tell him how to do his job!

It's like the story of the barber who became an artist. When asked why he changed professions, he replied, "A canvas doesn't tell me how to make it beautiful."

Neither do the meek.

That's why the announcement went first to the shepherds. They didn't ask God if he was sure he knew what he was doing. Had the angel gone to the theologians, they would have first consulted their commentaries. Had he gone to the elite, they would have looked around to see if anyone was watching. Had he gone to the successful, they would have first looked at their calendars.

So he went to the shepherds. Men who didn't have a reputation to protect or an ax to grind or a ladder to climb. Men who didn't know enough to tell God that angels don't sing to sheep and that messiahs aren't found wrapped in rags and sleeping in a feed trough.

A small cathedral outside Bethlehem marks the supposed birthplace of Jesus. Behind a high altar in the church is a cave, a little cavern lit by silver lamps.

You can enter the main edifice and admire the ancient church. You can also enter the quiet cave where a star embedded in the floor recognizes the birth of the King. There is one stipulation, however. You have to stoop. The door is so low you can't go in standing up.

The same is true of the Christ. You can see the world standing tall, but to witness the Savior, you have to get on your knees.

So . . .

       while the theologians were sleeping
         and the elite were dreaming
           and the successful were snoring,
             the meek were kneeling.
They were kneeling before the One only the meek will see.
They were kneeling in front of Jesus.

. . . for they will inherit the earth.

CHAPTER 8

The Bandit of Joy

He was a professional thief. His name stirred fear as the desert wind stirs tumbleweeds. He terrorized the Wells Fargo stage line for thirteen years, roaring like a tornado in and out of the Sierra Nevadas, spooking the most rugged frontiersmen. In journals from San Francisco to New York, his name became synonymous with the danger of the frontier.

During his reign of terror between 1875 and 1883, he is credited with stealing the bags and the breath away from twenty-nine different stagecoach crews. And he did it all without firing a shot.

His weapon was his reputation. His ammunition was intimidation.

A hood hid his face. No victim ever saw him. No artist ever sketched his features. No sheriff could ever track his trail. He never fired a shot or took a hostage.

He didn't have to. His presence was enough to paralyze.

Black Bart. A hooded bandit armed with a deadly weapon.

He reminds me of another thief—one who's still around. You know him. Oh you've never seen his face, either. You couldn't describe his voice or sketch his profile. But when he's near, you know it in a heartbeat.

If you've ever been in the hospital, you've felt the leathery brush of his hand against yours.

If you've ever sensed someone was following you, you've felt his cold breath down your neck.

If you've awakened late at night in a strange room, it was his husky whisper that stole your slumber.

You know him.

It was this thief who left your palms sweaty as you went for the job interview.

It was this con man who convinced you to swap your integrity for popularity.

And it was this scoundrel who whispered in your ear as you left the cemetery, "You may be next."

He's the Black Bart of the soul. He doesn't want your money. He doesn't want your diamonds. He won't go after your car. He wants something far more precious. He wants your peace of mind—your joy.

His name?

Fear.

His task is to take your courage and leave you timid and

trembling. His *modus operandi is* to manipulate you with the mysterious, to taunt you with the unknown. Fear of death, fear of failure, fear of God, fear of tomorrow—his arsenal is vast. His goal? To create cowardly, joyless souls.

He doesn't want you to make the journey to the mountain. He figures if he can rattle you enough, you will take your eyes off the peaks and settle for a dull existence in the flatlands.

A legend from India tells about a mouse who was terrified of cats until a magician agreed to transform him into a cat. That resolved his fear . . . until he met a dog, so the magician changed him into a dog. The mouse-turned-cat-turned-dog was content until he met a tiger—so, once again, the magician changed him into what he feared. But when the tiger came complaining that he had met a hunter, the magician refused to help. "I will make you into a mouse again, for though you have the body of a tiger, you still have the heart of a mouse."

Sound familiar? How many people do you know who have built a formidable exterior, only to tremble inside with fear? We tackle our anxieties by taking on the appearance of a tiger. We face our fears with force. Military power, security systems, defense strategy—all reflect a conviction that muscle creates security.

Or if we don't use force, we try other methods. We stock-pile wealth. We seek security in things. We cultivate fame and seek status.

But do these approaches work? Can power, possessions, or popularity really deliver us from our fears?

If power could, then Joseph Stalin should have been fear-less. Instead, this infamous Russian premier was afraid to go bed. He had seven different bedrooms. Each could be locked as tightly as a safe. In order to foil any would-be assassins, he slept in a different one each night. Five chauffeur-driven lim-ousines transported him wherever he went, each with curtains closed so no one would know which contained Stalin. So deep-seated were his apprehensions that he employed a ser-vant whose sole task was to monitor and protect his tea bags.[1]

If possessions conquered fear, the late billionaire Howard Hughes would have been fearless. But you probably know his story. His distrust of people and his paranoia of germs led this billionaire to Mexico, where he died a lonely death as a cadaverous hermit with a belly-length beard and corkscrew fingernails.[2]

What about popularity? Beatle John Lennon's fame as a singer, songwriter, and pop icon made him a household word, but his fears brought him misery. His biographers describe him as a frightened man, unwilling to sleep with the lights off and afraid to touch anything because of its filth.[3]

Though Stalin, Hughes, and Lennon are extreme cases, they are indicative ones. "Though you have the body of a tiger, you still have the heart of a mouse."

Parallel their stories with the life of a little-known but

gutsy young man named Paul Keating. On a cold night in February 1980, twenty-seven-year-old Keating was walking home in Manhattan's Greenwich Village when he saw two armed muggers robbing a college student. Keating, a gentle, much-admired photographer for *Time* magazine, had every reason to avoid trouble. He didn't know the student. No one knew he saw the crime. He was outnumbered. He had nothing to gain and much to lose by taking the risk, and yet he jumped on the muggers. The victim escaped and ran to a nearby deli to call for help. Moments later, two shots cracked the night, and the muggers fled. Paul Keating was found dead on the pavement.

The city of New York posthumously awarded him a medal of heroism. I think you'll agree with the commentary offered by Mayor Edward Koch at the ceremony: "Nobody was watching Paul Keating on the street that night. Nobody made him step forward in the time of crisis. He did it because of who he was."[4]

Well put.

Courage is an outgrowth of who we are. Exterior supports may temporarily sustain, but only inward character creates courage.

And it is those inward convictions that Jesus is building in the Beatitudes. Remember, Matthew 5 is not a list of proverbs or a compilation of independent sayings, but rather a step-by-step description of how God rebuilds the believer's heart.

The first step is to ask for help—to become "poor in spirit" and admit our need for a Savior.

The next step is sorrow: "Blessed are those who mourn. . . ." Those who mourn are those who know they are wrong and say they are sorry. No excuses. No justification. Just tears.

The first two steps are admittance of inadequacy and repentance for pride. The next step is the one of renewal: "Blessed are the meek. . . ." Realization of weakness leads to the source of strength—God. And renewal comes when we become meek—when we give our lives to God to be his tool.

The first two beatitudes pass us through the fire of purification; the third places us in the hands of the Master.

The result of this process? Courage: ". . . they shall inherit the earth." No longer shall the earth and its fears dominate us, for we follow the one who dominates the earth.

Could you use some courage? Are you backing down more than you are standing up? If so, let the Master lead you up the mountain again. Let him remind you why you should "fear not." Listen to the time Jesus scattered the butterflies out of the stomachs of his nervous disciples and see if his words help you.[5]

We need to remember that the disciples were common men given a compelling task. Before they were the stained-glassed saints in the windows of cathedrals, they were somebody's next-door-neighbors trying to make a living and raise a family. They weren't cut from theological cloth or raised on supernatural milk. But they were an ounce more devoted than they were afraid and, as a result, did some extraordinary things.

They would have done nothing, however, had they not learned to face their fears. Jesus knew that. That is why he spoke his words of courage.

The disciples are being sent out on their own. For a limited time they will go into the cities and do what Jesus has done—but without Jesus. Jesus assembles them to give them the final instructions. Perhaps the disciples look nervous, for they have reason to be nervous. What Jesus tells them would raise the pulse rate of the stoutest heart.

First Jesus tells them not to take any extra money or extra clothing on their journey.

"No money?"

Then he assures them that they are being sent out "like sheep among wolves."

"Uh, what do you mean, Jesus?"

His answer is not reassuring. He tells them they will be taken before the authorities (uh-oh), flogged (ouch), and arrested (groan).

And it gets worse before it gets better.

Jesus goes on to describe the impact their mission will have on people: "Brother will betray brother to death, and a father his child; children will rebel against their parents and have them put to death. All men will hate you because of me, but he who stands firm to the end will be saved."[6]

Some eyes duck. Some eyes widen. Someone swallows. Feet

shift. A brow is wiped. And though no one says it, you know someone is thinking, "Is it too late to get out of this?"

That's the setting for Jesus' paragraph on courage. Three times in five verses[7] he says, "Do not be afraid." Read the words and see his call and cause for courage. See the reason you should sleep well tonight:

"So do not be afraid of them. There is nothing concealed that will not be disclosed, or hidden that will not be made known."[8]

On the surface, those words would seem like a reason for panic rather than a source of peace. Who of us would like to have our secret thoughts made public? Who would want our private sins published? Who would get excited over the idea that every wrong deed we've ever done will be announced to everyone?

You're right, no one would. But we're told over and over that such a thing *will* happen:

Nothing in all creation is hidden from God's sight. Everything is uncovered and laid bare before the eyes of him to whom we must give account.

He reveals deep and hidden things;
    he knows what lies in darkness,
    and light dwells with him.

But I tell you that men will have to give account on the day of judgment for every careless word they have spoken.

You have set our iniquities before you,
    our secret sins in the light of your presence.

He will bring to light what is hidden in darkness and will expose the motives of men's hearts.[9]

To think of the disclosure of my hidden heart conjures up emotions of shame, humiliation, and embarrassment in me. There are things I've done that I want no one to know. There are thoughts I've thought I would never want to be revealed. So why does Jesus point to the day of revelation as a reason for *courage?* How can I take strength in what should be a moment of anguish?

The answer is found in Romans 2:16. Let out a sigh of relief as you underline the last three words of the verse: "This will take place on the day when God will judge men's secrets *through Jesus Christ.*"

Did you see it? Jesus is the screen through which God looks when he judges our sins. Now read another chorus of verses and focus on their promise:

Therefore, there is now no condemnation for those who are in Christ Jesus.

[God] justifies those who have faith in Jesus.

Through him everyone who believes is justified from everything.

For I will forgive their wickedness
    and will remember their sins no more.

For you died, and your life is now hidden with Christ in God.[10]

If you are in Christ, these promises are not only a source of joy. They are also the foundations of true courage. You are guaranteed that your sins will be filtered through, hidden in, and screened out by the sacrifice of Jesus. When God looks at you, he doesn't see you; he sees the One who surrounds you. That means that failure is not a concern for you. Your victory is secure. How could you not be courageous?

Picture it this way. Imagine that you are an ice skater in competition. You are in first place with one more round to go. If you perform well, the trophy is yours. You are nervous, anxious, and frightened.

Then, only minutes before your performance, your trainer rushes to you with the thrilling news: "You've already won! The judges tabulated the scores, and the person in second place can't catch you. You are too far ahead."

Upon hearing that news, how will you feel? Exhilarated!

And how will you skate? Timidly? Cautiously? Of course not. How about courageously and confidently? You bet you will. You will do your best because the prize is yours. You will skate like a champion because that is what you are! You will hear the applause of victory.

Hence, these words from Hebrews: "Therefore, brothers, since we have *confidence* to enter the Most Holy Place by the blood of Jesus . . . let us draw near to God with a sincere heart in *full assurance* of faith."[11]

The point is clear: the truth will triumph. The Father of truth will win, and the followers of truth will be saved.

As a result, Jesus says, don't be afraid:

What I tell you in the dark, speak in the daylight; what is whispered in your ear, proclaim from the roofs. Do not be afraid of those who kill the body but cannot kill the soul. Rather, be afraid of the One who can destroy both soul and body in hell.[12]

Earthly fears are no fears at all. All the mystery is revealed. The final destination is guaranteed. Answer the big question of eternity, and the little questions of life fall into perspective.

And by the way, remember Black Bart? As it turns out, he wasn't anything to be afraid of, either. When the hood came off, there was nothing to fear. When the authorities finally tracked down the thief, they didn't find a bloodthirsty bandit from Death Valley; they found a mild-mannered druggist from Decatur, Illinois. The man the papers pictured storming through the mountains on horseback was, in reality, so afraid of horses he rode to and from his robberies in a buggy. He was Charles E. Boles—the bandit who never once fired a shot, because he never once loaded his gun.[13]

Any false hoods in your world?

*Blessed are those who hunger and
thirst for righteousness . . .*

CHAPTER 9

A Satisfied Thirst

"Mommy, I'm so thirsty. I want a drink."

Susanna Petroysan heard her daughter's pleas, but there was nothing she could do. She and four-year-old Gayaney were trapped beneath tons of collapsed concrete and steel. Beside them in the darkness lay the body of Susanna's sister-in-law, Karine, one of the fifty-five thousand victims of the worst earthquake in the history of Soviet Armenia.

Calamity never knocks before it enters, and this time, it had torn down the door.

Susanna had gone to Karine's house to try on a dress. It was December 7, 1988, at 11:30 AM. The quake hit at 11:41. She had just removed the dress and was clad in stockings and a slip when the fifth-floor apartment began to shake. Susanna grabbed her daughter but had taken only a few steps before the floor opened up and they tumbled in. Susanna, Gayaney, and Karine fell into the basement with the nine-story apartment house crumbling around them.

"Mommy, I need a drink. Please give me something."

There was nothing for Susanna to give.

She was trapped flat on her back. A concrete panel eighteen inches above her head and a crumpled water pipe above her shoulders kept her from standing. Feeling around in the darkness, she found a twenty-four-ounce jar of blackberry jam that had fallen into the basement. She gave the entire jar to her daughter to eat. It was gone by the second day.

"Mommy, I'm so thirsty."

Susanna knew she would die, but she wanted her daughter to live. She found a dress, perhaps the one she had come to try on, and made a bed for Gayaney. Though it was bitter cold, she took off her stockings and wrapped them around the child to keep her warm.

The two were trapped for eight days.

Because of the darkness, Susanna lost track of time. Because of the cold, she lost the feeling in her fingers and toes. Because of her inability to move, she lost hope. "I was just waiting for death."

She began to hallucinate. Her thoughts wandered. A merciful sleep occasionally freed her from the horror of her entombment, but the sleep would be brief. Something always awakened her: the cold, the hunger, or—most often—the voice of her daughter.

"Mommy, I'm thirsty."

At some point in that eternal night, Susanna had an idea. She remembered a television program about an explorer in the Arctic who was dying of thirst. His comrade slashed open his hand and gave his friend his blood.

"I had no water, no fruit juice, no liquids. It was then I remembered I had my own blood."

Her groping fingers, numb from the cold, found a piece of shattered glass. She sliced open her left index finger and gave it to her daughter to suck.

The drops of blood weren't enough. "Please, Mommy, some more. Cut another finger." Susanna has no idea how many times she cut herself. She only knows that if she hadn't, Gayaney would have died. Her blood was her daughter's only hope.

"This cup is the new covenant in my blood," Jesus explained, holding up the wine.[1]

The claim must have puzzled the apostles. They had been taught the story of the Passover wine. It symbolized the lamb's blood that the Israelites, enslaved long ago in Egypt, had painted on the doorposts of their homes. That blood had kept death from their homes and saved their firstborn. It had helped deliver them from the clutches of the Egyptians.

For thousands of generations the Jews had observed the Passover by sacrificing the lambs. Every year the blood would be poured, and every year the deliverance would be celebrated.

The law called for spilling the blood of a lamb. That would be enough.

It would be enough to fulfill the law. It would be enough to satisfy the command. It would be enough to justify God's justice.

But it would not be enough to take away sin.

". . . because it is impossible for the blood of bulls and goats to take away sins."[2]

Sacrifices could offer temporary solutions, but only God could offer the eternal one.

So he did.

Beneath the rubble of a fallen world, he pierced his hands. In the wreckage of a collapsed humanity, he ripped open his side. His children were trapped, so he gave his blood.

It was all he had. His friends were gone. His strength was waning. His possessions had been gambled away at his feet. Even his Father had turned his head. His blood was all he had. But his blood was all it took.

"If anyone is thirsty," Jesus once said, "let him come to me and drink."[3]

Admission of thirst doesn't come easy for us. False fountains pacify our cravings with sugary swallows of pleasure. But there comes a time when pleasure doesn't satisfy. There comes a dark hour in every life when the world caves in and we are left trapped in the rubble of reality, parched and dying.

A Satisfied Thirst

Some would rather die than admit it. Others admit it and escape death.

"God, I need help."

So the thirsty come. A ragged lot we are, bound together by broken dreams and collapsed promises. Fortunes that were never made. Families that were never built. Promises that were never kept. Wide-eyed children trapped in the basement of our own failures.

And we are very thirsty.

Not thirsty for fame, possessions, passion, or romance. We've drunk from those pools. They are salt water in the desert. They don't quench—they kill.

"Blessed are those who hunger and thirst for righteousness. . . ."

Righteousness. That's it. That's what we are thirsty for. We're thirsty for a clean conscience. We crave a clean slate. We yearn for a fresh start. We pray for a hand which will enter the dark cavern of our world and do for us the one thing we can't do for ourselves—make us right again.[4]

"Mommy, I'm so thirsty," Gayaney begged.

"It was then I remembered I had my own blood," Susanna explained.

And the hand was cut, and the blood was poured, and the child was saved.

"God, I'm so thirsty," we pray.

"It is my blood, the blood of the new agreement," Jesus stated, "shed to set many free from their sins."[5]

And the hand was pierced,

and the blood was poured,

and the children are saved.

. . . *for they will be filled.*

CHAPTER 10

Life in the Pits

$\mathcal{I}$ took my two oldest daughters to
Sea World recently. My wife was out of town, so Jenna,
Andrea, and I went to spend the day watching the dolphins
dip, the walruses waddle, and the penguins paddle.

We had a great day. Hot dogs. Ice cream. Stuffed whales.
Toys, toys, and toys. The girls know their dad is a pushover
for a thirteen-letter "Pleeeeeeeease." I should have known
better. The average interest in amusement park memorabilia
is twelve minutes and thirty-two seconds. Then it is,
"Daddy, can you hold this? It's too heavy."

"Now, I told you not to buy it if you couldn't hold on to
it."

"Pleeeeeeeeease."

So by the end of the day I was carrying two pen-and-pencil sets, one set of sunglasses, an inflated penguin, a shark's tooth (complete with shark), a life-sized stuffed version of Shamu the killer whale, six balloons, and a live turtle. (OK, I'm exaggerating; there were only five balloons.) Add to that the heat, the rash from getting splashed with salt water, and the Eskimo Pie that melted down my shirt, and I was ready for a break.

That's why I was glad to see the plastic ball pit. This one activity is enough to convince you to keep your season pass current. It's a large, covered, shady, cool, soothing pavilion. Under the awning is a four-foot-deep pit the size of a backyard pool. But rather than being filled with water, it is loaded with balls—thousands and thousands of plastic, colorful, lightweight balls.

In the center of the pit is a sort of table with holes through which blow jets of air. Kids climb through the pit, grab balls, place them over the holes, and "Whee!"—up fly the balls.

The greatest part of the pit is the parents' area. While the kids roll and romp in the balls, the parents sit on the carpeted floor next to the pit and rest.

My oldest daughter, Jenna, did great. She dove in and made a beeline to the table.

Three-year-old Andrea, however, had a few difficulties. As soon as she took one step into the pit, she filled her arms with balls.

Now, it is hard enough to walk through the waisthigh pit of balls with your arms spread to keep your balance. It is *impossible* to do it with your arms full.

Andrea took a step and fell. She tried to wrestle her way up without releasing the balls. She couldn't. She began to cry. I walked over to the edge of the pit.

"Andrea," I said gently, "let go of the balls, and you can walk."

"No!" she screamed, wiggling and submerging herself beneath the balls. I reached in and pulled her up. She was still clutching her armful of treasures.

"Andrea," her wise, patient father said, "if you'll let the balls go, you'll be able to walk. Besides, there are plenty of balls near the table."

"No!"

She took two steps and fell again.

Parents aren't supposed to go into the pit. I tried to reach her from the edge, but I couldn't. She was somewhere under the balls, so I spoke toward the area where she had fallen. "Andrea, let go of the balls so you can get up."

I saw a movement under the balls. "Nooo!!"

"Andrea," spoke her slightly agitated father. "You could get up if you would let go of . . ."

"Nooooo!!!!!"

"Jenna, come here and help your sister up."

By now the other parents were beginning to look at me. Jenna waded through the balls toward her little sister. She reached down into the pit and tried to help Andrea onto her feet. Jenna wasn't strong enough, and Andrea couldn't help because she was still clutching the same balls she had grabbed when she first stepped into the pit.

Jenna straightened up and shook her head at me. "I can't get her up, Daddy."

"Andrea," her increasingly irritated father said loudly, "let go of the balls so you can get up!"

The cry from beneath the balls was muffled, but distinct. "Nooooo!!!!!"

"Great," I thought to myself. "She's got what she wants, and she's going to hold on to it if it kills her."

"Jenna," her visibly angered father said sternly. "Take those balls away from your sister."

Down Jenna dove, digging through the balls like a puppy digging through the dirt. I knew she had found her little sister and that the two were engaged in mortal combat when waves of balls began to move on the surface of the pit.

By now the other parents were whispering and pointing. I looked forlornly at the employee who was monitoring the pit. I didn't even have to say a word. "Go on in," he told me.

I waded through the balls to my two angels, broke the death-locks they had on each other, put one under each arm, and carried them to the center of the pit. I dropped them next to the table (all the other kids scrambled away when they saw me coming). Then I marched back to the side of the pit and sat down.

As I watched the girls play with the balls, I asked myself, "What is it that makes children immobilize themselves by clutching toys so tightly?"

I winced as a response surfaced. "Whatever it is, they learned it from their parents."

Andrea's determination to hold those balls is nothing compared to the vice-grips we put on life. If you think

Jenna's job of taking the balls away from Andrea was tough, try prying our fingers away from our earthly treasures. Try taking a retirement account away from a fifty-five-year-old. Or try convincing a yuppie to give up her BMW. Or test your luck on a clotheshorse and his or her wardrobe. The way we clutch our possessions and our pennies, you'd think we couldn't live without them.

Ouch.

Jesus' promise is comprehensive: "Blessed are those who hunger and thirst for righteousness, for they will be filled."

We usually get what we hunger and thirst for. The problem is, the treasures of earth don't satisfy. The promise is, the treasures of heaven do.

Blessed are those, then, who hold their earthly possessions in open palms. Blessed are those who, if everything they own were taken from them, would be, at most, inconvenienced, because their true wealth is elsewhere. Blessed are those who are totally dependent upon Jesus for their joy.

"Andrea," her father pleaded, "there are more than enough balls to play with at the table. Concentrate on walking."

"Max," the heavenly Father pleads, "there are more riches than you could ever dream at the banquet table. Concentrate on walking."

Our resistance to our Father is just as childish as Andrea's.

God, for our own good, tries to loosen our grip from something that will cause us to fall. But we won't let go.

"No, I won't give up my weekend rendezvous for eternal joy."

"Trade a life addicted to drugs and alcohol for a life of peace and a promise of heaven? Are you kidding?"

"I don't want to die. I don't want a new body. I want this one. I don't care if it is fat, balding, and destined to decay. I want this body."

And there we lie, submerged in the pits, desperately clutching the very things that cause us grief.

It's a wonder the Father doesn't give up.

Blessed are the merciful, for they will be shown mercy.

CHAPTER 11

The Father in the Face of the Enemy

March 24, 1989. A cold night off the coast of Alaska.

The captain of a tanker barked orders to a second mate. The orders were vague, the night was black, and the collision was disastrous. The tanker ship *Exxon Valdez* ran hard aground on Bligh Reef, dumping eleven million gallons of crude oil into one of the most scenic bodies of water in the world. Petroleum blackened everything from the surface of the sea, to beaches, to otters, to sea gulls. Alaska was infuriated, and Exxon, the company which owned the tanker, was humiliated.

The collision, terrible as it was, was mild compared to the ones that occur daily in our relationships. You've been there.

Someone doesn't meet your expectations. Promises go unful-filled. Verbal pistols are drawn, and a round of words is fired.

The result? A collision of the hull of your heart against the reef of someone's actions. Precious energy escapes, coating the surface of your soul with the deadly film of resentment. A black blanket of bitterness darkens your world, dims your sight, sours your outlook, and suffocates your joy.

Do you have a hole in your heart?

Perhaps the wound is old. A parent abused you. A teacher slighted you. A mate betrayed you. A business partner bailed out, leaving you a choice of bills or bankruptcy.

And you are angry.

Or perhaps the wound is fresh. The friend who owes you money just drove by in a new car. The boss who hired you with promises of promotions has forgotten how to pro-nounce your name. Your circle of friends escaped on a weekend getaway, and you weren't invited. The children you raised seem to have forgotten you exist.

And you are hurt.

Part of you is broken, and the other part is bitter. Part of you wants to cry, and part of you wants to fight. The tears you cry are hot because they come from your heart, and there is a fire burning in your heart. It's the fire of anger. It's blazing. It's consuming. Its flames leap up under a steaming pot of revenge.

And you are left with a decision. "Do I put the fire out or heat it up? Do I get over it or get even? Do I release it or resent it? Do I let my hurts heal, or do I let hurt turn into hate?"

That's a good definition of resentment: Resentment is when you let your hurt become hate. Resentment is when you allow what is eating you to eat you up. Resentment is when you poke, stoke, feed, and fan the fire, stirring the flames and reliving the pain.

Resentment is the deliberate decision to nurse the offense until it becomes a black, furry, growling grudge.

Grudge is one of those words that defines itself. Its very sound betrays its meaning.

Say it slowly: "Grr-uuuud-ge."

It starts with a growl. "Grr . . ." Like a bear with bad breath coming out of hibernation or a mangy mongrel defending his bone in an alley. "Grrr . . ."

Being near a resentful person and petting a growling dog are equally enjoyable.

Don't you just love being next to people who are nursing a grudge? Isn't it a delight to listen to them sing their songs of woe? They are so optimistic! They are so full of hope. They are bubbling with life.

You know better. You know as well as I that if they are bubbling with anything it is anger. And if they are full of anything, it is poisonous barbs of condemnation for all the people who have hurt them. Grudge bearers and angry animals are a lot alike. Both are irritable. Both are explosive.

Both can be rabid. Someone needs to make a sign that can be worn around the neck of the resentful: "Beware of the Grrrrudge Bearer."

Add an *M* to the second part of the word, and you will see what grudge bearers throw. Mud. It's not enough to accuse; the other person's character must be attacked. It's insufficient to point a finger; a rifle must be aimed. Slander is slung. Names are called. Circles are drawn. Walls are built. And enemies are made.

Remove a *GR* from the word *grudge* and replace it with *SL* and you have the junk that grudge bearers trudge through. Sludge. Black, thick, ankle-deep resentment that steals the bounce from the step. No joyful skips through the meadows. No healthy hikes up the mountain. Just day after day of walking into the storm, shoulders bent against the wind, and feet dragging through all the muck life has delivered.

Is this the way you are coping with your hurts? Are you allowing your hurts to turn into hates? If so, ask yourself: Is it working? Has your hatred done you any good? Has your resentment brought you any relief, any peace? Has it granted you any joy?

Let's say you get even. Let's say you get him back. Let's say she gets what she deserves. Let's say your fantasy of fury runs its ferocious course and you return all your pain with interest. Imagine yourself standing over the corpse of the one you have hated. Will you now be free?

The writer of the following letter thought she would be. She thought her revenge would bring release. But she learned otherwise.

The Father in the Face of the Enemy

I caught my husband making love to another woman. He swore it would never happen again. He begged me to forgive him, but I could not—would not. I was so bitter and so incapable of swallowing my pride that I could think of nothing but revenge. I was going to make him pay and pay dearly. I'd have my pound of flesh.

I filed for divorce, even though my children begged me not to.

Even after the divorce, my husband tried for two years to win me back. I refused to have anything to do with him. He had struck first; now I was striking back. All I wanted was to make him pay.

Finally he gave up and married a lovely young widow with a couple of small children. He began rebuilding his life—without me.

I see them occasionally, and he looks so happy. They all do. And here I am—a lonely, old, miserable woman who allowed her selfish pride and foolish stubbornness to ruin her life.

Unfaithfulness is wrong. Revenge is bad. But the worst part of all is that, without forgiveness, bitterness is all that is left.

Resentment is the cocaine of the emotions. It causes our blood to pump and our energy level to rise.

But, also like cocaine, it demands increasingly larger and more frequent dosages. There is a dangerous point at which anger ceases to be an emotion and becomes a driving force. A person bent on revenge moves unknowingly further and further away from being able to forgive, for to be without the anger is to be without a source of energy.

That explains why the bitter complain to anyone who will listen. They want—they need—to have their fire fanned. That helps explain the existence of the KKK, the Skinheads, and other hate organizations. Members of these groups feed each other's anger. And that is why the resentful often appear unreasonable. They are addicted to their bitterness. They don't want to surrender their anger, for to do so would be to surrender their reason to live.

Take bigotry from the racist, and what does he have left? Remove revenge from the heart of the zealot, and her life is empty. Extract chauvinism from the radical sexist, and what remains?

Resentment is like cocaine in another way, too. Cocaine can kill the addict. And anger can kill the angry.

It can kill physically. Chronic anger has been linked with elevated cholesterol, high blood pressure, and other deadly conditions. It can kill emotionally, in that it can raise anxiety levels and lead to depression.[1]

And it can be spiritually fatal, too. It shrivels the soul.

Hatred is the rabid dog that turns on its owner. Revenge is the raging fire that consumes the arsonist. Bitterness is the trap that snares the hunter.

And mercy is the choice that can set them all free.

"Blessed are the merciful," said Jesus on the mountain. Those who are merciful to others are the ones who are truly blessed. Why? Jesus answered the question: ". . . they will be shown mercy."

The merciful, says Jesus, are shown mercy. They witness grace. They are blessed because they are testimonies to a greater goodness. Forgiving others allows us to see how God has forgiven us. The dynamic of giving grace is the key to understanding grace, for it is when we forgive others that we begin to feel what God feels.

Jesus told the story of a king who decided to close out all his accounts with those who worked for him.[2] He called in his debtors and told them to pay. One man owed an amount too great to return—a debt that could never be repaid. But when the king saw the man and heard his story, his heart went out to him, and he erased the debt.

As the man was leaving the palace grounds, he encountered a fellow employee who owed him a small sum. He grabbed the debtor and choked him, demanding payment. When the fellow begged for mercy, no mercy was granted. Instead, the one who had just been forgiven had his debtor thrown into jail.

When word of this got to the king, he became livid. And Jesus says, "In anger his master turned him over to the jailers to be tortured, until he should pay back all he owed."[3]

Could someone actually be forgiven a debt of millions and be unable to forgive a debt of hundreds? Could a person be set free and then imprison another?

You don't have to be a theologian to answer those questions; you only have to look in the mirror. Who among us has not begged God for mercy on Sunday and then demanded justice on Monday? Who hasn't served as a bottleneck instead of a conduit of God's love? Is there anyone who doesn't, at one time or the other, "show contempt for the riches of his [God's] kindness, tolerance and patience, not realizing that God's kindness leads you towards repentance?"[4]

Notice what God does when we calibrate our compassion. He turns us over to be tortured. Tortured by anger. Choked by bitterness. Consumed by revenge.

Such is the punishment for one who tastes God's grace but refuses to share it.

But for the one who tastes God's grace and then gives it to others, the reward is a blessed liberation. The prison door is thrown open, and the prisoner set free is yourself.

Earlier in the book I mentioned Daniel, a dear friend of mine in Brazil. (Daniel was the one who took me to meet Anibal in prison.)

Daniel is big. He used to make his living by lifting weights and teaching others to do the same. His scrapbook is colorful with ribbons and photos of him in his prime, striking the muscle-man pose and flexing the bulging arms.

The only thing bigger than Daniel's biceps is his heart. Let me tell you about a time his heart became tender.

Daniel was living in the southern city of Porto Alegre. He

worked at a gym and dreamed of owning his own. The bank agreed to finance the purchase if he could find someone to cosign the note. His brother agreed.

They filled out all the applications and awaited the approval. Everything went smoothly, and Daniel soon received a call from the bank telling him he could come and pick up the check. As soon as he got off work, he went to the bank.

When the loan officer saw Daniel, he looked surprised and asked Daniel why he had come.

"To pick up the check," Daniel explained.

"That's funny," responded the banker. "Your brother was in here earlier. He picked up the money and used it to retire the mortgage on his house."

Daniel was incensed. He never dreamed his own brother would trick him like that. He stormed over to his brother's house and pounded on the door. The brother answered the door with his daughter in his arms. He knew Daniel wouldn't hit him if he was holding a child.

He was right. Daniel didn't hit him. But he promised his brother that if he ever saw him again he would break his neck.

Daniel went home, his big heart bruised and ravaged by the trickery of his brother. He had no other choice but to go back to the gym and work to pay off the debt.

A few months later, Daniel met a young American missionary named Allen Dutton. Allen befriended Daniel and taught him about Jesus Christ. Daniel and his wife soon became Christians and devoted disciples.

But though Daniel had been forgiven so much, he still found it impossible to forgive his brother. The wound was deep. The pot of revenge still simmered. He didn't see his brother for two years. Daniel couldn't bring himself to look into the face of the one who had betrayed him. And his brother liked his own face too much to let Daniel see it.

But an encounter was inevitable. Both knew they would eventually run into each other. And neither knew what would happen then.

The encounter occurred one day on a busy avenue. Let Daniel tell you in his own words what happened:

I saw him, but he didn't see me. I felt my fists clench and my face get hot. My initial impulse was to grab him around the throat and choke the life out of him.

But as I looked into his face, my anger began to melt. For as I saw him, I saw the image of my father. I saw my father's eyes. I saw my father's look. I saw my father's expression. And as I saw my father in his face, my enemy once again became my brother.

Daniel walked toward him. The brother stopped, turned, and started to run, but he was too slow. Daniel reached out and grabbed his shoulder. The brother winced, expecting the worst. But rather than have his throat squeezed by Daniel's hands, he found himself hugged by Daniel's big arms. And the two brothers stood in the middle of the river of people and wept.

Daniel's words are worth repeating: "When I saw the

image of my father in his face, my enemy became my brother."

Seeing the father's image in the face of the enemy. Try that. The next time you see or think of the one who broke your heart, look twice. As you look at his face, look also for his face—the face of the One who forgave you. Look into the eyes of the King who wept when you pleaded for mercy. Look into the face of the Father who gave you grace when no one else gave you a chance. Find the face of the God who forgives in the face of your enemy. And then, because God has forgiven you more than you'll ever be called on to forgive in another, set your enemy—and yourself—free.

And allow the hole in your heart to heal.

Blessed are the pure in heart . . .

CHAPTER 12

The State of the Heart

$\mathcal{I}$ can still remember the first time I saw one. I had gone to work with my dad—a big thrill for a ten-year-old whose father worked in the oil fields. I sat in the cab of the pickup as tall as I could, stretching to see the endless West Texas plain. The countryside was flat and predictable, boasting nothing taller than pumpjacks and windmills. Maybe that is why the thing seemed so colossal. It stood out on the horizon like a science-fiction city.

"What's that?"

"It's a refinery," Dad answered.

A jungle of pipes and tanks and tubes and generators—heaters, pumps, pipes, filters, valves, hoses, conduits, switches, circuits. It looked like a giant Tinker-Toy set.

The function of that maze of machinery is defined by its name: It refines. Gasoline, oil, chemicals—the refinery takes whatever comes in and purifies it so that it's ready to go out.

The refinery does for petroleum and other products what your "heart" should do for you. It takes out the bad and utilizes the good.

We tend to think of the heart as the seat of emotion. We speak of "heartthrobs," "heartaches," and "broken hearts."

But when Jesus said, "Blessed are the pure in heart," he was speaking in a different context. To Jesus' listeners, the heart was the totality of the inner person—the control tower, the cockpit. The heart was thought of as the seat of the character—the origin of desires, affections, perceptions, thoughts, reasoning, imagination, conscience, intentions, purpose, will, and faith.

Thus a proverb admonished, "Above all else, guard your heart, for it is the wellspring of life."[1]

To the Hebrew mind, the heart is a freeway cloverleaf where all emotions and prejudices and wisdom converge. It is a switch house that receives freight cars loaded with moods, ideas, emotions, and convictions and puts them on the right track.

And just as a low-grade oil or alloyed gasoline would cause you to question the performance of a refinery, evil acts and impure thoughts cause us to question the condition of our hearts.

But the things that come out of the mouth come from the heart, and these make a man "unclean." For out of the heart come evil thoughts, murder, adultery, sexual immorality, theft, false testimony, slander.[2]

> The good man brings good things out of the good stored up in his heart, and the evil man brings evil things out of the evil stored up in his heart. For out of the overflow of his heart his mouth speaks.[3]

These verses hammer home the same truth: The heart is the center of the spiritual life. If the fruit of a tree is bad, you don't try to fix the fruit; you treat the roots. And if a person's actions are evil, it's not enough to change habits; you have to go deeper. You have to go to the heart of the problem, which is the problem of the heart.

That is why the state of the heart is so critical. What's the state of yours?

When someone barks at you, do you bark back or bite your tongue? That depends on the state of your heart.

When your schedule is too tight or your to-do list too long, do you lose your cool or keep it? That depends on the state of your heart.

When you are offered a morsel of gossip marinated in slander, do you turn it down or pass it on? That depends on the state of your heart.

Do you see the bag lady on the street as a burden on society or as an opportunity for God? That, too, depends on the state of your heart.

The state of your heart dictates whether you harbor a grudge or give grace, seek self-pity or seek Christ, drink human misery or taste God's mercy.

No wonder, then, the wise man begs, "Above all else, guard your heart."

David's prayer should be ours: "Create in me a pure heart, O God."[4]

And Jesus' statement rings true: "Blessed are the pure in heart, for they shall see God."

Note the order of this beatitude: *first*, purify the heart, *then you* will see God. Clean the refinery, and the result will be a pure product.

We usually reverse the order. We try to change the inside by altering the outside. Let me give you an example.

When my family lived in Rio de Janeiro, I owned a ham radio. I kept it in the utility room on top of the freezer. When we traveled, I always unplugged the radio and disconnected the antenna.

Once, when we were leaving for a week-long trip, I remembered I hadn't unplugged the radio. I ran back in the house, pulled the plug, and dashed out again.

But I pulled the wrong plug. I unplugged the freezer. It was summertime, and summer in Rio redefines the word *hot.* Our apartment was on the top of a fourteen-floor apartment building, which adds another degree of intensity to the word *hot.* For seven days, then, a freezer full of food sat in a sweltering apartment with the power off. (Why are you groaning?)

When we came home, Denalyn decided to get some meat out of the freezer. As she opened the freezer door—well, I won't go into details as to what she saw, but I will say it was a moving experience.

Guess who got fingered as the one who had unplugged the freezer—and who therefore would be responsible for cleaning it? You got it. So I got to work.

What is the best way to clean out a rotten interior? I knew exactly what to do. I got a rag and a bucket of soapy water and began cleaning the outside of the appliance. I was sure the odor would disappear with a good shine, so I polished and buffed and wiped. When I was through, the freezer could have passed a Marine boot-camp inspection. It was sparkling.

But when I opened the door, that freezer was revolting.

(Are you wondering, "Now what kind of fool would do that?" Read on and you'll see.)

No problem, I thought. I knew what to do. This freezer needs some friends. I'd stink, too, if I had the social life of a machine in a utility room. So, I threw a party. I invited all the appliances from the neighborhood kitchens. It was hard work, but we filled our apartment with refrigerators, stoves, microwaves, and washing machines. It was a great party. A couple of toasters recognized each other from the appliance store. Everyone played pin the plug on the socket and had a few laughs about limited warranties. The blenders were the hit, though; they really mixed well.

I was sure the social interaction would cure the inside of my freezer, but I was wrong. I opened it up, and the stink was even worse!

Now what?

I had an idea. If a polish job wouldn't do it and a social life didn't help, I'd give the freezer some status!

I bought a Mercedes sticker and stuck it on the door. I painted a paisley tie down the front. I put a "Save the Whales" bumper sticker on the rear and installed a cellular phone on the side. That freezer was classy. It was stylish. It was . . . cool. I splashed it with cologne and gave it a credit card for clout.

Then I backed away and admired the high-class freezer. "You just might make the cover of *Popular Mechanics,*" I told it. It blushed. Then I opened the door, expecting to see a clean inside, but what I saw was putrid—a stinky and repulsive interior.

I could think of only one other option. My freezer needed some high-voltage pleasure! I immediately bought it some copies of *Playfridge* magazine—the publication that displays freezers with their doors open. I rented some films about foxy appliances. (My favorite was *The Big Chill.*) I even tried to get my freezer a date with the Westinghouse next door, but she gave him the cold shoulder.

After a few days of supercharged, after-hours entertainment, I opened the door. And I nearly got sick.

I know what you're thinking. The only thing worse than Max's humor is his common sense. Who would concentrate on the outside when the problem is on the inside?

Do you really want to know?

A homemaker battles with depression. What is the solution suggested by some well-meaning friend? Buy a new dress.

A husband is involved in an affair that brings him as much guilt as it does adventure. The solution? Change peer groups. Hang out with people who don't make you feel guilty!

A young professional is plagued with loneliness. His obsession with success has left him with no friends. His boss gives him an idea: Change your style. Get a new haircut. Flash some cash.

Case after case of treating the outside while ignoring the inside—polishing the case while ignoring the interior. And what is the result?

The homemaker gets a new dress, and the depression disappears . . . for a day, maybe. Then the shadow returns.

The husband finds a bunch of buddies who sanction his adultery. The result? Peace . . . until the crowd is gone. Then the guilt is back.

The young professional gets a new look and the people notice . . . until the styles change. Then he has to scurry out and buy more stuff so he won't appear outdated.

The exterior polished; the interior corroding. The outside altered; the inside faltering. One thing is clear: Cosmetic changes are only skin deep.

By now you could write the message of the beatitude. It's a clear one: You change your life by changing your heart.

How do you change your heart? Jesus gave the plan on the mountain. Back away from the beatitudes once more and view them in sequence.

The first step is an admission of poverty: "Blessed are the poor in spirit. . . ." God's gladness is not received by those who earn it, but by those who admit they *don't* deserve it. The joy of Sarah, Peter, and Paul came when they surrendered, when they pleaded for a lifeguard instead of a swimming lesson, when they sought a savior instead of a system.

The second step is sorrow: "Blessed are those who mourn. . . ." Joy comes to those who are sincerely sorry for their sin. We discover gladness when we leave the prison of pride and repent of our rebellion.

Sorrow is followed by meekness. The meek are those who are willing to be used by God. Amazed that God would save them, they are just as surprised that God could use them. They are a junior-high-school clarinet section playing with the Boston Pops. They don't tell the maestro how to conduct; they're just thrilled to be part of the concert.

The result of the first three steps? Hunger. Never have you seen anything like what is happening! You admit sin —you get saved. You confess weakness—you receive strength. You say you are sorry—you find forgiveness. It's a zany, unpredictable path full of pleasant encounters. For once in your life you're addicted to something positive—something that gives life instead of draining it. And you want more.

Then comes mercy. The more you receive, the more you give. You find it easier to give grace because you realize you have been given so much. What has been done to you is nothing compared to what you did to God.

For the first time in your life, you have found a permanent joy, a joy that is not dependent upon your whims and actions. It's a joy from God, a joy no one can take away from you.

A sacred delight is placed in your heart.

It is sacred because only God can grant it.

It is a delight because you would never expect it.

And though your heart isn't perfect, it isn't rotten. And though you aren't invincible, at least you're plugged in. And you can bet that he who made you knows just how to purify you—from the inside out.

. . . for they will see God.

CHAPTER 13

Nice Palace
but No King

Once, long ago, there lived a king who had many wives. As his kingdom flourished, so had his harem. But, of all his wives, he loved one most.

When the favorite wife died, the king grieved deeply. Devastated, he resolved to honor her by constructing a temple that would serve as her tomb. Her coffin was placed in the center of a large parcel of land, and construction of the temple began around it. No expense would be spared to make her final resting place magnificent.

But as the weeks turned into months, the king's grief was eclipsed by his passion for the project. He no longer mourned her absence. The construction consumed him. One day, while walking from one side of the construction site to the other, his leg bumped against a wooden box. The king's son brushed the dust off his leg and ordered the worker to throw the box out.

The king didn't know he had ordered the disposal of the coffin—now forgotten—hidden beneath layers of dust and time.

The one the temple was intended to honor was forgotten, but the temple was erected anyway.

Difficult to believe? Perhaps. But eerie nonetheless.

Could someone build a temple and forget why? Could someone construct a palace, yet forget the king? Could someone sculpt a tribute and forget the hero?

You answer those questions. Answer them in a church. The next time you enter an assembly of worship, position yourself where you can see the people. Then decide.

You can tell the ones who remember the slain one. They're wide-eyed and expectant. They're children watching the unwrapping of a gift. They're servants standing still as a king passes. You don't doze in the presence of royalty. And you don't yawn while receiving a gift, especially when the giver is the King himself!

You can also tell the ones who see only the temple. Their eyes wander. Their feet shuffle. Their hands doodle, and their mouths open—not to sing, but to yawn. For no matter how hard they try to stay amazed, their eyes start to glaze over. All temples lose their luster after a while.

The temple gazers don't mean to be bored. They love the church. They can cite its programs and praise its pastors. They don't mean to grow stale. They put on hats and hose and coats and ties and come every week. But still, something is missing. The One they once planned to honor hasn't been seen in a while.

But those who have seen him can't seem to forget him. They find him, often in spite of the temple rather than because of it. They brush the dust away and stand ever impressed before his tomb—his empty tomb.

The temple builders and the Savior seekers. You'll find them both in the same church, on the same pew—at times, even in the same suit. One sees the structure and says, "What a great church." The other sees the Savior and says, "What a great Christ!"

Which do you see?

*B*lessed are the peacemakers . . .

CHAPTER 14

Seeds of Peace

Want to see a miracle? Try this.

Take a seed the size of a freckle. Put it under several inches of dirt. Give it enough water, light, and fertilizer. And get ready. A mountain will be moved. It doesn't matter that the ground is a zillion times the weight of the seed. The seed will push it back.

Every spring, dreamers around the world plant tiny hopes in overturned soil. And every spring, their hopes press against impossible odds and blossom.

Never underestimate the power of a seed.

As far as I know, James, the epistle writer, wasn't a farmer. But he knew the power of a seed sown in fertile soil.

"Those who are peacemakers will plant seeds of peace and reap a harvest of goodness."[1]

The principle for peace is the same as the principle for crops: Never underestimate the power of a seed.

The story of Heinz is a good example. Europe, 1934. Hitler's plague of anti-Semitism was infecting a continent. Some would escape it. Some would die from it. But eleven-year-old Heinz would learn from it. He would learn the power of sowing seeds of peace.

Heinz was a Jew.

The Bavarian village of Furth, where Heinz lived, was being overrun by Hitler's young thugs. Heinz's father, a schoolteacher, lost his job. Recreational activities ceased. Tension mounted on the streets.

The Jewish families clutched the traditions that held them together—the observance of the Sabbath, of Rosh Hashanah, of Yom Kippur. Old ways took on new significance. As the clouds of persecution swelled and blackened, these ancient precepts were a precious cleft in a mighty rock.

And as the streets became a battleground, such security meant survival.

Hitler youth roamed the neighborhoods looking for trouble. Young Heinz learned to keep his eyes open. When he saw a band of troublemakers, he would step to the other side of the street. Sometimes he would escape a fight—sometimes not.

One day, in 1934, a pivotal confrontation occurred. Heinz found himself face-to-face with a Hitler bully. A beating appeared inevitable. This time, however, he walked away unhurt—not because of what he did, but because of what he said. He didn't fight back; he spoke up. He convinced the troublemakers that a fight was not necessary. His words kept battle at bay.

And Heinz saw firsthand how the tongue can create peace.

He learned the skill of using words to avoid conflict. And for a young Jew in Hitler-ridden Europe, that skill had many opportunities to be honed.

Fortunately, Heinz's family escaped from Bavaria and made their way to America. Later in life, he would downplay the impact those adolescent experiences had on his development.

But one has to wonder. For after Heinz grew up, his name became synonymous with peace negotiations. His legacy became that of a bridge builder. Somewhere he had learned the power of the properly placed word of peace. And one has to wonder if his training didn't come on the streets of Bavaria.

You don't know him as Heinz. You know him by his Anglicized name, Henry. Henry Kissinger.[2]

Never underestimate the power of a seed.

How good are you at sowing seeds of peace?

You may not be called on to ward off international conflict, but you will have opportunities to do something more vital: to bring *inner* peace to troubled hearts.

Jesus modeled this. We don't see him settling many disputes

or negotiating conflicts. But we *do* see him cultivating inward harmony through acts of love:

washing the feet of men he knew would betray him,

having lunch with a corrupt tax official,

honoring the sinful woman whom society had scorned.

He built bridges by healing hurts. He prevented conflict by touching the interior. He cultivated harmony by sowing seeds of peace in fertile hearts.

Do me a favor. Pause for a moment and think about the people who make up your world. Take a stroll through the gallery of faces that are significant to you. Mentally flip through the scrapbook of snapshots featuring those you deal with often.

Can you see their faces? Your spouse. Your best friend. Your golf buddies. Your friends at PTA. Your kids. Your aunt across the country. Your neighbor across the street. The receptionist at work. The new secretary in the next office.

Freeze-frame those mental images for a moment while I tell you how some of them are feeling.

I went to our family doctor not long ago. I went for my first check-up since the one required for high school football seventeen years ago.

Since I was way overdue, I ordered the works. One nurse put me on a table and stuck little cold suction cups to my chest. Another nurse wrapped a heavy band around my arm and squeezed a black bulb until my arm tingled. Then they pricked my finger (which always hurts) and told me to fill up a cup (which is always awkward). Then, with all the preliminaries done, they put me in a room and told me to take off my shirt and wait on the doctor.

There is something about being poked, pushed, measured, and drained that makes you feel like a head of lettuce in the produce department. I sat on a tiny stool and stared at the wall.

May I tell you something you know, but may have forgotten? Somebody in your world feels like I felt in that office. The daily push and shove of the world has a way of leaving us worked over and worn out. Someone in your gallery of people is sitting on a cold aluminum stool of insecurity, clutching the backside of a hospital gown for fear of exposing what little pride he or she has left. And that person desperately needs a word of peace.

Someone needs you to do for them what Dr. Jim did for me.

Jim is a small-town doctor in a big city. He still remembers names and keeps pictures of babies he delivered on his office bulletin board. And though you know he's busy, he makes you feel you are his only patient.

After a bit of small talk and a few questions about my medical history, he put down my file and said, "Let me take off my doctor hat for a minute and talk to you as a friend."

The chat lasted maybe five minutes. He asked me about my family. He asked me about my work load. He asked me about my stress. He told me he thought I was doing a good job at the church and that he loved to read my books.

Nothing profound, nothing probing. He went no deeper than I allowed. But I had the feeling he would have gone to the bottom of the pit with me had I needed him to.

After those few minutes, Dr. Jim went about his task of tapping my knee with his rubber hammer, staring down my throat, looking in my ear, and listening to my chest. When he was all done, as I was buttoning up my shirt, he took his doctor hat off again and reminded me not to carry the world on my shoulders. "And be sure to love your wife and hug those kids, because when it all boils down to it, you're not much without them."

"Thanks, Jim," I said.

And he walked out as quickly as he'd come in—a seed sower in a physician's smock.

Want to see a miracle? Plant a word of love heartdeep in a person's life. Nurture it with a smile and a prayer, and watch what happens.

An employee gets a compliment. A wife receives a bouquet of flowers. A cake is baked and carried next door. A widow is hugged. A gas-station attendant is honored. A preacher is praised.

Sowing seeds of peace is like sowing beans. You don't know why it works; you just know it does. Seeds are planted, and topsoils of hurt are shoved away.

Don't forget the principle. Never underestimate the power of a seed.

God didn't. When his kingdom was ravaged and his people had forgotten his name, he planted his seed.

When the soil of the human heart had grown crusty, he planted his seed. When religion had become a ritual and the temple a trading post, he planted his seed.

Want to see a miracle? Watch him as he places the seed of his own self in the fertile womb of a Jewish girl.

Up it grew, "like a tender green shoot, sprouting from a root in dry and sterile ground."³ The seed spent a lifetime pushing back the stones that tried to keep it underground. The seed made a ministry out of shoving away the rocks that cluttered his father's soil.

The stones of legalism that burdened backs.

The stones of oppression that broke bones.

The stones of prejudice that fenced out the needy.

But it was the final stone that proved to be the supreme test of the seed. The stone of death—rolled by humans and sealed by Satan in front of the tomb. For a moment it appeared the seed would be stuck in the earth. For a moment, it looked like this rock was too big to be budged.

But then, somewhere in the heart of the earth, the seed of God stirred, shoved, and sprouted. The ground trembled, and the rock of the tomb tumbled. And the flower of Easter blossomed.

Never underestimate the power of a seed.

. . . for they will be called sons of God.

CHAPTER 15

The Greasy Pole
of Power

The push for power has come to shove.

You know the power lingo. You know the power plays. You have a power wardrobe.

You think you have everything you need for power? Think twice and come to dinner. Now there are power table manners.

"Manners will take you where your money can't," states the "Queen of Courtesy," Marjabelle Stewart. This crusader for couth has developed a seminar to help you eat your way to the top. For six thousand dollars you can sit in on a seminar and learn the manners that have clout.

Here are a few examples of what Stewart calls "power failures":

- Never tuck your napkin into your collar.
- Never leave a lipstick mark on the rim of a glass.
- Never mash or stir your food.
- Never haggle over the bill.
- Never, ever, hand your plate to the waiter.
- Never read the menu like a Bible. You aren't there to eat, but to do business.
- Never stoop down to retrieve dropped silver.[1]

In fact, the primary rule of thumb in the quest for power is never to stoop down for anything.

Never stoop to appear weak. Never stoop to admit mistakes. Never stoop to help someone who could never help you. Never stoop to any level that might loosen your grip on your rung of the ladder.

Add "power etiquette" to "name dropping," "card flashing," and "title touting." Put it on the long list of games we play to make a name for ourselves.

"Power moves" are simply "King of the Mountain" on an adult level.

Remember playing that game as a kid? The object of the game is to get high on the heap and stay there. You push, claw, and climb until you get to the top. And once you get there, you fight to hold your position. Don't even think about sitting down. Forget enjoying the view. Slack up for even a minute, and you'll be slapped down to the bottom of the hill. And then you'll have to start all over again.

As grown-ups we still play "King of the Mountain," but now the stakes are higher. Harrison Ford in the movie *Working Girl* put it this way:

> One lost deal is all it takes to get canned these days. The line buttons on my phone all have an inch of little pieces of tape piled on—the names of new guys over the names of old guys—good men who aren't at the other end of the line anymore all because of one lost deal. I don't want to get buried under a little piece of tape.

The push for power has come to shove. And most of us are either pushing or being pushed.

I might point out the difference between a passion for excellence and a passion for power. The desire for excellence is a gift of God, much needed in society. It is characterized by respect for quality and a yearning to use God's gifts in a way that pleases him. Recall the words of Antonio Stradivari, the seventeenth-century violin maker whose name in its Latin form, Stradivarius, has become synonymous with excellence:

> When any master holds 'twixt chin and hand a violin of mine, he will be glad that Stradivari lived, made violins and made them of the best. . . . If my hand slacked I should rob God—since he is the fullest good. . . . But he could not make Antonio Stradivari's violins without Antonio.[2]

He was right. God could not make Stradivarius violins without Antonio Stradivari. Certain gifts were given to that craftsman that no other violin maker possessed.

In the same vein, there are certain things you can do that no one else can. Perhaps it is parenting, or constructing houses, or encouraging the discouraged. There are things that *only you* can do, and you are alive to do them. In the great orchestra we call life, you have an instrument and a song, and you owe it to God to play them both sublimely.

But there is a canyon of difference between doing your best to glorify God and doing whatever it takes to glorify yourself. The quest for excellence is a mark of maturity. The quest for power is childish.

It might interest you to know that the first power play happened not on Wall Street nor on a battlefield, but in a garden. The first promise of prestige was whispered with a hiss, a wink, and a snakish grin by a fallen angel.

Standing in the shadow of the tree of the knowledge of good and evil, Satan knew what to offer Eve to convince her to eat the apple. It wasn't pleasure. It wasn't health. It wasn't prosperity. It was . . . well, you read his words and look for his lure:

"God knows that when you eat of it your eyes will be opened, and you will be like God, knowing good and evil."[3]

The words found a soft spot.

"You will be like God. . . ."

Eve stroked her chin as she replayed the promise.

"You will be like God. . . ."

The snake pulled back the curtain to the throne room and invited Eve to take a seat. Put on the crown. Pick up the scepter. Put on the cape. See how it feels to have power. See how it feels to have a name. See how it feels to be in control!

Eve swallowed the hook. The temptation to be *like* God eclipsed her view of God, and the crunch of an apple echoed in the kingdom. You know the rest of the story.

Now, perhaps your flirtations with power haven't been so blatant. No doubt, you were amused at the thought of spending six grand on a table manners seminar. No doubt you've shaken your head in amazement at the buy-outs staged by the barons of Wall Street. No doubt you've been cha-grined by the murders ordered by drug lords and kingpins. That type of power play has no attraction for you. If the snake were to woo you with promises of status, you'd send him back to the pit, right?

Or would you? "King of the Mountain" comes in many forms.

It's the boss who won't compliment her employees. After all, workers need to be kept in their place.

It's the husband who refuses to be kind to his wife. He knows if he does he will lose his most powerful weapon—her fear of his rejection.

It's the employee who places personal ambition over per-sonal integrity.

It's the wife who withholds sex both to punish and per-suade.

It might be the taking of someone's life, or it might be the taking of someone's turn. It might be manipulation with a pistol, or it might be manipulation with a pout. It might be the takeover of a nation by a politician, or the takeover of a church by a preacher.

But they are all spelled the same: P-O-W-E-R.

All have the same goal: "I will get what I want at your expense."

All have the same game plan: push, shove, take, and lie.

All have listened to the same snake, the same lying Lucifer who whispers into the ears of anyone who will listen, "You will be like God."

And all have the same end: futility. Please note carefully what I am about to say. Absolute power is unreachable. The pole to the top is greasy, and the ladder rungs are made of cardboard. When you stand at the top—if there is a top—the only way to go is down. And the descent is often painful.

Ask Muhammed Ali.

You know Ali, the unprecedented three-time world heavyweight boxing champion. His face has appeared on the cover of *Sports Illustrated* more times than any other athlete. When he was "floating like a butterfly and stinging like a bee," he was king of his profession. An entourage of reporters, trainers, and support staff tailed this comet as he raced around the world.

But that was yesterday. Where is Muhammed Ali today? Sportswriter Gary Smith went to find out.

Ali escorted Smith to a barn next to his farmhouse. On the floor, leaning against the walls, were mementos of Ali in his prime. Photos and portraits of the champ punching and dancing. Sculpted body. Fist punching the air. Championship belt held high in triumph. "The thrilla in Manila."

But on the pictures were white streaks—bird droppings. Ali looked into the rafters at the pigeons who had made his gym their home. And then he did something significant. Perhaps it was a gesture of closure. Maybe it was a statement of despair. Whatever the reason, he walked over to the row of pictures and turned them, one by one, toward the wall. He then walked to the door, stared at the countryside, and mumbled something so low that Smith had to ask him to repeat it. Ali did.

"I had the world," he said, "and it wasn't nothin'. Look now."[4]

The pole of power is greasy.

The Roman emperor Charlemagne knew that. An interesting story surrounds the burial of this famous king. Legend has it that he asked to be entombed sitting upright in his throne. He asked that his crown be placed on his head and his scepter in his hand. He requested that the royal cape be draped around his shoulders and an open book be placed in his lap.

That was A.D. 814. Nearly two hundred years later, Emperor Othello determined to see if the burial request had been carried out. He allegedly sent a team of men to open the tomb and make a report. They found the body just as Charlemagne had requested. Only now, nearly two centuries later, the scene was gruesome. The crown was tilted, the mantle moth-eaten, the body disfigured. But open on the skeletal thighs was the book Charlemagne had requested—

the Bible. One bony finger pointed to Matthew 16:26: "What good will it be for a man if he gains the whole world, yet forfeits his soul?"[5]

You can answer that one.

As these thoughts on power were beginning to take shape, I found myself at a banquet.

Now, on my list of favorite things to do on a free evening, attending a banquet is pretty close to the bottom. The thought conjures up images of cold food, hot rooms, poor sound systems, long-winded speakers, and gravy spots on my tie. Forgive my social maladjustment, but I'll take a good movie or baseball game anytime.

This particular banquet was doing little to change my opinion. It was an awards ceremony that had been overbooked and had begun late. The master of ceremonies was having a hard time keeping everyone's attention. He competed against a squad of waiters that darted in and dashed out every thirteen seconds. The awards were presented with meticulous detail. They were received with explicit—and verbose—gratitude. I began looking at my watch and munching on ice cubes.

That's when the king was introduced.

"A king?" I looked around, thinking I would see a cape and a crown. I didn't. I did see a nicely dressed young man escorted to the platform.

"So that is what a king looks like," I thought. Others must have been just as intrigued. The place was silent.

King Goodwill was his name. He is a seventh-generation king of the Zulu tribe in Africa. Impressive title. But more significant was the fact that King Goodwill himself had a King. Goodwill was a believer. He had embraced Christ as his Lord and was encouraging his nation to do the same.

Though King Goodwill's entire speech was noteworthy, it was his first phrase that I copied in my date book: "I am a king, but I greet you as my brothers."

A king who considers me his brother. A ruler who welcomes me into his family. Royalty freely granted.

His words reminded me of another King who did the same.

"Blessed are the peacemakers, for they will be called sons of God."

"Be a power broker," the snake lied, "and you will be like God."

"Be a peacemaker," the King promised, "and you will be a son of God."

Which would you prefer? To be king of the mountain for a day? Or to be a child of God for eternity?

There is a side benefit to sonship. If you are a child of God, then what does the world have to offer? Can you have any greater title than the one you have?

Answer this: A thousand years from now, will it matter what title the world gave you? No, but it will make a literal hell of a difference whose child you are.

One final note about that banquet. After it was over, I

stuck around, hoping to meet the king. At first I couldn't find him. Then I came across him and his wife and assistants in a side hall. Guess what they were doing? Laughing! Somebody must have told a whopper of a joke, because this group could barely stand up.

A king in stitches. What a delight.

A belly laugh is not what I would call a power play. It could better be described as a good time. I guess when you're a king, you don't have to worry about being proper for the sake of status; you already have all you need.

That goes for children of the King, too.

Next time I eat, I think I'll tuck my napkin in my collar.

Blessed are those who are persecuted
because of righteousness . . .

CHAPTER 16

The Dungeon of Doubt

He was a child of the desert. Leathery face. Tanned skin. Clothing of animal skins. What he owned fit in a pouch. His walls were the mountains and his ceiling the stars.

But not anymore. His frontier is walled out, his horizon hidden. The stars are memories. The fresh air is all but forgotten. And the stench of the dungeon relentlessly reminds the child of the desert that he is now a captive of the king.[1]

In anyone's book, John the Baptist deserves better treatment than this. After all, isn't he the forerunner of the Christ? Isn't he a relative of the Messiah? At the very least, isn't his the courageous voice of repentance?

But most recently that voice, instead of opening the

door of renewal, has opened the door to his own prison cell.

John's problems began when he called a king on the carpet.

On a trip to Rome, King Herod succumbed to the enticements of his brother's wife, Herodias. Deciding Herodias was better off married to him, Herod divorced his wife and brought his sister-in-law home.

The gossip columnists were fascinated, but John the Baptist was infuriated. He pounced on Herod like a desert scorpion, denouncing the marriage for what it was—adultery.

Herod might have let him get away with it. But not Herodias. This steamy seductress wasn't about to have her social climbing exposed. She told Herod to have John pulled off the speaking circuit and thrown into the dungeon. Herod hemmed and hawed until she whispered and wooed. Then Herod gave in.

But that wasn't enough for this mistress. She had her daughter strut before the king and his generals at a stag party. Herod, who was as easily duped as he was aroused, promised to do anything for the pretty young thing in the G-string.

"Anything?"

"You name it," he drooled.

She conferred with her mother, who was waiting in the wings, then returned with her request.

"I want John the Baptist."

"You want a date with the prophet?"

"I want his head," replied the dancer. And then, reassured by a nod from her mother, she added, "On a silver platter, if you don't mind."

Herod looked at the faces around him. He knew it wasn't fair, but he also knew everyone was looking at him. And he *had* promised "anything." Though he personally had nothing against the country preacher, he valued the opinion polls much more than he valued John's life. After all, what's more important—to save face or to save the neck of an eccentric prophet?

The story reeks with inequity.

John dies because Herod lusts.

The good is murdered while the bad smirk.

A man of God is killed while a man of passion is winking at his niece.

Is this how God rewards his anointed? Is this how he honors his faithful? Is this how God crowns his chosen? With a dark dungeon and a shiny blade?

The inconsistency was more than John could take. Even before Herod reached his verdict, John was asking his questions. His concerns were outnumbered only by the number of times he paced his cell asking them. When he had a chance to get a message to Jesus, his inquiry was one of despair:

"When John heard in prison what Christ was doing, he sent his disciples to ask him, 'Are you the one who was to come, or should we expect someone else?'"[2]

Note what motivated John's question. It was not just the dungeon or even death. It was the problem of unmet expectations

—the fact that John was in deep trouble and Jesus was conducting business as usual.

Is this what messiahs do when trouble comes? Is this what God does when his followers are in a bind?

Jesus' silence was enough to chisel a leak into the dam of John's belief. "Are you the one? Or have I been following the wrong Lord?"

Had the Bible been written by a public relations agency, they would have eliminated that verse. It's not good PR strategy to admit that one of the cabinet members has doubts about the president. You don't let stories like that get out if you are trying to present a unified front.

But the Scriptures weren't written by personality agents; they were inspired by an eternal God who knew that every disciple from then on would spend time in the dungeon of doubt.

Though the circumstances have changed, the questions haven't.

They are asked anytime the faithful suffer the consequences of the faithless. Anytime a person takes a step in the right direction, only to have her feet knocked out from under her, anytime a person does a good deed but suffers evil results, anytime a person takes a stand, only to end up flat on his face . . . the questions fall like rain:

"If God is so good, why do I hurt so bad?"

"If God is really there, why am I here?"

"What did I do to deserve this?"

"Did God slip up this time?"

"Why are the righteous persecuted?"

In his book *Disappointment with God,* Philip Yancey quotes a letter that articulates the problem of unmet expectations in all its excruciating reality. Meg Woodson lost two children to cystic fibrosis, and her daughter's death at age twenty-three was particularly traumatic. The following words speak of her pain and doubt as she struggled to cope with what happened:

> I was sitting beside her bed a few days before her death when suddenly she began screaming. I will never forget those shrill, piercing, primal screams. . . . It's against this background of human beings falling apart . . . that God, who could have helped, looked down on a young woman devoted to Him, quite willing to die for Him to give Him glory, and decided to sit on His hands and let her death top the horror charts for cystic fibrosis deaths.[3]

Does God sometimes sit on his hands? Does God sometimes choose to do nothing? Does God sometimes opt for silence even when I'm screaming my loudest?

Some time ago, I took my family to the bicycle store to purchase a bike for five-year-old Jenna. She picked out a shiny "Starlett" with a banana seat and training wheels. And Andrea, age three, decided she wanted one as well.

I explained to Andrea that she was too young. I told her she was still having trouble with a tricycle and was too small for a two-wheeler. No luck; she still wanted a bike. I explained to her that when she was a bit older, she would get a bike, too. She just stared at me. I tried to tell her that a big bike would bring her more pain than pleasure, more scrapes than thrills. She turned her head and said nothing.

Finally I sighed and said this time her daddy knew best. Her response? She screamed it loud enough for everyone in the store to hear:

"Then I want a *new* daddy!"

Though the words were from a child's mouth, they carried an adult's sentiments.

Disappointment demands a change in command. When we don't agree with the One who calls the shots, our reaction is often the same as Andrea's—the same as John's. "Is he the right one for this job?" Or, as John put it, "Are you the one? Should we look for another?"

Andrea, with her three-year-old reasoning powers, couldn't believe that a new bike would be anything less than ideal for her. From her vantage point, it would be the source of eternal bliss. And from her vantage point, the one who could grant that bliss was "sitting on his hands."

John couldn't believe that anything less than his release would be for the best interest of all involved. In his opinion, it was time to exercise some justice and get some action. But the One who had the power was "sitting on his hands."

I can't believe that God would sit in silence while a missionary is kicked out of a foreign country or a Christian loses a promotion because of his beliefs or a faithful wife is abused by an unbelieving husband. These are just three of many items that have made their way onto my prayer list —all prayers that seem to have gone unanswered.

Rule of thumb: Clouds of doubt are created when the warm, moist air of our expectations meets the cold air of God's silence.

If you've heard the silence of God, if you've been left standing in the dungeon of doubt, then don't put this book down until you read the next chapter. You may learn, as John did, that the problem is not as much in God's silence as it is in your ability to hear.

. . . for theirs is the kingdom of heaven.

CHAPTER 17

The Kingdom Worth Dying For

$\mathcal{G}$o back and report to John what you hear and see: The blind receive sight, the lame walk, those who have leprosy are cured, the deaf hear, the dead are raised, and the good news is preached to the poor."[1]

This was Jesus' answer to John's agonized query from the dungeon of doubt: "Are you the one who was to come, or should we expect someone else?"[2]

But before you study what Jesus said, note a couple of things he didn't say.

First, he didn't get angry. He didn't throw up his hands in disgust. He didn't scream, "What in the world do I have to do for John? I've already become flesh! I've already been sinless for three decades. I let him baptize me. What else does he want? Go and tell that ungrateful locust eater I am shocked at his disbelief."

He could have done that. (I would have done that.)

But Jesus didn't. Underline that fact: *God has never turned away the questions of a sincere searcher.* Not Job's nor Abraham's nor Moses' nor John's nor Thomas's nor Max's nor yours.

But note also that Jesus didn't save John. The One who had walked on water could have easily walked on Herod's head, but he didn't. The One who cast out the demons had the power to nuke the king's castle, but he didn't. No battle plan. No SWAT teams. No flashing swords. Just a message —a kingdom message.

"Tell John that everything is going as planned. The kingdom is being inaugurated."

Jesus' words are much more than a statement from Isaiah.[3] They are the description of a heavenly kingdom being established.

A unique kingdom. An invisible kingdom. A kingdom with three distinct traits.

First of all, it is a kingdom where the rejected are received.

"The blind receive sight, the lame walk, those who have leprosy are cured, the deaf hear. . . ."

None were more shunned by their culture than the blind, the lame, the lepers, and the deaf. They had no place. No name. No value. Canker sores on the culture. Excess baggage on the side of the road. But those whom the people called trash, Jesus called treasures.

In my closet hangs a sweater that I seldom wear. It is too small. The sleeves are too short, the shoulders too tight. Some of the buttons are missing, and the thread is frazzled. I should throw that sweater away. I have no use for it. I'll never wear it again. Logic says I should clear out the space and get rid of the sweater.

That's what *logic* says.

But *love* won't let me.

Something unique about that sweater makes me keep it. What is unusual about it? For one thing, it has no label. Nowhere on the garment will you find a tag that reads, "Made in Taiwan," or "Wash in Cold Water." It has no tag because it wasn't made in a factory. It has no label because it wasn't produced on an assembly line. It isn't the product of a nameless employee earning a living. It's the creation of a devoted mother expressing her love.

That sweater is unique. One of a kind. It can't be replaced. Each strand was chosen with care. Each thread was selected with affection.

And though the sweater has lost all of its use, it has lost none of its value. It is valuable not because of its function, but because of its maker.

That must have been what the psalmist had in mind when he wrote, "you knit me together in my mother's womb."[4]

Think on those words. You were knitted together. You aren't an accident. You weren't mass-produced. You aren't an assembly-line product. You were deliberately planned, specifically gifted, and lovingly positioned on this earth by the Master Craftsman.

"For we are God's workmanship, created in Christ Jesus to

do good works, which God prepared in advance for us to do."⁵

In a society that has little room for second fiddles, that's good news. In a culture where the door of opportunity opens only once and then slams shut, that is a revelation. In a system that ranks the value of a human by the figures of his salary or the shape of her legs . . . let me tell you something: Jesus' plan is a reason for joy!

Jesus told John that a new kingdom was coming—a kingdom where people have value not because of what they do, but because of *whose* they are.

The second characteristic of the kingdom is as potent as the first: "The dead have life." The grave has no power.

The year 1899 marked the deaths of two well-known men —Dwight L. Moody, the acclaimed evangelist, and Robert Ingersoll, the famous lawyer, orator, and political leader.

The two men had many similarities. Both were raised in Christian homes. Both were skilled orators. Both traveled extensively and were widely respected. Both drew immense crowds when they spoke and attracted loyal followings. But there was one striking difference between them—their view of God.

Ingersoll was an agnostic and a follower of naturalism; he had no belief in the eternal, but stressed the importance of living only in the here and now. Ingersoll made light of the

Bible, stating that "free thought will give us truth." To him the Bible was "a fable, an obscenity, a humbug, a sham and a lie."[6] He was a bold spokesman against the Christian faith. He claimed that a Christian "creed [was] the ignorant past bullying the enlightened present."[7]

Ingersoll's contemporary, Dwight L. Moody, had different convictions. He dedicated his life to presenting a resurrected King to a dying people. He embraced the Bible as the hope for humanity and the cross as the turning point of history. He left behind a legacy of written and spoken words, institutions of education, churches, and changed lives.

Two men. Both powerful speakers and influential leaders. One rejected God; the other embraced him. The impact of their decisions is seen most clearly in the way they died. Read how one biographer parallels the two deaths.

Ingersoll died suddenly. The news of his death stunned his family. His body was kept at home for several days because his wife was reluctant to part with it. It was eventually removed for the sake of the family's health.

Ingersoll's remains were cremated, and the public response to his passing was altogether dismal. For a man who put all his hopes on this world, death was tragic and came without the consolation of hope.

Moody's legacy was different. On December 22, 1899, Moody awoke to his last winter dawn. Having grown increasingly weak during the night, he began to speak in slow measured words. "Earth recedes, heaven opens before me!" Son Will, who was nearby, hurried across the room to his father's side.

"Father, you are dreaming," he said.

"No. This is no dream, Will," Moody said. "It is beautiful. It is like a trance. If this is death, it is sweet. God is calling me, and I must go. Don't call me back."

At that point, the family gathered around, and moments later the great evangelist died. It was his coronation day—a day he had looked forward to for many years. He was with his Lord.

The funeral service of Dwight L. Moody reflected that same confidence. There was no despair. Loved ones gathered to sing praise to God at a triumphant home-going service. Many remembered the words the evangelist had spoken earlier that year in New York City: "Someday you will read in the papers that Moody is dead. Don't you believe a word of it. At that moment I shall be more alive than I am now. . . . I was born of the flesh in 1837, I was born of the Spirit in 1855. That which is born of the flesh may die. That which is born of the Spirit shall live forever."[8]

Jesus looked into the eyes of John's followers and gave them this message. "Report to John . . . the dead are raised." Jesus wasn't oblivious to John's imprisonment. He wasn't blind to John's captivity. But he was dealing with a greater dungeon than Herod's; he was dealing with the dungeon of death.

But Jesus wasn't through. He passed on one other message to clear the cloud of doubt out of John's heart: "The good news is preached to the poor."

Some months ago I was late to catch a plane out of the San Antonio airport. I wasn't terribly late, but I was late enough to be bumped and have my seat given to a stand-by passenger.

When the ticket agent told me that I would have to miss the flight, I put to work my best persuasive powers.

"But the flight hasn't left yet."

"Yes, but you got here too late."

"I got here before the plane left; is that too late?"

"The regulation says you must arrive ten minutes before the flight is scheduled to depart. That was two minutes ago."

"But, ma'am," I pleaded, "I've got to be in Houston by this evening."

She was patient but firm. "I'm sorry, sir, but the rules say passengers must be at the gate ten minutes before scheduled departure time."

"I know what the rules say," I explained. "But I'm not asking for justice; I'm asking for mercy."

She didn't give it to me.

But God does. Even though by the "book" I'm guilty, by God's love I get another chance. Even though by the law I'm indicted, by mercy I'm given a fresh start.

"For it is by grace you have been saved . . . not by works, so that no one can boast."[9]

No other world religion offers such a message. All others demand the right performance, the right sacrifice, the right chant, the right ritual, the right seance or experience. Theirs is a kingdom of trade-offs and barterdom. You do this, and God will give you that.

The result? Either arrogance or fear. Arrogance if you think you've achieved it, fear if you think you haven't.

Christ's kingdom is just the opposite. It is a kingdom for the poor. A kingdom where membership is *granted*, not *purchased*. You are placed into God's kingdom. You are "adopted." And this occurs not when you do enough, but when you admit you *can't* do enough. You don't earn it; you simply accept it. As a result, you serve, not out of arrogance or fear, but out of gratitude.

I recently read a story of a woman who for years was married to a harsh husband. Each day he would leave her a list of chores to complete before he returned at the end of the day. "Clean the yard. Stack the firewood. Wash the windows. . . ."

If she didn't complete the tasks, she would be greeted with his explosive anger. But even if she did complete the list, he was never satisfied; he would always find inadequacies in her work.

After several years, the husband passed away. Some time later she remarried, this time to a man who lavished her with tenderness and adoration.

One day, while going through a box of old papers, the wife discovered one of her first husband's lists. And as she read the sheet, a realization caused a tear of joy to splash on the paper.

"I'm still doing all these things, and no one has to tell me. I do it because I love him."

That is the unique characteristic of the new kingdom. Its subjects don't work in order to go to heaven; they work *because* they are going to heaven. Arrogance and fear are replaced with gratitude and joy.

※

That's the kingdom Jesus proclaimed: a kingdom of acceptance, eternal life, and forgiveness.

We don't know how John received Jesus' message, but we can imagine. I like to think of a slight smile coming over his lips as he heard what his Master said.

"So that's it. That is what the kingdom will be. That is what the King will do."

For now he understood. It wasn't that Jesus was silent; it was that John had been listening for the wrong answer. John had been listening for an answer to his earthly problems, while Jesus was busy resolving his heavenly ones.

That's worth remembering the next time you hear the silence of God.

If you've asked for a mate, but are still sleeping alone . . . if you've asked for a child, but your womb stays barren . . . if you've asked for healing, but are still hurting . . . don't think God isn't listening. He is. And he is answering requests you are not even making.

Saint Teresa of Avila was insightful enough to pray, "Do not punish me by granting that which I wish or ask." [10]

The apostle Paul was honest enough to write, "We do not know what we ought to pray for."[11]

The fact is, John wasn't asking too much; he was asking too little. He was asking the Father to resolve the temporary, while Jesus was busy resolving the eternal. John was asking for immediate favor, while Jesus was orchestrating the eternal solution.

Does that mean that Jesus has no regard for injustice? No. He cares about persecutions. He cares about inequities and hunger and prejudice. And he knows what it is like to be punished for something he didn't do. He knows the meaning of the phrase, "It's just not right."

For it wasn't right that people spit into the eyes that had wept for them. It wasn't right that soldiers ripped chunks of flesh out of the back of their God. It wasn't right that spikes pierced the hands that formed the earth. And it wasn't right that the Son of God was forced to hear the silence of God.

It wasn't right, but it happened.

For while Jesus was on the cross, God *did* sit on his hands. He did turn his back. He did ignore the screams of the innocent.

He sat in silence while the sins of the world were placed upon his Son. And he did nothing while a cry a million times bloodier than John's echoed in the black sky: "My God, my God, why have you forsaken me?"[12]

Was it right? No.

Was it fair? No.

Was it love? Yes.

In a world of injustice, God once and for all tipped the scales in the favor of hope. And he did it by sitting on his hands so that we could know the kingdom of God.

Rejoice and be glad, because great is
your reward. . . .

CHAPTER 18

The Applause of Heaven

I'm almost home. After five days, four hotel beds, eleven restaurants, and twenty-two cups of coffee, I'm almost home. After eight airplane seats, five airports, two delays, one book, and five hundred thirteen packages of peanuts, I'm almost home.

The plane resonates under me. A baby cries behind me. Businessmen converse around me. Cool air blows from a hole above me. But all that matters is what is before me—home.

Home. It was my first thought when I awoke this morning. It was my first thought when I stepped down from the last podium. It was my first thought when I said good-bye to my last host at the last airport.

There's no door like the one to your own house. There's

no better place to put your feet than under your own table. There's no coffee like coffee out of your own mug. There's no meal like the one at your own table. And there's no embrace like the one from your own family.

Home. The longest part of going home is the last part —the plane's taxiing to the terminal from the runway. I'm the fellow the flight attendant always has to tell to sit down. I'm the guy with one hand on my briefcase and the other on my seat belt. I have learned that there is a critical split second in which I can bolt down the aisle into the first-class section before the tributaries of people begin emptying into the main aisle.

I don't do that on every flight. Only when I'm going home.

There is a leap of the heart as I exit the plane. I almost get nervous as I walk up the ramp. I step past people. I grip my satchel. My stomach tightens. My palms sweat. I walk into the lobby like an actor walking onto a stage. The curtain is lifted, and the audience stands in a half-moon. Most of the people see that I'm not the one they want and look past me.

But from the side I hear the familiar shriek of two little girls. "Daddy!" I turn and see them—faces scrubbed, standing on chairs, bouncing up and down in joy as the man in their life walks toward them. Jenna stops bouncing just long enough to clap. She applauds! I don't know who told her to do that, but you can bet I'm not going to tell her to stop.

Behind them I see a third face—little Sara, only a few months old. Deeply asleep, she furrows her brow slightly in reaction to the squealing.

And then I see a fourth face—my wife's face. Somehow, she has found time to comb her hair, put on a new dress, put on that extra sparkle. Somehow, though wrung out and done in, she will make me feel that my week is the only week worth talking about.

Faces of home.

That is what makes the promise at the end of the Beatitudes so compelling: "Rejoice and be glad, because great is your reward in heaven."

What is our reward? Home.

The Book of Revelation could be entitled the Book of Homecoming, for in it we are given a picture of our heavenly home.

John's descriptions of the future steal your breath. His depiction of the final battle is graphic. Good clashes with evil. The sacred encounters the sinful. The pages howl with the shrieks of dragons and smolder with the coals of fiery pits. But in the midst of the battlefield there is a rose. John describes it in chapter 21:

> Then I saw a new heaven and a new earth, for the first heaven and the first earth had passed away, and there was no longer any sea. I saw the Holy City, the new Jerusalem, coming down out of heaven from God, prepared as a bride

beautifully dressed for her husband. And I heard a loud voice from the throne saying, "Now the dwelling of God is with men, and he will live with them. They will be his people, and God himself will be with them and be their God. He will wipe every tear from their eyes. There will be no more death or mourning or crying or pain, for the old order of things has passed away. He who was seated on the throne said, "I am making everything new!"[1]

John is old when he writes these words. His body is weary. The journey has taken its toll. His friends are gone. Peter is dead. Paul has been martyred. Andrew, James, Nathaniel . . . they are fuzzy figures from an early era.

As he hears the voice from the throne, I wonder, does he remember the day he heard it on the mountain? For it is the same John and the same Jesus. The same feet that followed Jesus up the mount so long ago now stand to follow him again. The same eyes that watched the Nazarene teach on the summit watch for him again. The same ears that heard Jesus first describe sacred delight listen to it revealed again.

In this final mountaintop encounter, God pulls back the curtain and allows the warrior to peek into the homeland. When given the task of writing down what he sees, John chooses the most beautiful comparison earth has to offer. The Holy City, John says, is like "a bride beautifully dressed for her husband."

What is more beautiful than a bride? One of the side benefits of being a minister is that I get an early glimpse of the bride as she stands at the top of the aisle. And I have to say that I have never seen an ugly bride. I've seen some grooms that could use an alteration or two, but never a bride. Maybe it is the aura of whiteness that clings to her as dew clings to a rose. Or perhaps it is the diamonds that glisten in her eyes. Or maybe it's the blush of love that pinks her cheeks or the bouquet of promises she carries. Whatever it is, there is the feeling that when you see a bride you are seeing the purest beauty the world can boast.

A bride. A commitment robed in elegance. "I'll be with you forever." Tomorrow bringing hope to today. Promised purity faithfully delivered.

When you read that our heavenly home is similar to a bride, tell me, doesn't it make you want to go home?

The world I woke up to this morning couldn't be described as a bride beautifully dressed for her husband, could yours?

Part of the world to which I awoke was grieving. A teenager took his life in the predawn darkness. No note. No explanation. Just a dumbstruck mother and a bewildered father who will forever be hounded by questions they cannot answer.

Part of the world to which I awoke was disillusioned. Another national leader has been accused of dishonesty. He blinked back tears and swallowed anger on network news. A generation ago, we would have given him the benefit of the doubt. Not now.

A part of the world to which I awoke this morning was devastated. A three-year-old's throat was cut open by her own father. A pre-med student was butchered and sacrificed by Satan worshipers. A husband of thirty years ran off with another man. (No, not a woman, a man.)

When you look at this world, stained by innocent blood and smudged with selfishness, doesn't it make you want to go home?

Me, too.

The old saint tells us that when we get home, God himself will wipe away our tears.

When I was a young man, I had plenty of people to wipe away my tears. I had two big sisters who put me under their wings. I had a dozen or so aunts and uncles. I had a mother who worked nights as a nurse and days as a mother—exercising both professions with tenderness. I even had a brother three years my elder who felt sorry for me occasionally.

But when I think about someone wiping away my tears, I think about Dad. His hands were calloused and tough, his fingers short and stubby. And when my father wiped away a tear, he seemed to wipe it away forever. There was something in his touch that took away more than the drop of hurt from my cheek. It also took away my fear.

John says that someday God will wipe away your tears. The same hands that stretched the heavens will touch your cheeks. The same hands that formed the mountains will caress your face. The same hands that curled in agony as the Roman spike cut through will someday cup your face and brush away your tears. Forever.

When you think of a world where there will be no reason to cry, ever, doesn't it make you want to go home?

"There will be no more death . . ." John declares. Can you

imagine it? A world with no hearses or morgues or cemeteries or tombstones? Can you imagine a world with no spades of dirt thrown on caskets? No names chiseled into marble? No funerals? No black dresses? No black wreaths?

If one of the joys of the ministry is a bride descending the church aisle, one of the griefs is a body encased in a shiny box in front of the pulpit. It's never easy to say good-bye. It's never easy to walk away. The hardest task in this world is to place a final kiss on cold lips that cannot kiss in return. The hardest thing in this world is to say good-bye.

In the next world, John says, "good-bye" will never be spoken.

Tell me, doesn't that make you want to go home?

The most hopeful words of that passage from Revelation are those of God's resolve: "I am making everything new."

It's hard to see things grow old. The town in which I grew up is growing old. I was there recently. Some of the buildings are boarded up. Some of the houses are torn down. Some of my teachers are retired; some are buried. The old movie house where I took my dates has "For Sale" on the marquee, long since outdated by the newer theaters that give you eight choices. The only visitors to the drive-in theater are tumbleweeds and rodents. Memories of first dates and senior proms are weather-worn by the endless rain of years.

High school sweethearts are divorced. A cheerleader died of an aneurysm. Our fastest halfback is buried only a few plots from my own father.

I wish I could make it all new again. I wish I could blow the dust off the streets. I wish I could walk through the familiar neighborhood, and wave at the familiar faces, and pet the familiar dogs, and hit one more home run in the Little League park. I wish I could walk down Main Street and call out the merchants that have retired and open the doors that have been boarded up. I wish I could make everything new . . . but I can't.

My mother still lives in the same house. You couldn't pay her to move. The house that seemed so big when I was a boy now feels tiny. On the wall are pictures of Mom in her youth—her hair autumn-brown, her face irresistibly beautiful. I see her now—still healthy, still vivacious, but with wrinkles, graying hair, slower step. Would that I could wave the wand and make everything new again. Would that I could put her once again in the strong embrace of the high-plains cowboy she loved and buried. Would that I could stretch out the wrinkles and take off the bifocals and restore the spring to her step. Would that I could make everything new . . . but I can't.

I can't. But God can. "He restores my soul,"[2] wrote the shepherd. He doesn't reform; he restores. He doesn't camouflage the old; he restores the new. The Master Builder will pull out the original plan and restore it. He will restore the vigor. He will restore the energy. He will restore the hope. He will restore the soul.

When you see how this world grows stooped and weary and then read of a home where everything is made new, tell me, doesn't that make you want to go home?

What would you give in exchange for a home like that? Would you really rather have a few possessions on earth than eternal possessions in heaven? Would you really choose a life of slavery to passion over a life of freedom? Would you honestly give up all of your heavenly mansions for a second-rate sleazy motel on earth?

"Great," Jesus said, "is your reward in heaven." He must have smiled when he said that line. His eyes must have danced, and his hand must have pointed skyward.

For he should know. It was his idea. It was his home.

I'll be home soon. My plane is nearing San Antonio. I can feel the nose of the jet dipping downward. I can see the flight attendants getting ready. Denalyn is somewhere in the parking lot, parking the car and hustling the girls toward the terminal.

I'll be home soon. The plane will land. I'll walk down that ramp and hear my name and see their faces. I'll be home soon.

You'll be home soon, too. You may not have noticed it, but you are closer to home than ever before. Each moment is a step taken. Each breath is a page turned. Each day is a mile marked, a mountain climbed. You are closer to home than you've ever been.

Before you know it, your appointed arrival time will come; you'll descend the ramp and enter the City.

You'll see faces that are waiting for you. You'll hear your name spoken by those who love you. And, maybe, just maybe —in the back, behind the crowds—the One who would rather die than live without you will remove his pierced hands from his heavenly robe and . . . applaud.

Notes

CHAPTER 1 · SACRED DELIGHT
1. 1 Timothy 1:11.
2. 1 Timothy 6:15.

CHAPTER 2 · THE SUMMIT
1. "How Americans Are Running out of Time," *Time*, 24 April 1989, 74–76.
2. Matthew 11:28.
3. Walter Burkhardt, *Tell the Next Generation* (Ramsey, NJ: Paulist, 1982), 80, quoted in Brennan Mannin, *Lion and Lamb* (Old Tappan, NJ: Chosen, Revell, 1986), 129.

CHAPTER 3 · THE AFFLUENT POOR
1. His story is told in Matthew 19, Mark 10, and Luke 18.
2. Luke 18:27.
3. Mark 10:23.
4. Matthew 7:22.
5. Matthew 7:23.
6. Romans 8:3.
7. Frederick Dale Bruner clarifies this as he interprets Matthew 5:3: "Blessed are those who feel their poverty . . . and so cry out to heaven." *The Christbook: Matthew 1–12* (Waco, TX: Word, 1987), 135.
8. The word Jesus used for "poor" is a word which, when used in its most basic sense, "would not indicate the pauper, one so poor that he must daily work for his living, but the beggar, one who is dependent upon others for support." William Hendricksen, *Exposition of the Gospel of Matthew* (Grand Rapids, MI: Baker, 1973), 269.

CHAPTER 4 · THE KINGDOM OF THE ABSURD
1. See Genesis 16–18, 21.
2. See Luke 5.
3. 2 Corinthians 12:9, LB.
4. Philippians 3:4–6, LB.
5. 1 Timothy 1:15.
6. Acts 22:16.
7. 1 Corinthians 1:23.
8. 1 Corinthians 1:23; Ephesians 2:8.
9. 1 Corinthians 5:14, NEB.

CHAPTER 5 · THE PRISON OF PRIDE
1. 1 John 1:9, emphasis mine.
2. Bruner states it admirably: "God helps those who cannot help themselves and he helps those who try to help others, but he does not in any beatitude help those who think they can help themselves—an often ungodly and antisocial conception." *The Christbook*, 152.
3. Matthew 14:28.

CHAPTER 6 · TOUCHES OF TENDERNESS
1. Matthew 6:28–33.
2. Matthew 7:11.

CHAPTER 7 · THE GLORY IN THE ORDINARY
1. See Exodus 4:1–4.
2. See 1 Samuel 17.
3. See John 9:1–6.

CHAPTER 8 · THE BANDIT OF JOY
1. Ian Grey, *Stalin* (Garden City, NY: Doubleday, 1979), 457, and Alex De Jonge, *Stalin and the Shaping of the Soviet Union* (New York: William Morrow, 1986), 450.
2. "The Secret Life of Howard Hughes," *Time*, 13 December 1976, 22–41.
3. "John Lennon: In the Hard Day's Light," *People Weekly*, 15 August 1989, 68–69.
4. "In Praise of Courage," *Quest*, November 1980, 23.

Notes

5. See Matthew 10:1–28.
6. Matthew 10:21–22.
7. Matthew 10:26–31.
8. Matthew 10:26.
9. Hebrews 4:13, Daniel 2:22, Matthew 12:36, Psalm 90:8, 1 Corinthians 4:5.
10. Romans 8:1, 3:26, Acts 13:39, Hebrews 8:12, Colossians 3:3.
11. Hebrews 10:19, 22, emphasis mine.
12. Matthew 10:27–28.
13. Paul Harvey, *Paul Harvey's The Rest of the Story* (New York, NY: Bantam, 1977), 117.

CHAPTER 9 · A SATISFIED THIRST
1. Luke 22:20.
2. Hebrews 10:4.
3. John 7:37.
4. "It is not sufficient that we merely want righteousness unless we have a downright famine for it . . ." —St. Jerome, quoted in Bruner, *The Christbook*, 142.
5. Matthew 26:28, PHILLIPS.

CHAPTER 11 · THE FATHER IN THE FACE OF THE ENEMY
1. Archibald Hart, *The Hidden Link between Adrenaline and Stress* (Waco, TX: Word, 1986), 101, 142–45.
2. Matthew 18:21–35.
3. Matthew 18:34.
4. Romans 2:4.

CHAPTER 12 · THE STATE OF THE HEART
1. Proverbs 4:23.
2. Matthew 15:18–19.
3. Luke 6:45.
4. Psalms 51:10.

CHAPTER 14 · SEEDS OF PEACE
1. James 3:18, LB.
2. Paul Harvey, *Paul Harvey's The Rest of the Story* (New York, NY: Bantam, 1977), 49.

3. Isaiah 53:2, LB.

CHAPTER 15 · THE GREASY POLE OF POWER
1. *USA Today*, 22 March 1988, 5D.
2. Henry Emerson Fosdick, quoted in *A Guide to Prayer for Ministers and Other Servants* (Nashville: The Upper Room, 1983), 263.
3. Genesis 3:5.
4. Gary Smith, "Ali and His Entourage," *Sports Illustrated*, 16 April 1988, 48–49.
5. Paul Lee Tan, ed., *Encyclopedia of 7700 Illustrations* (Rockville, MD: Assurance Publishers, 1979), 1213–14.

CHAPTER 16 · THE DUNGEON OF DOUBT
1. Matthew 14:1–12.
2. Matthew 11:3–4.
3. Philip Yancey, *Disappointment with God* (Grand Rapids, MI: Zondervan, 1988), 158.

CHAPTER 17 · THE KINGDOM WORTH DYING FOR
1. Matthew 11:4–5.
2. Matthew 11:3–4.
3. Isaiah 35:5; 61:1.
4. Psalm 139:13.
5. Ephesians 2:10.
6. George Sweeting and Donald Sweeting, "The Evangelist and the Agnostic," *Moody Monthly*, July/August 1989, 69.
7. Ibid., 67.
8. Ibid., 69.
9. Ephesians 2:8–9.
10. Quoted in *A Guide to Prayer for Ministers and Other Servants*, 345.
11. Romans 8:26.
12. Matthew 27:46.

CHAPTER 18 · THE APPLAUSE OF HEAVEN
1. Revelation 21:1–5.
2. Psalm 23:3.

Meeting Christ
on the Mountain

$\mathcal{T}$his book is not an end in itself.

If it does its job, it will lead you toward your own encounter with Christ on the mountain. And the following guide is intended to help you make that connection between reading a book and meeting the Christ.

This, then, is not so much a study of a book but a study of Christ's message and a catalyst for helping the book bring his message into the core of your life. It does not proceed chapter by chapter, but beatitude by beatitude, using the insights of the chapters as springboards for your own study and meditation.

There are ten study "sessions" here. If you are meeting together in a group, you might try to work through one a week. (Note to group leaders: since some of the questions in the guide are very personal, "sharing" answers should always be optional.) If you are studying on your own, go at your own pace, taking the time to let each beatitude work its transforming way into your attitude and character.

To each encounter, I suggest you bring your Bible and a notebook for writing down your own thoughts and observations. More important, bring a prayerful spirit and an expectant attitude. And when you come, plan to be surprised with the sacred delight of meeting Christ on the mountain.

Session 1 · Chapters 1 & 2
Now when he saw the crowds, he went up on a moun-
tainside and sat down. . . . and he began to teach them,
saying: Blessed . . .

1. Describe the happiest moment you can remember. Jot
   down some of the circumstances surrounding it—who
   was involved, when it happened, how long your happiness lasted. Now, recall the time in your life that you
   were most miserable. What was happening then? How
   have the circumstances of your life contributed to your
   happiness or unhappiness?

2. What is the difference between "choosing to be
   cheerful," as Beverly Sills describes it, and putting on a
   cheerful facade to cover up or deny misery? Under what
   circumstances, if any, could "choosing to be cheerful" be
   a negative choice?

3. The following Old Testament passages reveal some of
   the ideas about happiness Jesus' listeners had grown up
   on. How does each passage describe a happy (blessed)
   person?

   • Psalm 1:1–6
   • Psalm 2:10–12
   • Psalm 32:1–2, 5–7, 10–11
   • Psalm 41:1–3

- Psalm 84:4–5, 11–12
- Psalm 94:12–13
- Psalm 112:1–9
- Proverbs 8:1–2, 32–36 (note who is "speaking")

4. Chapter 1 states that the Greek word Jesus used for "blessed" in the Beatitudes (*makarios*) is the same one used by Paul to describe God. It was used in other ancient literature to describe the "happy state of the gods above earthly sufferings" and to denote "a transcendent happiness of a life beyond care, labor and death" (*Theological Dictionary of the New Testament*, 4:362). What does Jesus' use of this powerful word say about the kind of happiness he is promising?

5. Read Matthew 4:23–25. What events in Jesus' ministry immediately preceded Jesus' withdrawing to the mountain? What do you think was the significance of this order of events? Why did Jesus withdraw to the mountain with his disciples at this particular time?

6. What are the best times and places for you to "go to the mountain"? What specific activities and responsibilities tend to stand in the way of your getting there?

7. Chapter 1 states that "you are one decision away from joy." Chapter 2 says that "the mountain is only a decision away." Specifically, what decision is this?

Session 2 · Chapters 3 & 4

Blessed are the poor in spirit, for theirs is the kingdom of heaven.

1. How does chapter 3 interpret being "poor in spirit"? How does this compare with any previous ideas you had about what this beatitude means?

2. Luke's version of this beatitude (found in Luke 6:20, 24) omits the "in spirit" idea entirely; it simply states that "the rich" have their reward here and therefore cannot expect a reward in heaven. And Jesus tells the rich young ruler directly that "it is hard for a rich man to enter the kingdom of heaven" (Matthew 19:23–24). Do you think the first beatitude applies especially to those who are poor in material possessions? If not, why does Matthew make these specific comments about material wealth? (You may find some ideas in the end notes for this chapter.)

3. List three reasons why being poor in spirit as described in these two chapters is difficult for most of us. Why do we have such a hard time admitting our own inadequacy and failures even to God and ourselves?

4. List what you consider your five greatest strengths and your five greatest weaknesses. Then examine your list in light of chapter 3. Does being poor in spirit mean denying your strengths or not trying to improve your

weaknesses? Does it mean being "down on yourself"?
Why or why not?

5. Is it possible to be both arrogant and insecure at the
   same time? What do you think are the motives behind
   the rich young ruler's self-justification and overachieve-
   ment?

6. What is the difference between trying to achieve salvation and trying to please God? Between being poor in
   spirit and being a poor steward of your God-given gifts?

7. Read the following parables describing the "kingdom of
   heaven": Matthew 13:24–33, 44–50. What additional
   insight do these parables give about the nature of the
   "kingdom" in which the poor in spirit will live?

8. Read Matthew 16:13–20, which tells the circumstances
   under which Peter's name was changed and he was given
   the "keys to the kingdom of heaven." What elements of
   this account point to Peter's being poor in spirit? What
   does this passage tell you about the nature of the
   kingdom?

9. What sort of positive change would you like in your
   life? According to these two chapters, what would be
   your best strategy for such change?

Session 3 · Chapters 5 & 6

Blessed are those who mourn, for they will be comforted.

1 After reading these two chapters, complete the sentence: "Blessed are those who mourn for." What specific kind of grief do these chapters speak of?

2. Can you think of cases in which admitting failure can become a cop-out—an excuse to stop trying? What (if any) is the difference between "mourning" and giving in to failure?

3. Most of our everyday situations aren't as dramatic as that of Anibal or Peter; the life-or-death nature of our decisions isn't as obvious. How can we be more aware of our need for Jesus in noncrisis situations?

4. Read Hosea 7:14 and 2 Corinthians 7:9–11. What kind of mourning do they describe? Is it included under Jesus' blessing in the second beatitude?

5. To what things, people, or activities (adult versions of the hug, the Band-Aid, the flashlight) do you tend to turn for comfort? Do they work? In your opinion, is anything inherently wrong with such "security blankets"?

6. Practically speaking, what does God's comfort feel like? What form does it take, and how does it come to us? Have you ever felt it? (For ideas, see Genesis 5:29, 24:67; 1 Chronicles 7:22; Job 6:10; Psalms 23:4, 71:21, 77,

119:50–52, 40:1–5; Isaiah 52:70–9, 57:14–19; John 11:19, 15:15–22, 14:1–6; 2 Corinthians 1:3–4, 7:6–7.)

7. Why do you think so many of us come to think that God doesn't want to hear about our problems or gets tired of forgiving us?

8. Read 2 Corinthians 1:3–4. Under what circumstances are we called upon to be agents of God's comfort to those who mourn?

9. List three ways we can comfort others effectively. What are some tactics that do *not* work? Describe a situation in which you were able to provide comfort.

10. What is the relationship between "mourning" and being poor in spirit? How are the two alike? How are they different?

Session 4 · Chapters 7 & 8
Blessed are the meek, for they will inherit the earth.

1. How does chapter 7 interpret the word meek? How does that definition differ from your previous ideas of "meekness."

2. Do you think of yourself as "ordinary"? Why or why not? Do you find that description comforting or insulting?

3. What are some synonyms for the word meek as it is used in the Beatitudes? For ideas, look up Numbers 12:3, Psalm 25:9, Isaiah 11:4, 61:1, Matthew 11:29, and 1 Peter 3:4 in the King James Version and another translation.

4. Practically speaking, what does it mean to be meek in the sense of letting God use you? If he doesn't speak through an angel or a burning bush, how do you know what he wants you to do?

5. In practical terms, how do you avoid taking over or "telling God how to do his job"—and still get something done?

6. Chapter 6 interprets "inherit the earth" as not being intimidated or afraid of any earthly power or person. In your mind, is this a satisfactory definition? Would you be more comfortable saying, "Blessed are the meek, for theirs is the kingdom of heaven?" Why do you think Jesus specified "the earth" in this beatitude?

7. Psalm 37:11 also states that the meek will inherit the earth. Read Psalm 37:1–17 to understand this verse in context. What is the message of the psalm? Is its thrust basically similar or different from the third beatitude? What new perspective does Psalm 37 give to Jesus' statement?

8. Describe one time in your life when you let fear keep you from doing something you knew you should do.

9. According to chapter 8, what are the three ways we seek to handle our fears? To which of these three are you more likely to turn? (Don't be misled by the 'big guy' examples; these defense mechanisms take many forms—major and minor!). Give an example of a time when you have taken refuge in one of these defenses.

10. What reason did Jesus give the disciples for not being afraid? Why can this be taken as a source of courage?

11. What would you do tomorrow if you were guaranteed you couldn't fail and that nothing could hurt you? Write down and/or share one example.

Session 5 · Chapters 9 & 10

Blessed are those who hunger and thirst for righteousness, for they will be filled.

1. A "how to write fiction" computer software program currently on the market begins its instruction with a question: "What does_____want?" The idea is that all plots (and therefore, all stories) arise from people's basic needs and desires. If you were writing a novel about yourself, how would you answer that starting question? What "hungers and thirsts" motivate you most?

2. How does chapter 9 interpret the idea of righteousness? What would your own definition be?

3 Read Matthew 23:27–28. What was there about the Pharisees' attitude about righteousness that made Jesus so angry?

4. Read Romans 3:10–31. What do this passage and Matthew 23:27–28 tell us about trying to be righteous in our own right, boasting about our righteousness, or assuming we are righteous because we "keep all the rules"? How are these attitudes different from "hungering and thirsting" for righteousness?

5. According to chapters 9 and 10 and Romans 3:21–31, what is the only way our "hunger and thirst for righteousness" can be "satisfied"?

6. According to chapter 9, what is the ultimate reason that those who hunger and thirst after righteousness will be filled?

7. What does "hungering and thirsting after righteousness" have to do with "holding earthly possessions in open palms" and being dependent on Jesus for joy (chapter 10)?

8. Chapter 10 intimates that our fullest experience of "being filled" will be in heaven. But do we ever experience such satisfaction here on earth? If so, how?

9. Look back over the first three beatitudes. What do they have in common? How is this fourth beatitude like them? How is it different?

Session 6 · Chapter 11
Blessed are the merciful, for they will be shown mercy.

1. According to chapter 11, what is the opposite of mercy?
2. Read Matthew 6:12 and 7:1–2. What light do these passages from later in the Sermon on the Mount throw on the idea of the merciful receiving mercy?
3. Is mercy synonymous with forgiveness? Why or why not?
4. Why is it so hard to give up resentments? What does mercy cost us?
5. In what ways does resentment harm us? List three specific negative effects.
6. According to chapter 12, what makes it possible for us to be merciful and forgiving?
7. Write one to five things to do in the next week either to make restitution for hurts you have caused or to reach out in forgiveness to those who have hurt you. (Be honest with yourself. If you cannot bring yourself yet to forgive those who have hurt you or to accept God's forgiveness for hurts you have caused, simply write down that you will pray for the ability to do these things.)

Session 7 · Chapters 12 & 13

Blessed are the pure in heart, for they will see God.

1. Does the fact that "what comes out of us" makes us good or evil mean that what goes in doesn't matter much? Why or why not?

2. Look up 1 Kings 18:26–28 and Acts 22:3. Is purity the same as sincerity or good intentions? Can a person be both pure and wrong?

3. Look up 1 Peter 1:22, 1 Timothy 1:5–8, and John 8:31–32. What principles determine purity of heart?

4. Now back up and read Matthew 22:34. What, according to this passage, is the key to achieving purity of heart?

5. Must we always wait until our "insides are clean" before we start to act right—and before we see God? Why or why not?

6. Look up John 14:5–14. What does John have to say about how we come to 'see God'? What different perspective does that give to the idea of being pure in heart?

7. According to chapter 13, what is the difference between "temple builders" and "Savior seekers"?

8. Give an example of a time you, or someone you know, got so caught up in a project you forgot the whole point of it. Have you ever been so involved in church or religious activities that you got out of touch with God?

9. At what time in your life have you been most aware of "seeing God"? At what times have you been able to "see" him only in retrospect? What is the difference between "temple building" and the "dry times" every Christian experiences?

10. If "Savior seekers" often must find Jesus "in spite of" the temple, what is the purpose of the organized church? What can we do better in community that we cannot do as individual seekers?

Session 8 · *Chapters 14 & 15*

Blessed are the peacemakers, for they will be called sons of God.

1. How would you define peace as it is portrayed in chapter 14? How does this concept of peace differ from more common ideas about peace?

2. Commentator Dale Bruner writes, "We can almost translate the key word here, 'peacemakers,' with the word 'wholemakers.' . . . Biblical *shalom* conveys the picture of a circle; it means comprehensive well-being in every direction and relation. . . . If we could translate 'blessed are the circle makers' and make sense, we would. To make peace, in Scripture, is to bring community. 'Peacemakers are reconcilers'" (*The Christbook*, 149). How do the examples of peacemaking given in this chapter fit Bruner's definition?

3. Read at least three of the following scriptures: Numbers 6:24–26, Psalm 29:11, Luke 1:76–79, John 14:27, 16:33, Romans 5:1, 1 Corinthians 14:33, Galatians 5:22, Ephesians 2:14–17, and Philippians 4:7. According to these passages and to chapter 14, what is the ultimate source of peace?

4. Read James 3:13–18. What are some of the "prerequisites" for peacemaking? What must happen inside us before we can be peacemakers?

5. Read Matthew 10:34–39. Are there times when peace-

making in the larger sense involves accepting conflict rather than avoiding it? Does it ever involve *initiating* conflict? If possible, give a biblical or contemporary example.

6. Is it enough simply to plant seeds of peace? Are there ways we can nurture them and help them grow?

7. Is the "push for power" a basic part of human nature? Can it ever be a positive thing? How can we avoid it?

8. How does power relate to peacemaking? Can power ever be used in the *service* of peacemaking? Why or why not?

9. Write down the names of three people in your life who could use a word or act of peace from you. Beside each person's name, write an idea for a "seed" of peace. Finally, write down a specific date and time to plant your seed and commit to that schedule. If you are meeting in a group, be prepared to share your "peace seed" (not necessarily the results) at the next meeting. If you are on your own, consider sharing your peace initiatives with a friend and asking to be held accountable.

Session 9 · Chapters 16 & 17
Blessed are those who are persecuted because of right-eousness, for theirs is the kingdom of God.

1. According to chapter 16, why did John send word to ask Jesus if he was really the Messiah?
2. Name a situation in which you have felt persecuted for doing what was right. What was the outcome of your experience?
3. What are some of the explanations you've heard for times when God seems silent? Which explanations seemed most satisfactory? Which didn't satisfy you?
4. Do persecution and "God's silence" always go hand in hand, or are they two separate things? Why do you think so?
5. What are some ways (subtle and overt) that Christians are persecuted "because of righteousness"?
6. Read Proverbs 21:2 and Jeremiah 17:9. What do these passages suggest about how we can interpret the bad things that happen to us? If we are in trouble, how can we be sure that our persecution is "because of righteous-ness"—that we are in trouble for the right reasons?
7. Chapter 17 states, "God has never turned away the ques-tions of a sincere searcher." Do you feel comfortable with this idea of questioning God? Why or why not? When you get to heaven, what are some questions you want to ask him?
8. The Book of Job is another biblical account of a person

who suffered from God's seeming silence in the face of injustice. When struck with numerous, undeserved afflictions, he, too, questioned God. But Job's questions were different, as were the answers he received and the outcome of the story.

- Read Job 3:23, 7:20–21, 10:2–7, 13:20–24, 24:1–12. What questions did Job ask God?
- Read Job 38:1–21, 40:1–14, and 42:1–6. What was God's answer? How was it similar to Jesus' answer to John? How was it different?

9. Write down the three characteristics of Christ's kingdom that are implied in Jesus' answer to John. In what ways have you seen these characteristics continuing in your lifetime?

10. Chapter 17 relates this beatitude back to the first one, "Blessed are the poor in spirit," which also states "for theirs is the kingdom of heaven." Why do you think the phrase was repeated? How does being poor in spirit relate to being persecuted for the sake of righteousness?

11. Read Jesus' familiar model prayer cited in Matthew 6:9–13. In your opinion, how do Jesus' instructions on how to pray relate to the way we respond to persecution and doubt?

Session 10 · Chapter 18

Rejoice and be glad, because great is your reward. . . .

1. According to chapter 18, what is the ultimate joy promised to those who follow Jesus?

2. Describe the happiest homecoming you have ever experienced. Who was there? Why were you (or someone else) coming home? Where had you (or the homecomer) been? Why was this particular experience so happy?

3. According to chapter 18, what biblical images does the Book of Revelation use to describe our "homeland"? What do these biblical pictures say about our future with Christ?

4. What kinds of experiences (personal or second hand) in this world make you "want to go home" to a world made new? How do you picture your heavenly home?

5. What do the Beatitudes tell us about how we receive "the applause of heaven" while still on earth?

6. Read Luke's version of the Beatitudes as given in Luke 6:20–26. How do the two versions differ? Where do they agree? What different perspective does Luke's account give to Jesus' picture of sacred delight?

7. Most of us tend to think of the beatitudes as cause-and-effect statements: If you become poor in spirit, then—as a result—you will see God. If you mourn your sins, then you will be comforted. They therefore tend to

be thought of as requirements—"rules to live by" that are almost impossible to live up to. For a different perspective, conclude this study by turning the "cause and effect" idea around a bit. Think of all the beatitudes as effects—descriptions of what happens when we accept Christ. If you look at each beatitude this way, the two parts of each beatitude can be seen as two stages or dimensions: the immediate, earthly effect and the ultimate or spiritual effect. With this idea in mind, fill in the chart for each beatitude, using the chapters of this book for a resource. The first is filled in below to give an example.

Beatitude	Cause	Result	Ultimate Result
Blessed are the poor in spirit for theirs is the kingdom of God.	We truly respond to the reality of who Christ is and who we are . . .	. . . we become acutely aware of where we fall short; we become poor in spirit.	. . . we become citizens of Christ's heavenly kingdom; we receive a new name and identity

Beatitude	Cause	Result	Ultimate Result
Blessed are those who mourn, for they will be comforted.	We truly respond to the reality of who Christ is and who we are . . .		
Blessed are the meek, for they shall inherit the earth	We truly respond to the reality of who Christ is and who we are . . .		
Blessed are those who hunger and thirst for righteousness, for they will be comforted	We truly respond to the reality of who Christ is and who we are . . .		
Blessed are the merciful, for they will be shown mercy.	We truly respond to the reality of who Christ is and who we are . . .		
Blessed are the pure in heart, for they will see God.	We truly respond to the reality of who Christ is and who we are . . .		
Blessed are the peacemakers, for they will be called sons of God.	We truly respond to the reality of who Christ is and who we are . . .		
Blessed are those who are persecuted because of righteousness.	We truly respond to the reality of who Christ is and who we are . . .		

Also Available from Max Lucado

A LOVE WORTH GIVING

Finding it hard to love? Someone in your world is hard to forgive? Is patience an endangered species? Kindness a forgotten virtue? If so, you may have forgotten an essential first step. Living loved. God loves you. Personally. Powerfully. Passionately.

Spanish edition available

AN ANGEL'S STORY

Was the birth of Jesus a quietly profound event? Come along as Lucado takes us on a journey into his imagination—pulling back the curtain as we see what might have taken place in *An Angel's Story* (previously titled *Cosmic Christmas*).

THE APPLAUSE OF HEAVEN

Max Lucado believes that the Beatitudes provide what we need to discover the joy of God. Much more than a how-to book on happiness, *The Applause of Heaven* is an encounter with the Source of Joy.

Spanish edition available

THE CHRISTMAS CHILD

A Chicago journalist finds himself in a small Texas town on Christmas eve. Lonely and alone, he encounters old faces and new facts...a handcarved manger, a father's guilt, a young girl's faith. The trip into the past holds his key to the future, and a scarlet cross shows him the way home.

THOMAS NELSON
Since 1798

A GENTLE THUNDER

What if God moved you to another land? (As He did Abraham.) What if He called you out of retirement? (Remember Moses?) God does what it takes to get our attention. That's the message of this book: the relentless pursuit of God.

Spanish edition available

THE GREAT HOUSE OF GOD

Using the Lord's Prayer as a floor plan for *The Great House of God*, Max Lucado introduces us to a God who desires his children to draw close to him. No house is more complete, no foundation more solid. So come to the house built just for you, *The Great House of God*.

Spanish edition available

HE CHOSE THE NAILS
Available in Large Print

Christ's sacrifice has defined the very essence of mankind's faith for the past 2000 years. Now Max Lucado invites you to examine the cross, contemplate its purpose, and celebrate its significance.

HE STILL MOVES STONES

Why does the Bible contain so many stories of hurting people? Though their situations vary, their conditions don't. Lucado reminds us that the purpose of these portraits isn't to tell us what Jesus *did*—but rather to remind us what Jesus still *does*.

Spanish edition available

THOMAS NELSON
Since 1798

In the Eye of the Storm

If you know what it means to be caught in life's storms . . . if you've ever ridden the roller coaster of sorrow and celebration . . . if you've ever wondered if God in heaven can relate to you on earth, then this book will encourage and inspire you.

Spanish edition available

In the Grip of Grace
Available in Large Print

Max Lucado shows how you can't fall beyond God's love. "God doesn't condone our sin, nor does He compromise His standard. Rather than dismiss our sin, He assumes our sin and incredibly, sentences Himself. God is still holy. Sin is still sin. And we are redeemed."

Spanish edition available

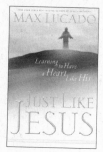

Just Like Jesus
Available in Large Print

"What if, for one day, Jesus became you?" asks master storyteller Max Lucado. With this simple premise, Lucado tells how God loves you just the way you are, but He refuses to leave you there. He wants you to have a heart like His. He wants you to be just like Jesus.

Spanish edition available

Just Like Jesus Devotional

This personal month-long journey with the Savior offers Scripture, practical devotions and application sessions to pattern one's life after Christ. As readers begin to think more like Christ, they are challenged to put words into action as the journey escalates into a full force, radical retracing and renewal of what it means to be a follower of Christ.

THOMAS NELSON
Since 1798

NEXT DOOR SAVIOR

We applaud men for doing good things. We enshrine God for doing great things. But what about a man who does God things? One thing is certain. We can't ignore him. If these moments are factual, if the claim of Christ is actual, then he was, at once, man and God.

Spanish edition available

TRAVELING LIGHT
Available in Large Print

No wonder we get so weary—we're worn out from carrying excess spiritual baggage. With the twenty-third Psalm as our guide, we learn to release some of the burdens we were never intended to bear. Learn to lighten your load, as Max Lucado embraces what it really means to say, "The Lord is my Shepherd."

Spanish edition available

WHEN CHRIST COMES

Thoughts of the Second Coming are unsettling. Open graves and occupied clouds. Sins revealed and evil unveiled. Yet, for Max Lucado, the coming of Christ will be "the beginning of the very best."

Spanish edition available

WHEN GOD WHISPERS YOUR NAME
Available in Large Print

Did you realize that your name is written on the hand of God (Is. 49:16)? Perhaps you've never seen your name honored. And you can't remember when you heard it spoken with kindness. In this book, Lucado offers the inspiration to believe that God has already bought the ticket with your name on it.

Spanish edition available

THOMAS NELSON
Since 1798